IMAGES
of America

COMMUNITIES OF THE PALMER DIVIDE

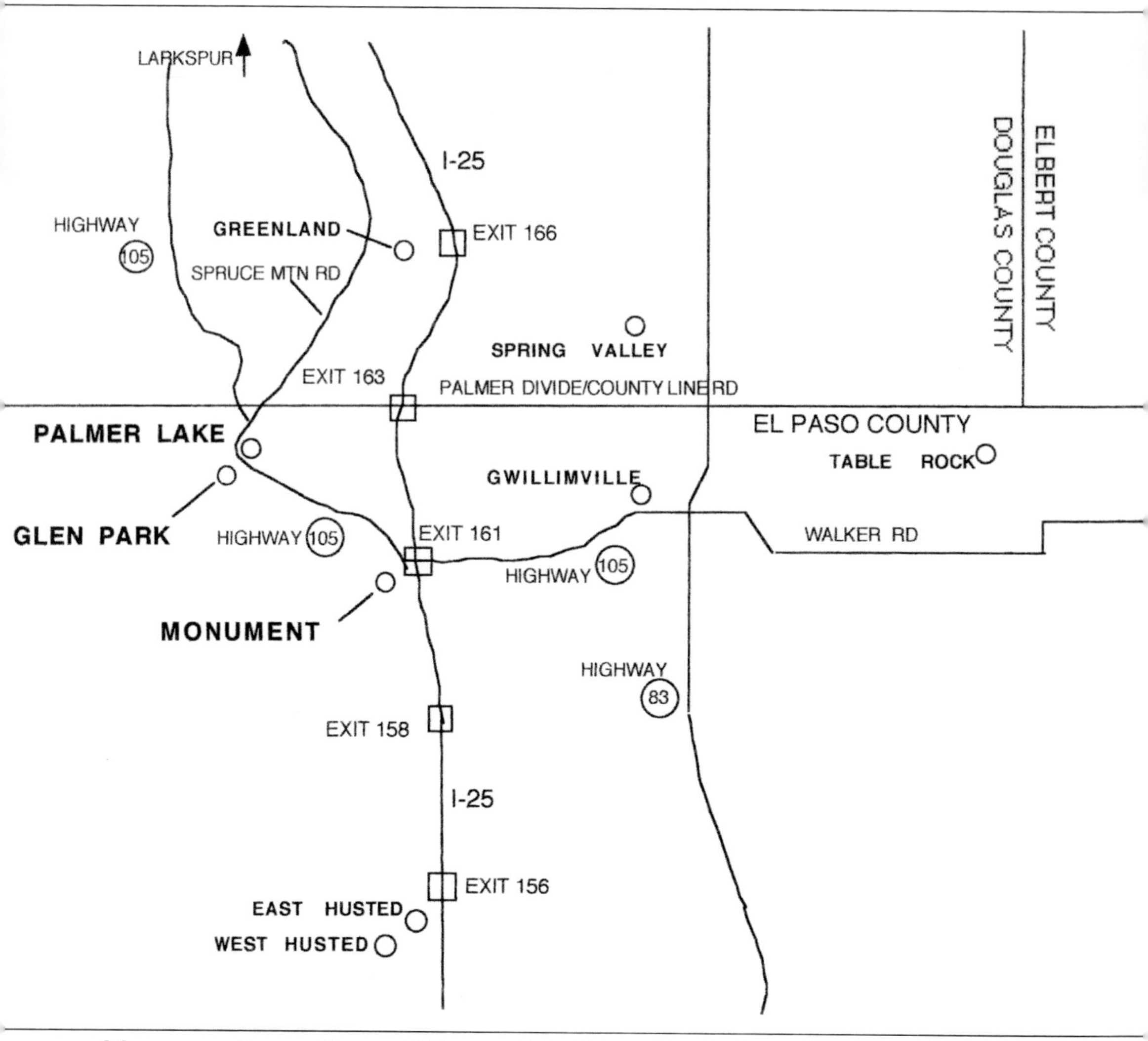

Map of the Palmer Divide. This map of the Palmer Divide shows the relative locations of the communities discussed in this book. Monument, Palmer Lake, and Glen Park have their own chapters. Smaller, once-vibrant towns or communities that have disappeared or diminished in size include Husted, Greenland, Gwillimville, Spring Valley, and Table Rock. (Courtesy of Bob Kirby.)

On the Cover: The Palmer Divide contains many geologic formations that attracted local residents as well as visiting tourists. The ice caves, formed by falling boulders in the mountains above the town of Palmer Lake, were a popular destination. After a long hike, travelers could enjoy a cool respite in the caves before beginning the return journey down the mountain. (Courtesy of Palmer Lake Historical Society and the Lucretia Vaile Museum.)

IMAGES
of America

COMMUNITIES OF THE PALMER DIVIDE

Palmer Lake Historical Society
and the Lucretia Vaile Museum

ARCADIA
PUBLISHING

ISBN 978-0-7385-8190-3

Published by Arcadia Publishing
Charleston, South Carolina

Printed in the United States of America

Library of Congress Control Number: 2010934825

For all general information, please contact Arcadia Publishing:
Telephone 843-853-2070
Fax 843-853-0044
E-mail sales@arcadiapublishing.com
For customer service and orders:
Toll-Free 1-888-313-2665

Visit us on the Internet at www.arcadiapublishing.com

This book is dedicated to lovers of local history everywhere, but especially to the Palmer Lake Historical Society, its founders, patrons, and volunteers—past, present, and future.

Contents

ACKNOWLEDGMENTS

The Palmer Lake Historical Society is indebted to the many volunteers and local residents who gave freely of their time and historical knowledge to make this book possible. We would like to acknowledge Dave Futey for planting the seed for this effort and providing guidance and direction, as well as the volunteers who spent many hours researching local history and assembling relevant photographs. These volunteers include Phyllis Bonser, Kim Braun, Rogers Davis, Dan Edwards, Herbert Edwards, Judy Harrington, Sharon Jarnigan, Dee and Bob Kirby, Mary Meyer, and Al and Rhetta Walter.

We especially would like to thank the local residents who shared their knowledge and photographs of early life on the Palmer Divide, including Fern (Wissler) Britt, Rogers and Susan Davis, Ethel (Lavelett) Engel, Norma (Younger) Lavelett, Barbara (Thompson) Morehead, Bill Noe, Jean (Schubarth) Rathburn, Jim Sawatzki, Darren Schubarth, and Dee Younger.

Finally, we should acknowledge the two authors of the local historical books that served as important resources for corroborating the accuracy of the information contained in this book. Lucille (Hagedorn) Lavelett and Marion Savage Sabin were instrumental in capturing the early history of the Palmer Divide and preserving it for us and for future generations.

Unless otherwise noted, all images appear courtesy of the Palmer Lake Historical Society and the Lucretia Vaile Museum.

Due diligence was used to verify the historical accuracy of information provided by local residents, which, in some cases, was based on their best recollections.

INTRODUCTION

Through *Communities of the Palmer Divide*, we provide a historical glimpse of the beginnings and growth of communities on the geologic anomaly named the Palmer Divide, which in the 1860s was known as the "Divide Country." More importantly, we present an insight into what makes the area a unique place to live and raise a family, and the spirit of community that has endured from the days of the early settlers to the present time.

In the early days, residents gathered at McShane's Fort to defend against marauding Native American tribes. Later, residents joined in annual potato bake festivals to celebrate successful potato harvests. More recently, annual events such as the Yule Log Festival and the lighting of the star on the mountainside above the town of Palmer Lake continue to bring the community together to celebrate and honor traditions established many years ago. There is much to tell about the people and places that make up the history of the Palmer Divide. Join us on a memorable journey through time as we discover the roots of the communities and the area of Colorado we call home.

Cresting at over 7,600 feet in the pineries (or the Black Forest, as the area has also been called since the beginning of the 20th century), the Palmer Divide is the highest point between Denver and Colorado Springs. The Palmer Divide extends eastward from the Front Range near the town of Palmer Lake and turns southeast near Table Rock, until it fades into the Great Plains of eastern Colorado. Location and altitude greatly influence weather conditions on the Palmer Divide, which can be markedly different from weather experienced by areas just a few miles away. While blizzards driven by high winds can be pummeling the Palmer Divide, nearby Colorado Springs can be experiencing relatively calm, sunny conditions.

Little recorded history exists concerning the early inhabitants of the area, although there is some evidence that Native Americans from the Ute tribe and Plains tribes traversed the Palmer Divide and may have briefly lived here. The earliest known homesteaders settled on the Palmer Divide around 1860 in the area of present day Monument. More settlers followed, which led to an influx of businesses providing goods and services to support the growing population. Towns began, lived, and died on the Palmer Divide.

The arrival of the railroad in the early 1870s allowed ranching, farming, ice and timber harvests, and tourism to flourish, helping to fuel the growth of small towns in the area. Many people came to the area to enjoy the fresh air and mountain scenery. The climate and rich soil promoted a robust potato industry that survived into the late 1800s, when blight decimated that crop. A timber industry prospered by providing railroad ties and fuel for the railroads that crisscrossed the Palmer Divide. An annual ice harvest on local lakes provided ice shipped by the railroads throughout the Front Range. However, as time passed and the railroads declined, commerce on a large scale decreased and only the towns of Monument and Palmer Lake survived.

The Monument area thrived as a center of commerce. Both the Denver & Rio Grande and the Santa Fe Railroads built depots in Monument and provided a means to transport local goods, produce, and timber. A collection of stores offered everything from dry goods to caskets. Livery stables served the needs of livestock, while a hotel, saloon, and billiard parlor filled the needs of travelers and local residents. Churches were active in the area as early as the mid-1870s, and one-room schoolhouses sprung up to educate the children. In 1879, the town of Monument was incorporated and elected its first mayor.

The town of Palmer Lake, a few miles north of Monument and higher up the Palmer Divide, owes its beginnings to Gen. William J. Palmer and his dream to build a railroad from Denver to Colorado Springs. Palmer Lake, a natural body of water at the apex of the Palmer Divide, served as a water stop for the Denver & Rio Grande and Santa Fe Railroads to replenish the steam engines that pulled the passenger and freight trains up and over the divide. The area west of the lake was envisioned as ideally suited to be a summer resort where tourists could embrace the beauty of the mountains, the fresh air, and the forests and streams that were now easily accessible due to the arrival of the railroad.

Tourism became the central industry in the area and slowly a town was born. The town also attracted an increasing number of travelers who sought relief from respiratory ailments and benefitted from the cool, dry mountain air. In 1889, the town of Palmer Lake was incorporated and a mayor elected. The famous Rockland Hotel was built to accommodate the influx of tourists and for more than 30 years enjoyed a reputation as the best summer getaway in the Rocky Mountains. Alas, with the advent of the automobile, the destruction of the Rockland Hotel by fire, and the decline in railroad passengers, the town of Palmer Lake was no longer the tourist destination that it had been in earlier times.

In 1874, the Chautauqua movement began in New York state and quickly spread across the nation. The first Rocky Mountain Chautauqua Assembly was held in Glen Park in Palmer Lake in 1887, offering challenging, educational, and inspirational stimulation. Many individuals and families from Colorado and neighboring states traveled by train to Palmer Lake to attend these assemblies, which lasted several weeks. Lectures, music, art, and theater were staples of Chautauqua assemblies and at their peak, more than 45 million people across the country had attended a Chautauqua event. The last Chautauqua assembly in Palmer Lake was held in 1910, and the Great Depression in the 1930s eventually brought an end to most of the assemblies across the nation.

No history of the Palmer Divide is complete without mentioning the settlers who inhabited the outlying ranches, farms, and small settlements that dotted the area. The final chapter of our journey begins in the southern part of the Palmer Divide, where the Schubarths and Youngs settled and raised their families, and where the town of Husted briefly existed. We then travel north, to the town of Greenland, which served as the hub for many large ranches in the area, including the Noe ranch. Finally, we turn eastward toward the Great Plains. This area was settled by hardy souls like the Thompsons, Geigers, Gwillims, Youngers, and others who ranched, farmed, and raised their families near settlements such as Spring Valley and Table Rock.

The early settlers of the Palmer Divide braved hardships and dangers to venture into the unknown and build a life and a community for themselves, their families, and the countless people who followed. These early settlers not only laid the foundation for the towns and communities that survived, but they instilled a spirit of community that exists and flourishes to this day. The Palmer Lake Historical Society and the Lucretia Vaile Museum are proud to tell the stories of these pioneers.

One

Geology and Early Exploration

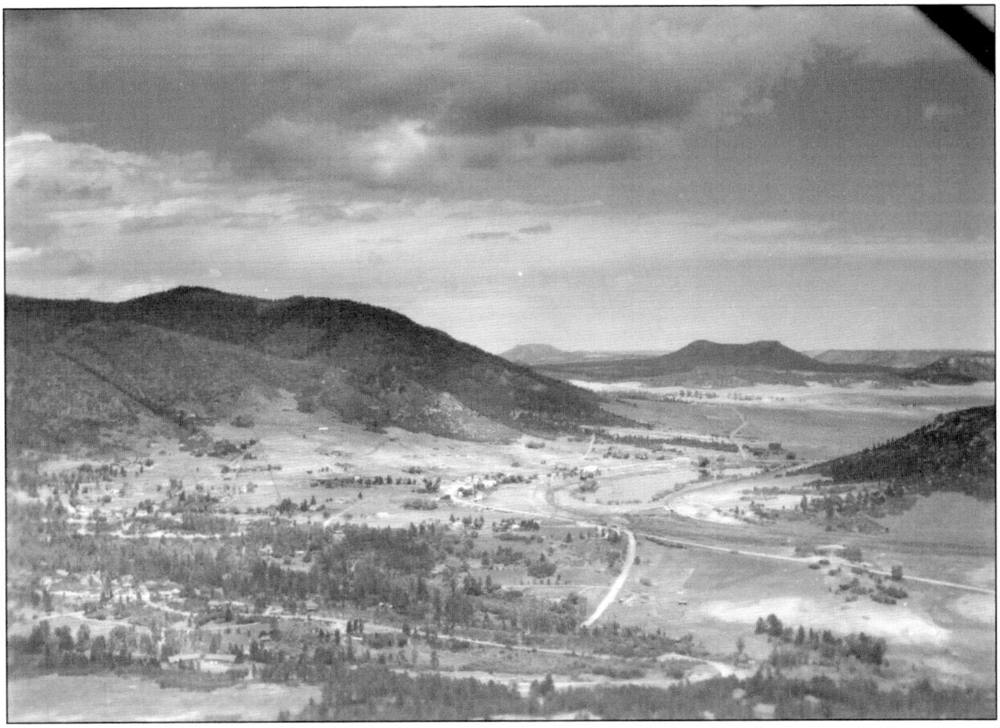

Aerial View of the Palmer Divide. The Palmer Divide is a ridge that begins near the town of Palmer Lake and extends southeast into the plains of eastern Colorado. Cresting at over 7,600 feet, the Palmer Divide acts as a watershed between the South Platte and Arkansas River systems and has a profound effect on weather in its vicinity. (Courtesy of Reba Bradley.)

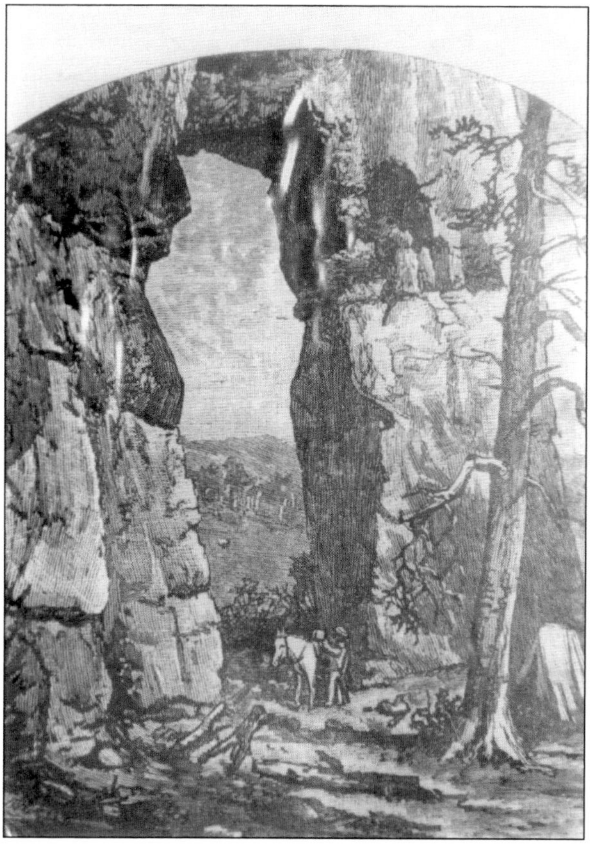

Elephant Rock. In 1820, Maj. Stephen H. Long led the first expedition to explore the Platte, Arkansas, and Red River systems. The 19-man expedition arrived in the area of the Palmer Divide on July 11, 1820. Pictured at left is a sketch of the area by Samuel Seymour, a member of the expedition and a landscape painter. Dr. Edwin James, a botanist with the expedition, noted in his journal that, "One of the singular hills, of which Mr. Seymour has preserved a sketch, was called Castle Rock, on account of its striking resemblance to a work of art. It has columns, and porticos, and arches, and, when seen from a distance, has an astonishingly regular and artificial appearance." Pictured below is the "Castle Rock" mentioned in James's account. It is now referred to as Elephant Rock.

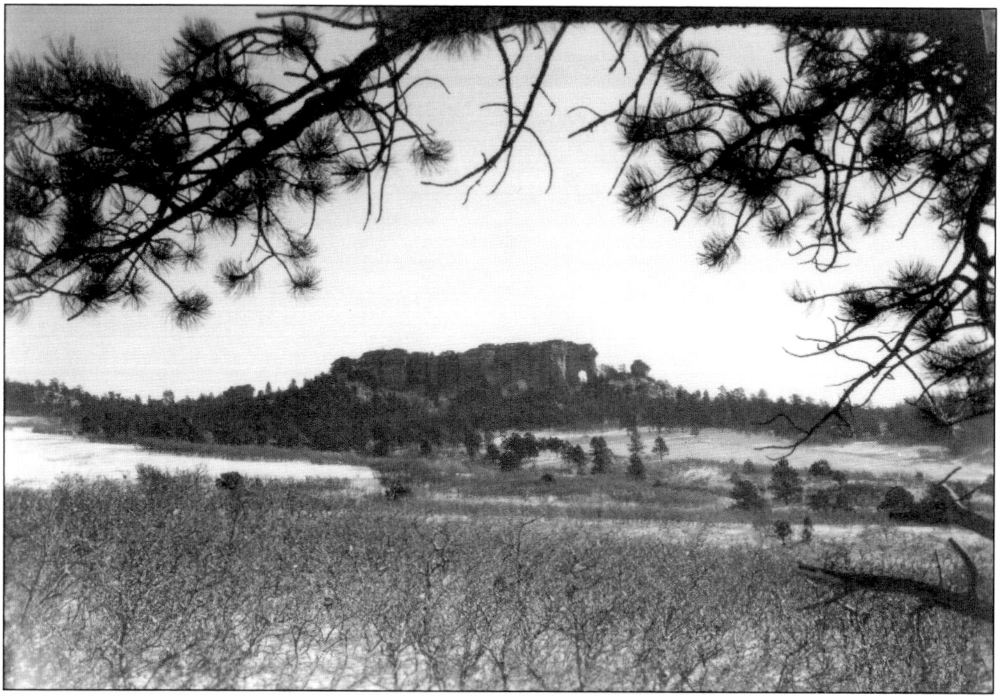

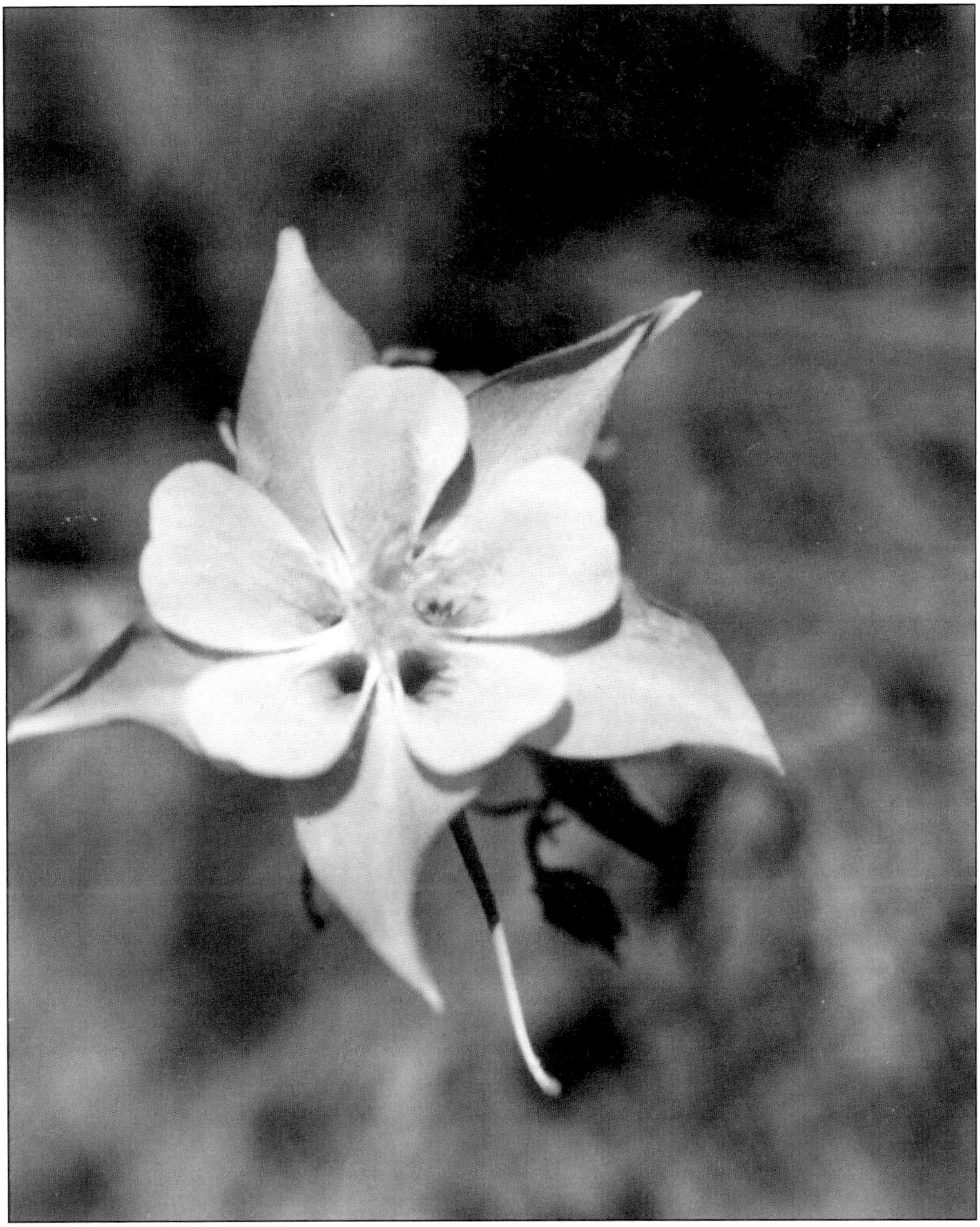

Rocky Mountain Columbine. While exploring areas around what is now Palmer Lake, Dr. Edwin James encountered a white and sky-blue flower. James named the flower *Aquilegia coerulea*, due to its blue color and its similar appearance to the known species of Columbine flower. The flower is now commonly referred to as the Colorado Blue Columbine or the Rocky Mountain Columbine. In 1899, this flower was adopted as Colorado's state flower. During his expedition through the area in 1843, Lt. John Fremont noted that flowers near the "dividing ridge" made a "mountain garden" as the "whole valley was radiant with flowers; blue, yellow, pink, white, scarlet, and purple, vying with each other in splendor." Once the railroads were constructed through the town of Palmer Lake in the 1870s, these flowers became a summertime attraction for tourists from Denver.

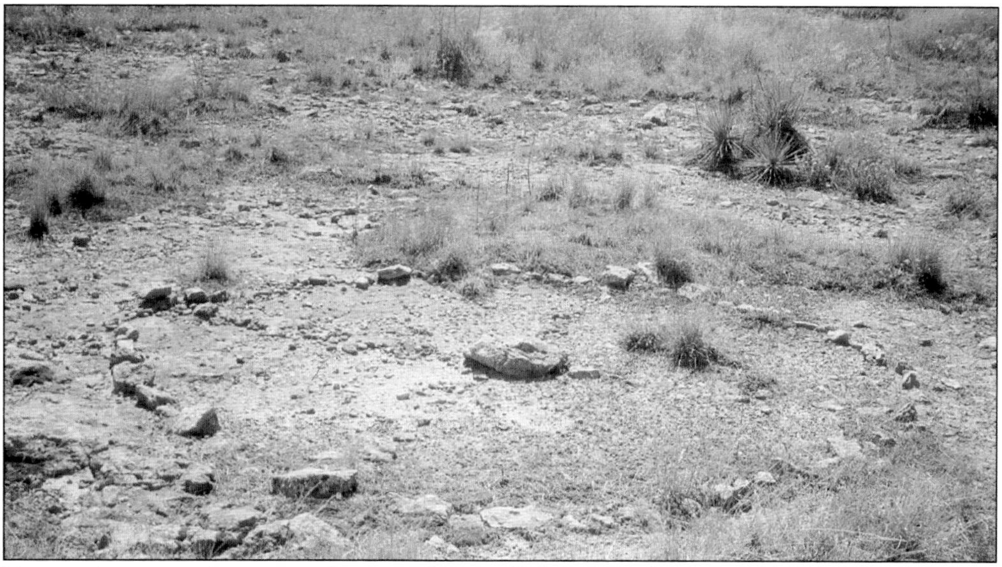

Native American Artifacts. Plains Indians including Arapahoe, Kiowa, and Cheyenne, along with Utes, who lived in the adjacent Rocky Mountains, most likely traversed the Palmer Divide. Remnants of Native American activity in the area of the Palmer Divide have been discovered. Pictured above is a medicine wheel near the Table Rock area east of Palmer Lake and Monument. A Native American grave was discovered on the Table Rock formation and an Indian cave was located on Ben Lomond Mountain in the town of Palmer Lake. Pictured below are arrowheads found on the Thompson Ranch near Table Rock. (Above, courtesy of Jim Sawatzki; below, courtesy of the Thompson Family.)

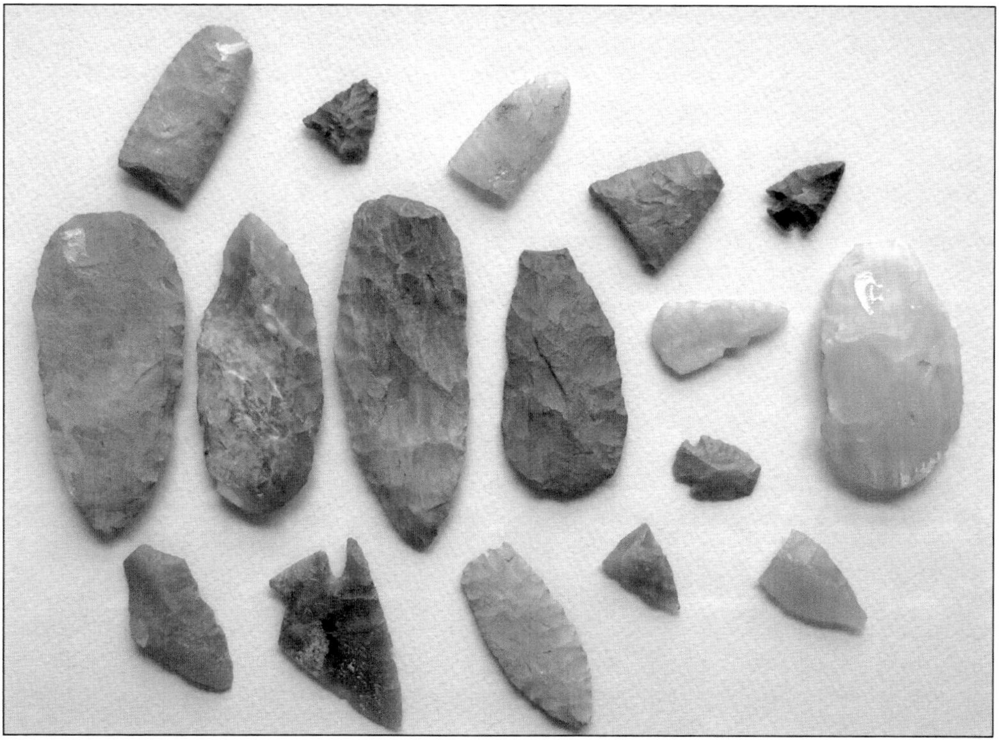

Two

Town of Monument

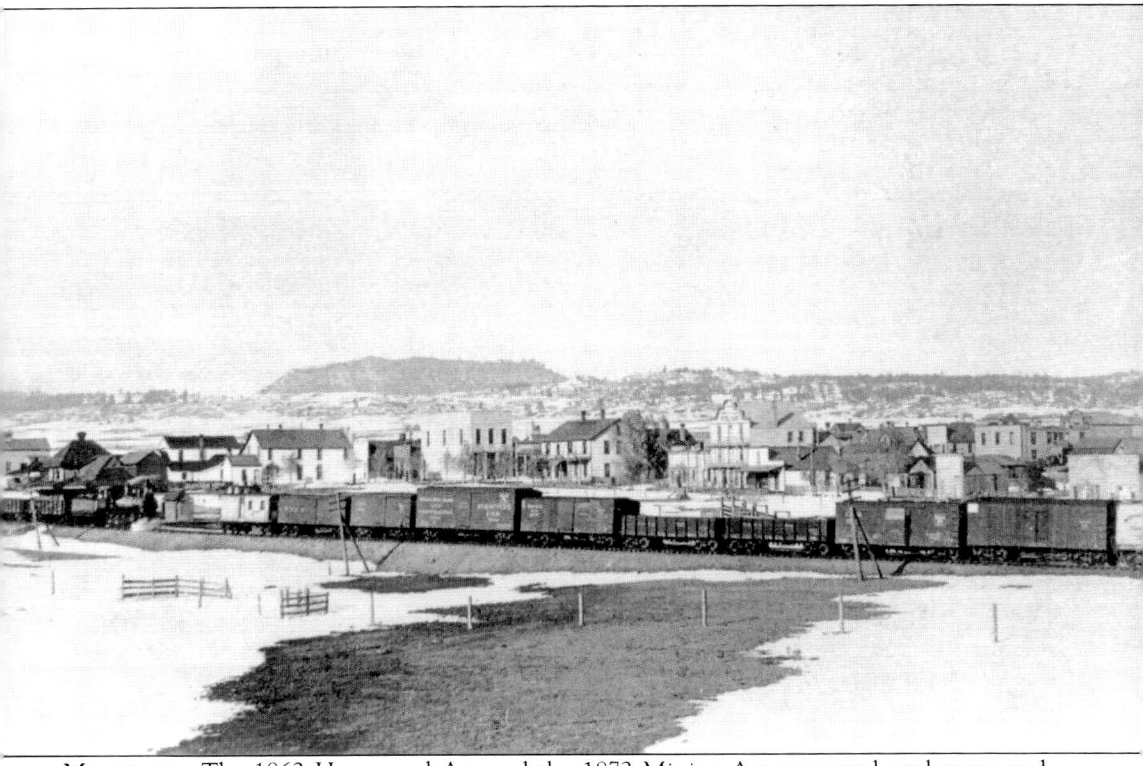

Monument. The 1862 Homestead Act and the 1872 Mining Act promoted settlement and development of agriculture, ranching, and mining in the west. In 1872, the Denver & Rio Grande Railroad opened the Palmer Divide to easier access. Subsequently, migration of settlers into the area began in earnest. As small communities sprang into life, Monument was positioned to become the transportation and commercial center of the region.

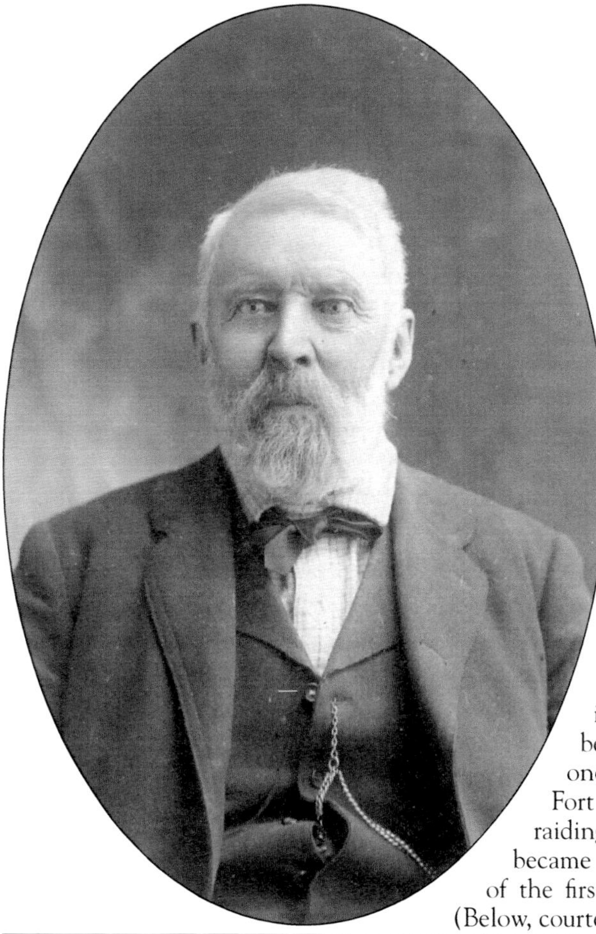

DAVID MCSHANE. David McShane, at left, first came to Colorado in 1861 in an unsuccessful search for gold. In 1865, he brought his family to the Palmer Divide and claimed 160 acres in the area of present day Monument. He noted it was "the best grazing country on earth." During 1868, a band of Cheyenne and Arapahoe raided settlements in the area and killed a number of settlers. Pictured below is McShane's Fort, which was used between 1865 and 1868. Reportedly, on one occasion, 40 people used McShane's Fort as a safe haven for protection from raiding Native Americans. McShane became the first postmaster in 1869 and one of the first commissioners of El Paso County. (Below, courtesy of Violetta Fauver.)

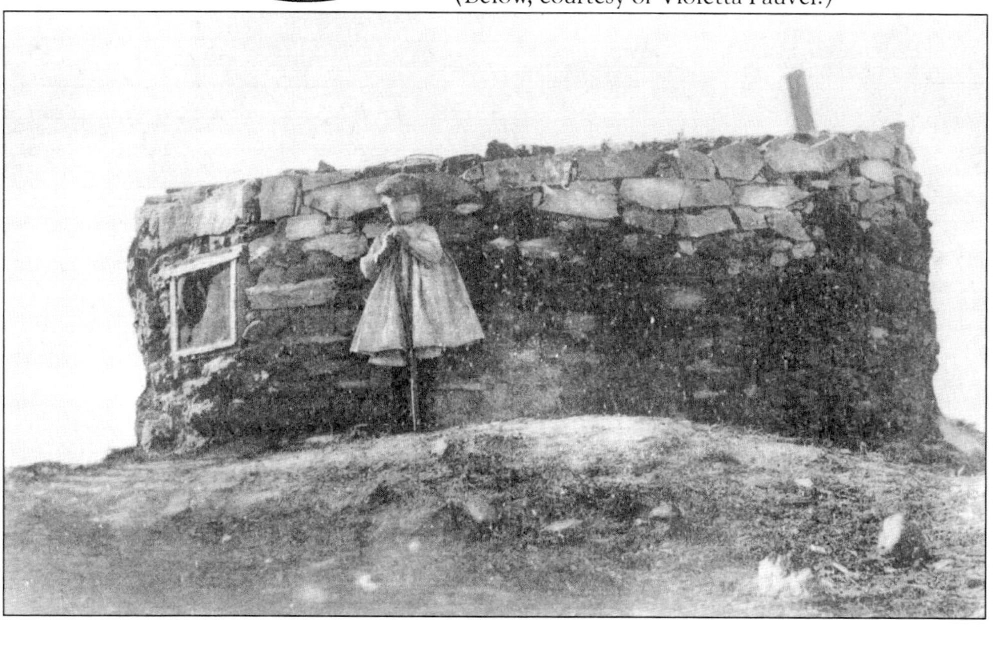

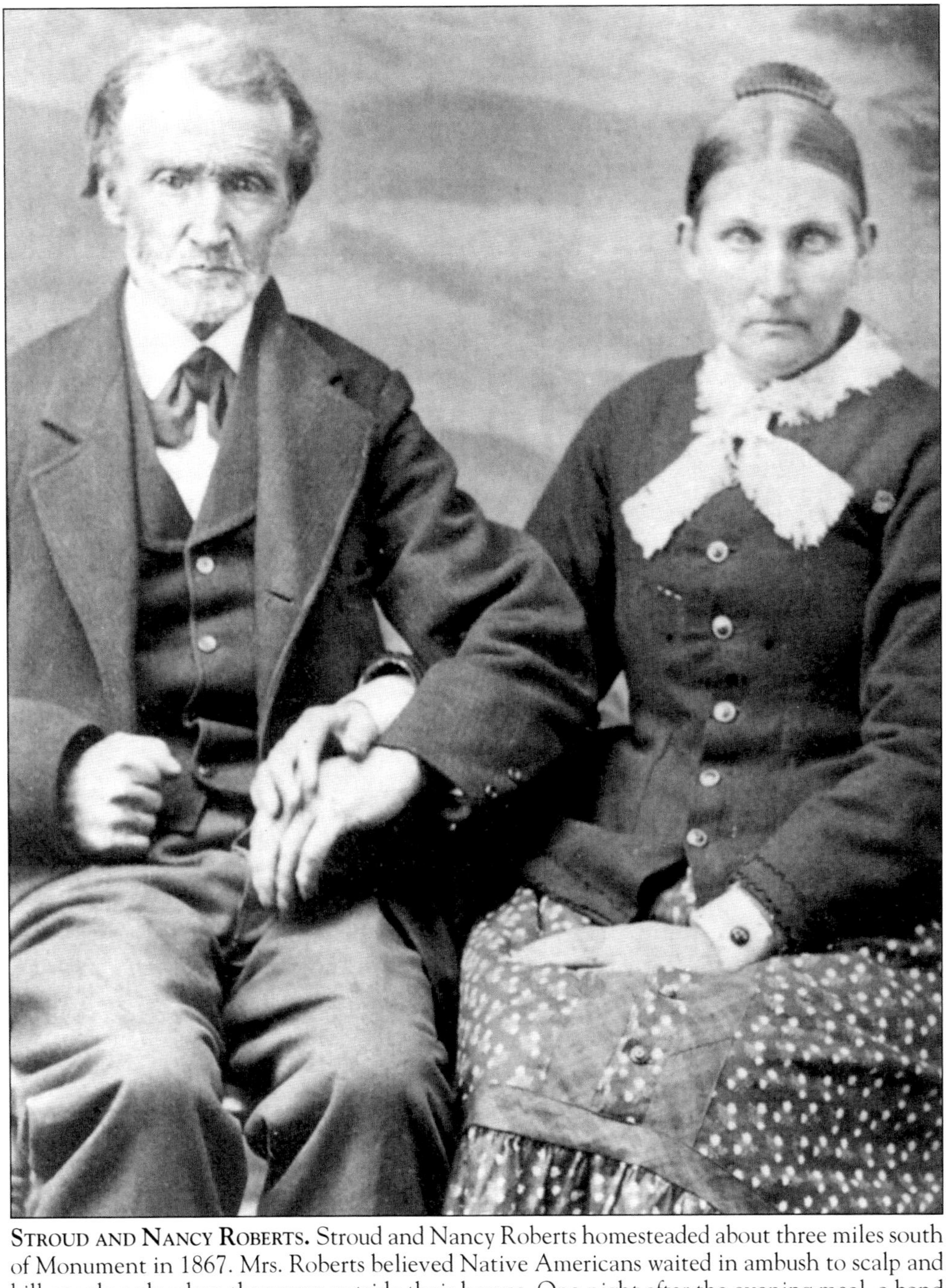

STROUD AND NANCY ROBERTS. Stroud and Nancy Roberts homesteaded about three miles south of Monument in 1867. Mrs. Roberts believed Native Americans waited in ambush to scalp and kill people only when they were outside their homes. One night after the evening meal, a band of Native Americans burst into the cabin demanding food, flour, and cooking utensils. Nancy attempted to slip away for help but was forced back into the house by an angry and menacing brave brandishing a revolver. The terrified family slipped into bed fully dressed. Late in the night, they crept from the cabin carrying their shoes and fled on foot to a neighbor's place a mile away, owned by Levi Welty. Fearful that the baby would cry, "she [Roberts] just about smothered the poor little thing," said granddaughter Nora Simpson Freeman.

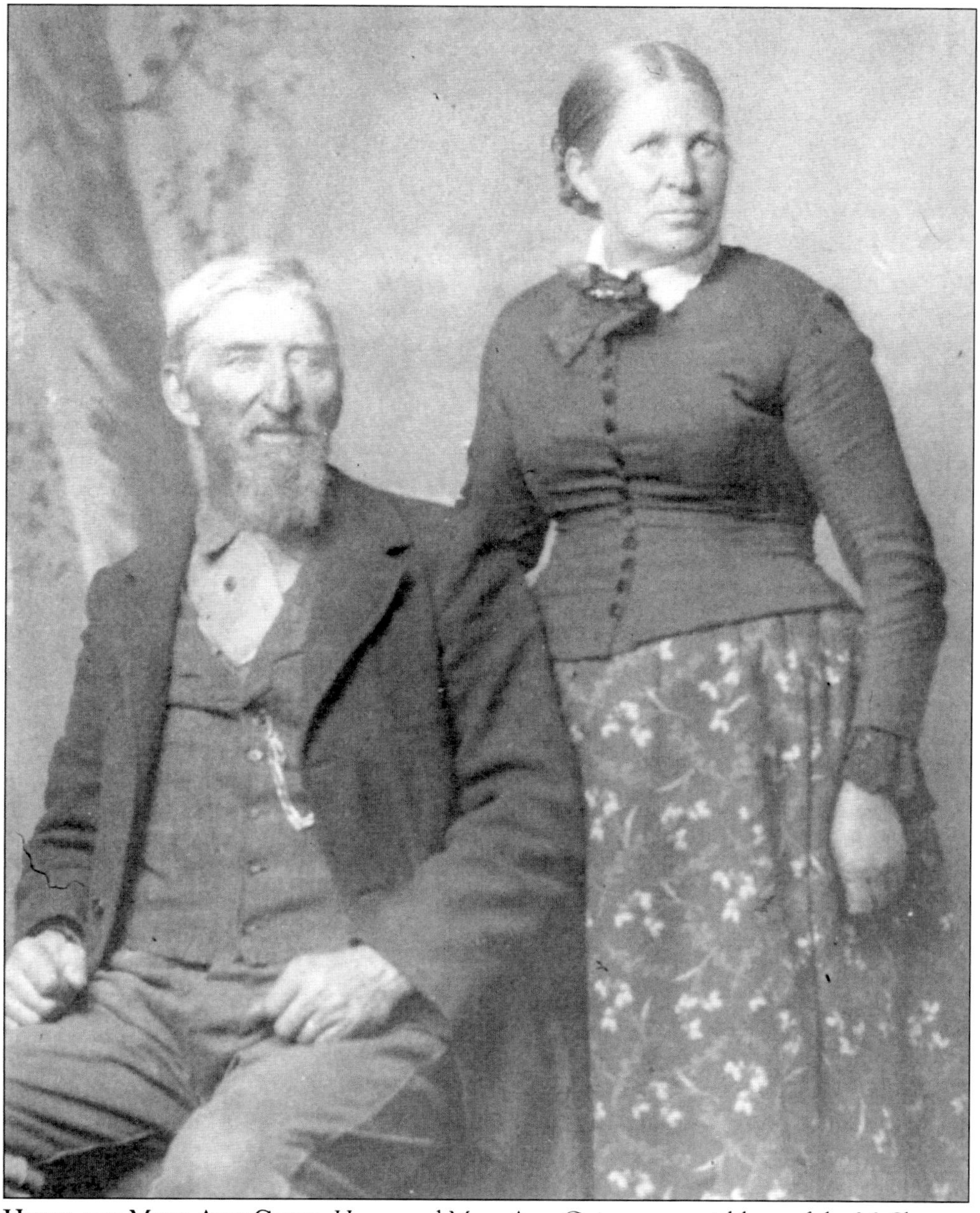

Henry and Mary Ann Guire. Henry and Mary Ann Guire were neighbors of the McShanes. They came to Colorado by wagon train in the summer of 1864. During their journey, Native Americans and wagon breakdowns were daily concerns. Once, the wagon flipped with their daughter, Alice Guire, in the back. Fortunately, she was unhurt. When Mary Ann put milk in containers stored in the back of the wagon, the milk churned into butter by the end of the day. She brought along her candle molds, coffee mill, and long handled fireplace waffle iron, but her most precious household possessions were her quilts in democratic rose and sunburst designs and her marriage pledge of 1854, the cover of which was decorated with hearts, flowers, and birds by Henry's penknife. Inside on its blue pages were the names of their children. The Guires had the first decorated community Christmas tree at their home, where children received gifts of cookies, candy, and apples.

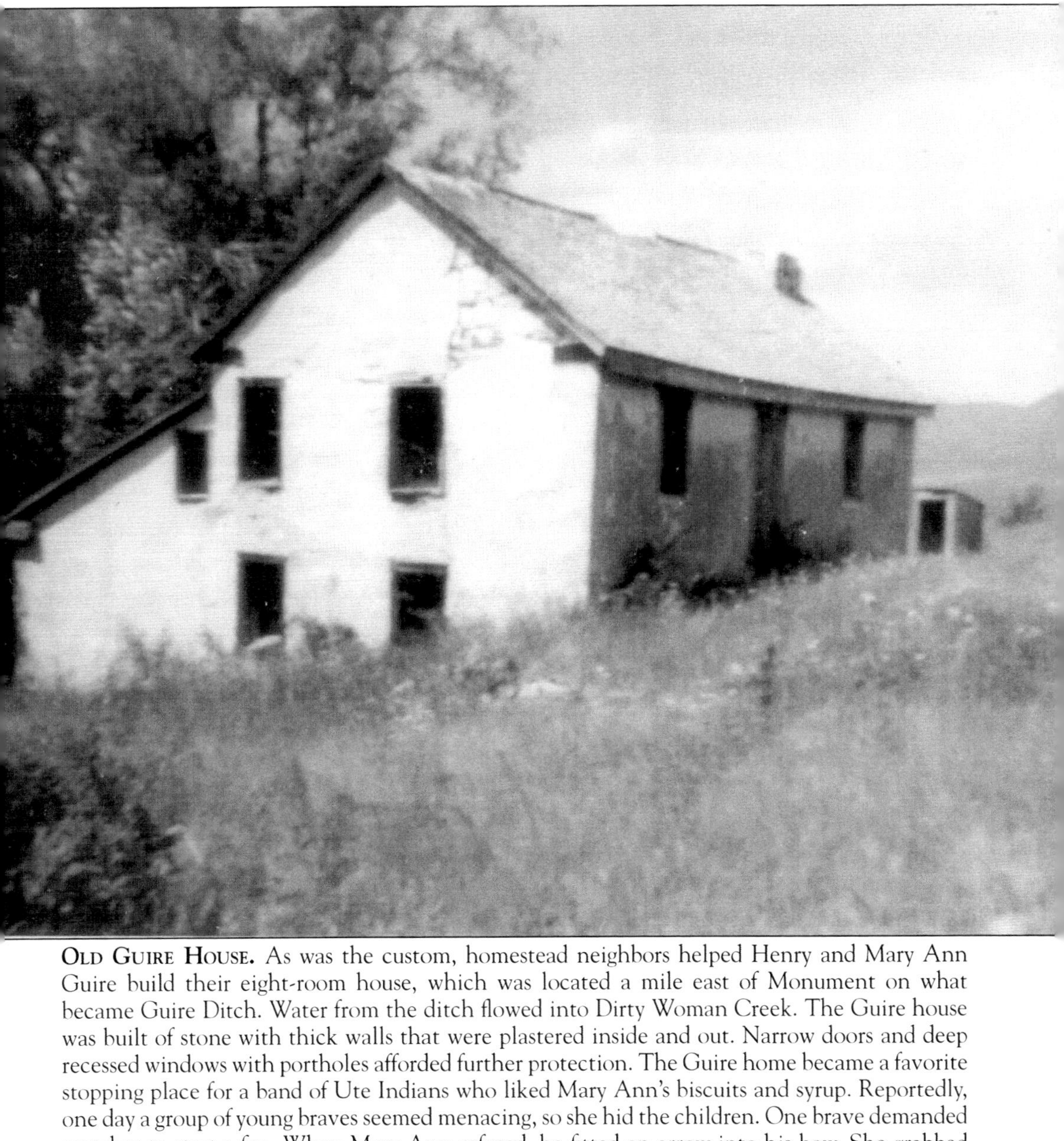

Old Guire House. As was the custom, homestead neighbors helped Henry and Mary Ann Guire build their eight-room house, which was located a mile east of Monument on what became Guire Ditch. Water from the ditch flowed into Dirty Woman Creek. The Guire house was built of stone with thick walls that were plastered inside and out. Narrow doors and deep recessed windows with portholes afforded further protection. The Guire home became a favorite stopping place for a band of Ute Indians who liked Mary Ann's biscuits and syrup. Reportedly, one day a group of young braves seemed menacing, so she hid the children. One brave demanded matches to start a fire. When Mary Ann refused, he fitted an arrow into his bow. She grabbed a flat iron from the stove and threatened to throw it at him. The brave ducked and yelled as he fled through the door, "Heap big brave squaw!"

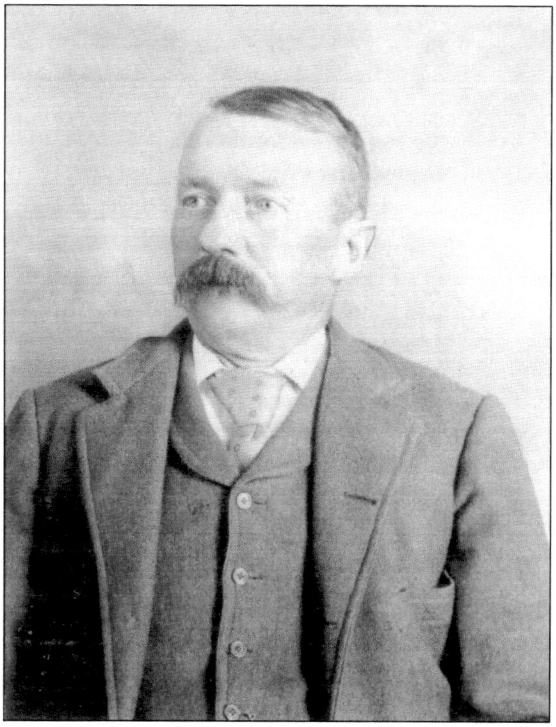

HENRY LIMBACH AND PIUTE JIM. Henry Limbach, at left, was born in Germany, arrived in the United States in 1863, and served with the 41st New York Volunteer Infantry during the Civil War. Limbach came west in 1866 as a member of the 8th Cavalry to fight in the Indian War. He and his mother-in-law, Maria Linder, owned land in the Monument area. About 1879, Limbach opened and ran a barbershop and saloon. The liquor license cost him $250 per year. Limbach and his wife, Caroline, raised six children. Later in life, Limbach became very close friends with Chief Ignacio, leader of the Ute Weeminuche band. Pictured below are Piute Jim and his squaw, whom Limbach also befriended. Limbach moved to Denver in 1909 and died on June 1, 1918. Monument's Limbach Park is named in honor of him and his wife.

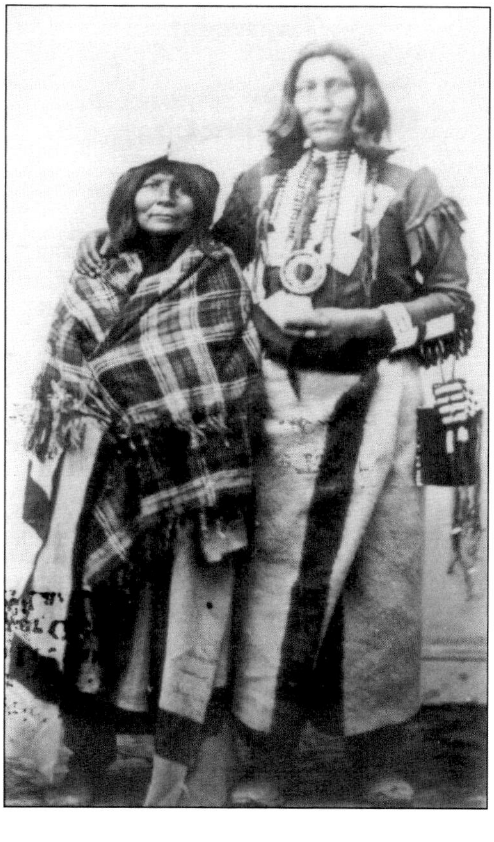

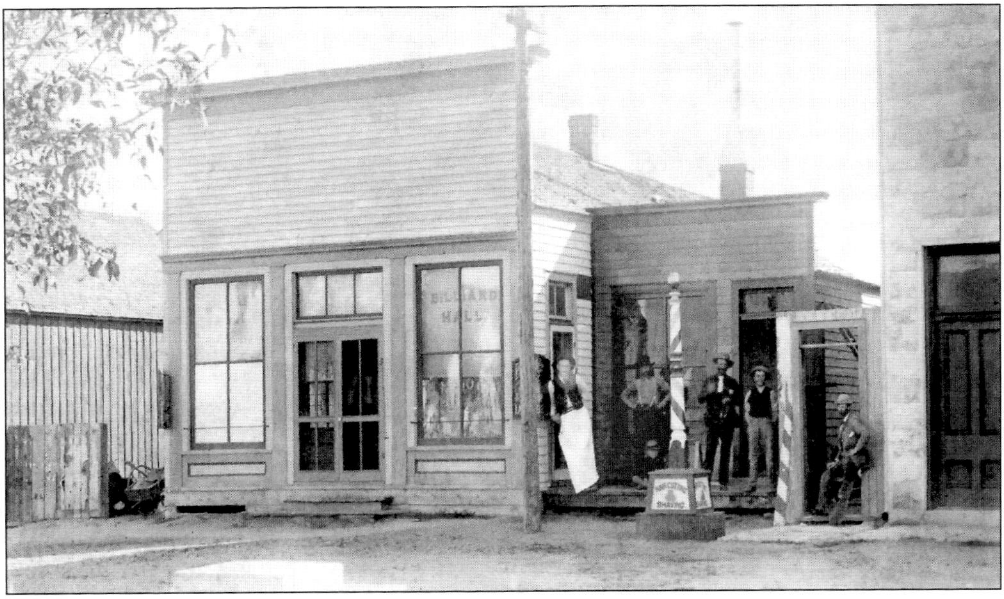

Murders in Monument. Two men were murdered in Monument in separate incidents. In 1876, an ongoing feud over a mining claim between Daniel Davidson and Francis Brown resulted in Davidson shooting Brown in the Limbach store. Davidson claimed he fired in self-defense, but was found guilty of manslaughter. The verdict was appealed all the way to the Supreme Court. Ironically, in 1881, Davidson, then on the town board, promoted an ordinance prohibiting shooting guns in town. In 1909, Rube Pribble killed William Neff at the Limbach Saloon, after accusing him of stealing a plow. The next day, Pribble said, "I have killed my best friend." Pictured above is Limbach's Saloon on Front Street. Pictured below is Burrell's Billiard Hall, formerly Limbach's Saloon, about 1915. Jeff Pribble, Rube's brother, is on the right.

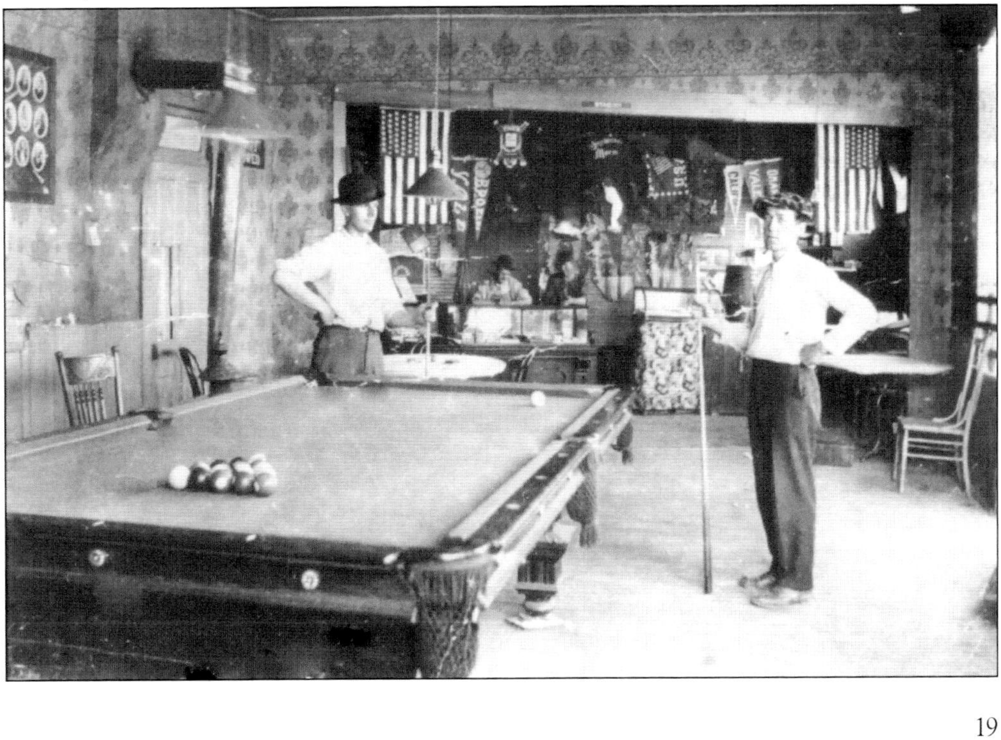

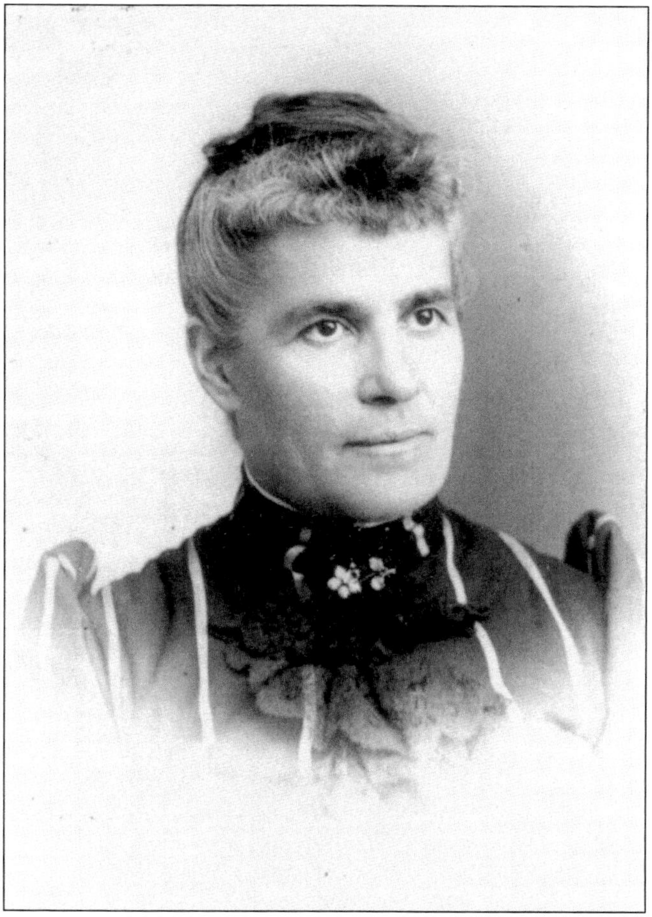

CAROLINE LIMBACH. Caroline Limbach, pictured at left, was born in Germany in 1842. She and her mother arrived in America in May of 1872. After she married her childhood sweetheart, Henry Limbach, in St. Louis, the three traveled to Limbach's Monument ranch, which was called Henry's Station and served the Denver & Rio Grande Railroad. Caroline was one of the first women to reside in Monument. Her firstborn child, Edward, became a curiosity to the Native Americans, as he was the first white baby many had seen. The Limbachs had six children. Pictured below is the family dry goods, millinery, and dressmaking store, which she managed for 12 years. Her store stood on the west comer of Front Street north of 2nd Street. Caroline died on May 3, 1894, at the age of 51.

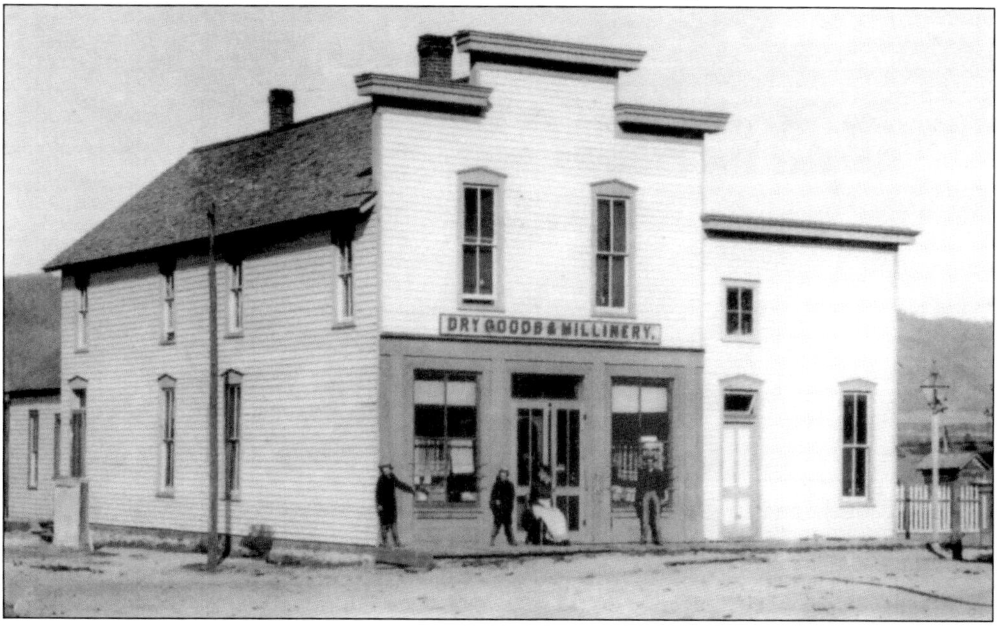

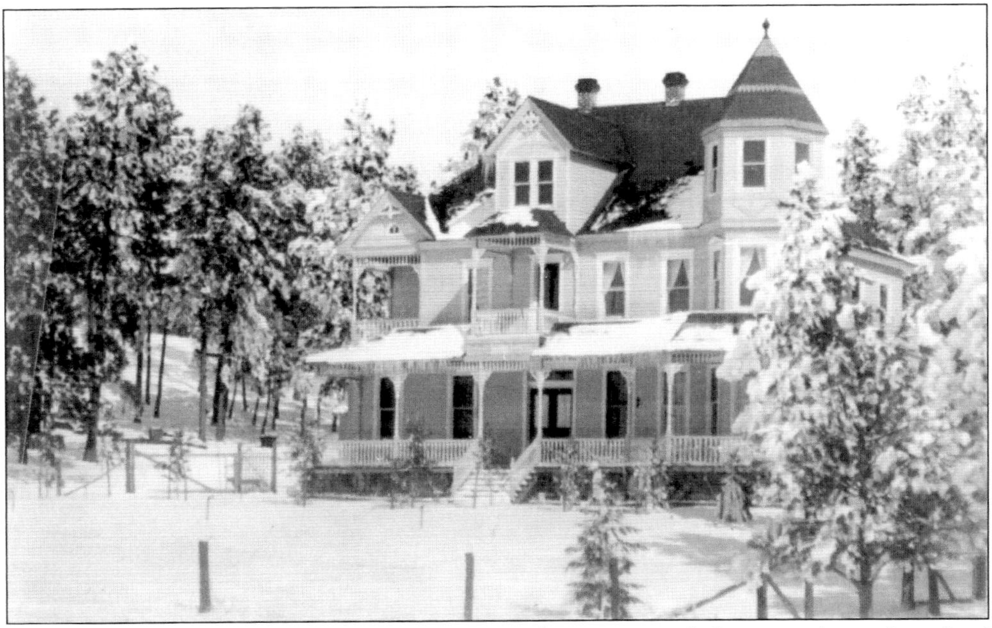

SCHUETT HOUSE, C. 1900. The elegant Victorian house pictured above was located north of the intersection of what is now Woodmoor Drive and Furrow Road, formerly Cemetery Road. It was built about 1900 by the three Schuett brothers, who were old-world craftsmen. The Schuett property encompassed land north of what would eventually become the Woodmoor Golf Course. Pictured below are Dora Schuett and her three unidentified brothers. None of the Schuetts ever married. The house was still standing when the Woodmoor community was first developed. Eventually, it became vacant, fell into disrepair, and was set on fire by vandals.

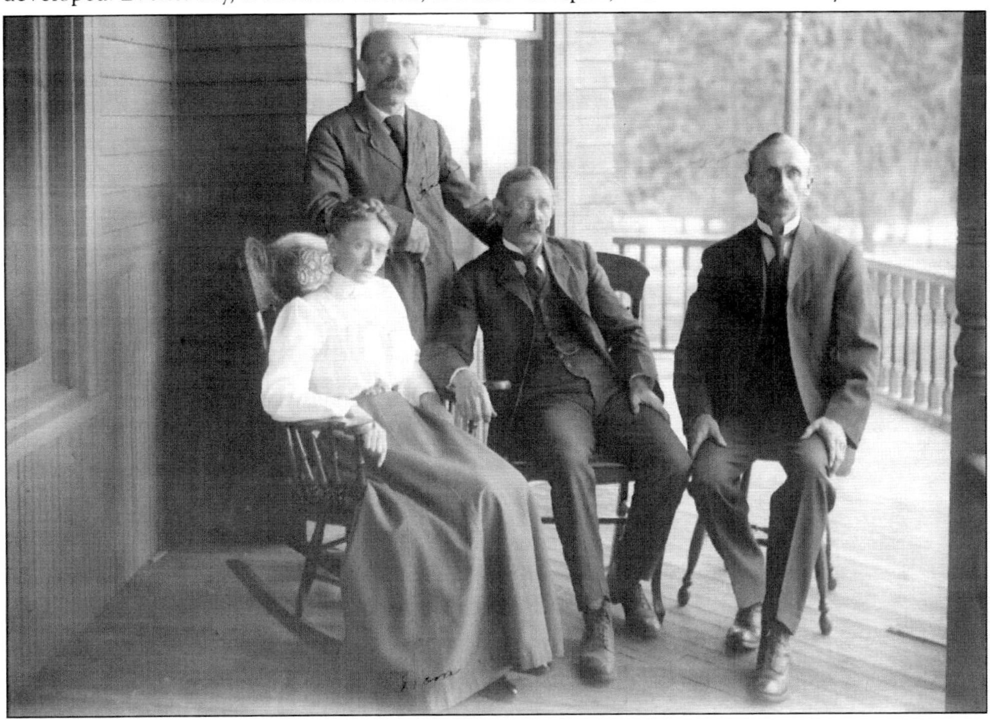

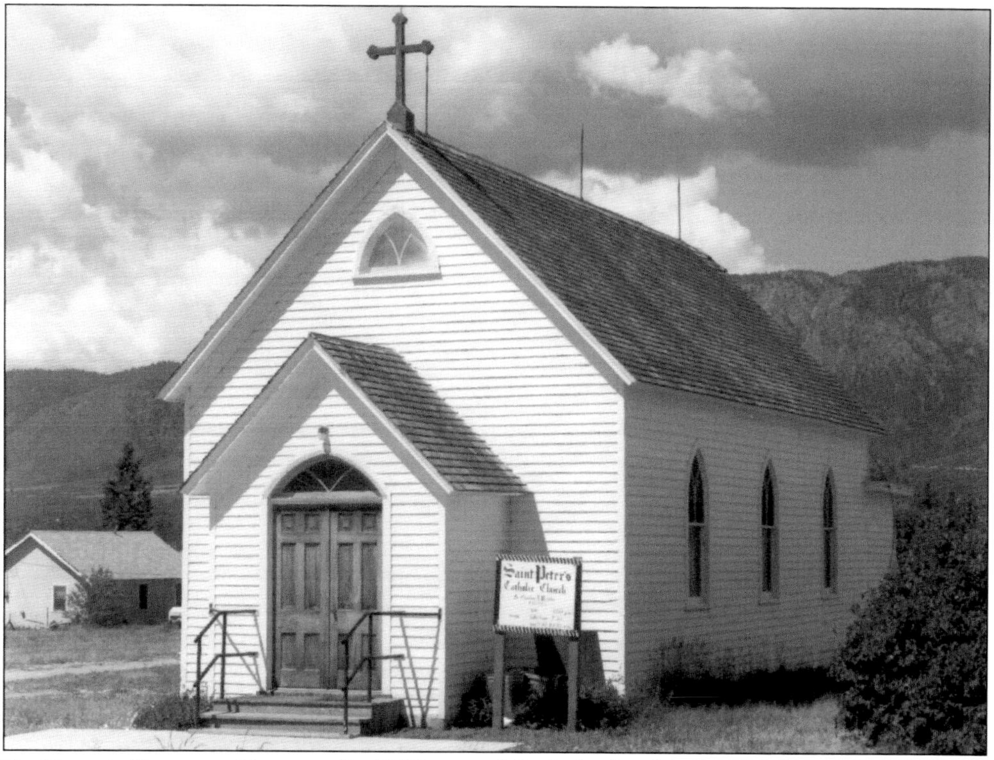

ST. PETER'S CATHOLIC CHURCH. By 1900, several Catholic families lived in Monument. A priest came from Colorado Springs to serve Sunday mass. In 1911, local carpenter Fred Schuett built St. Peter's. Charter members were Mitchell Lavelett, Jule Aubuchon, Sophia Wiscamb, Louise Ruppert, John Dolan, Patrick Murphy, Jim Pettigrew, Joe Lorraine, Ruel Aubuchon, Mary Brady, and Tom Long. The original church is located at 155 Jefferson Street in Monument.

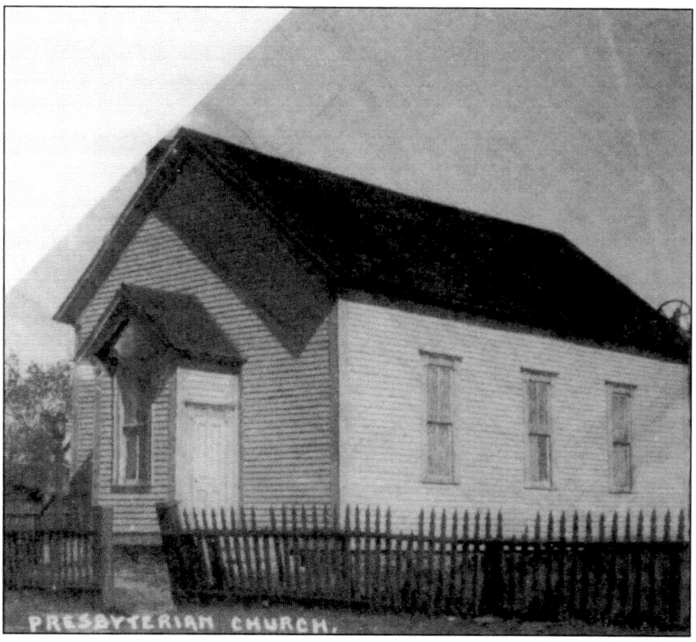

PRESBYTERIAN CHURCH, C. 1879. Monument's Presbyterian, Methodist, and Episcopal churches were active as early as 1874. The large bell on the Presbyterian church doubled as the town's fire alarm. When one of the area's pioneers died, the bell tolled once a minute for each year of his or her life. It tolled for the last time in 1914 upon the death of Christina Olfs. She died at age 71.

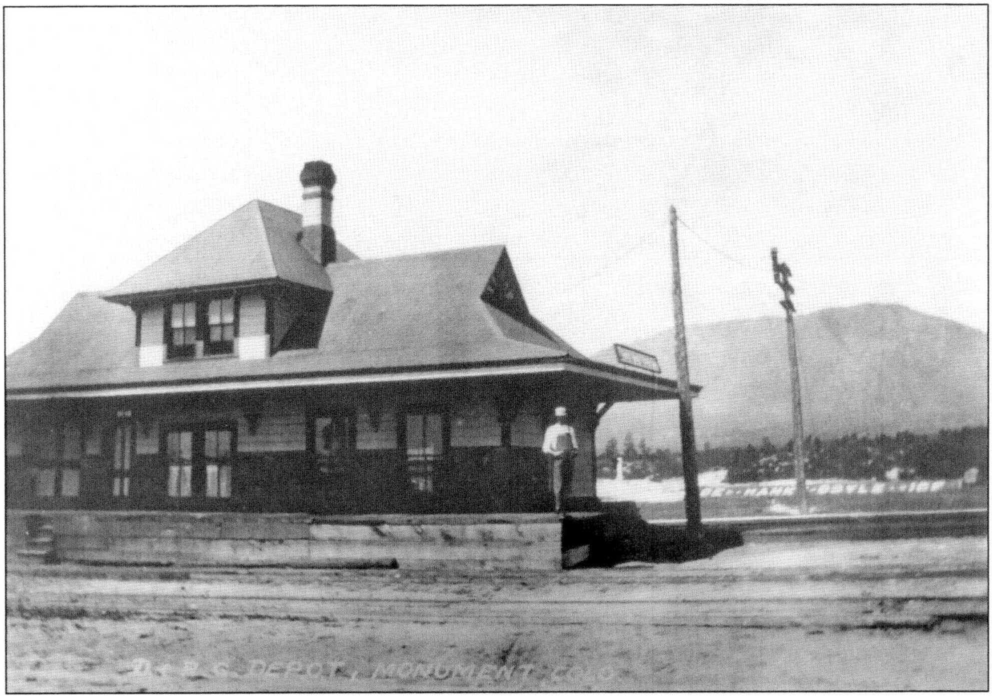

MONUMENT RAILROAD DEPOTS. In the late 1800s, two depots opened in Monument to accommodate the railroads. The Rio Grande Railroad Depot, pictured above, was built about 1872. Pictured below is the Santa Fe Depot in about 1939. The Santa Fe Railroad extended its line from Pueblo to Denver in 1887 and received the right of way to pass through Monument. Each depot had an agent and two "trick" operators who worked eight-hour shifts, six days a week. Both railroads also maintained stockyards that could hold several hundred head of cattle. The cattle were driven to town by area ranchers after roundup and held in the yards to be shipped to market by train.

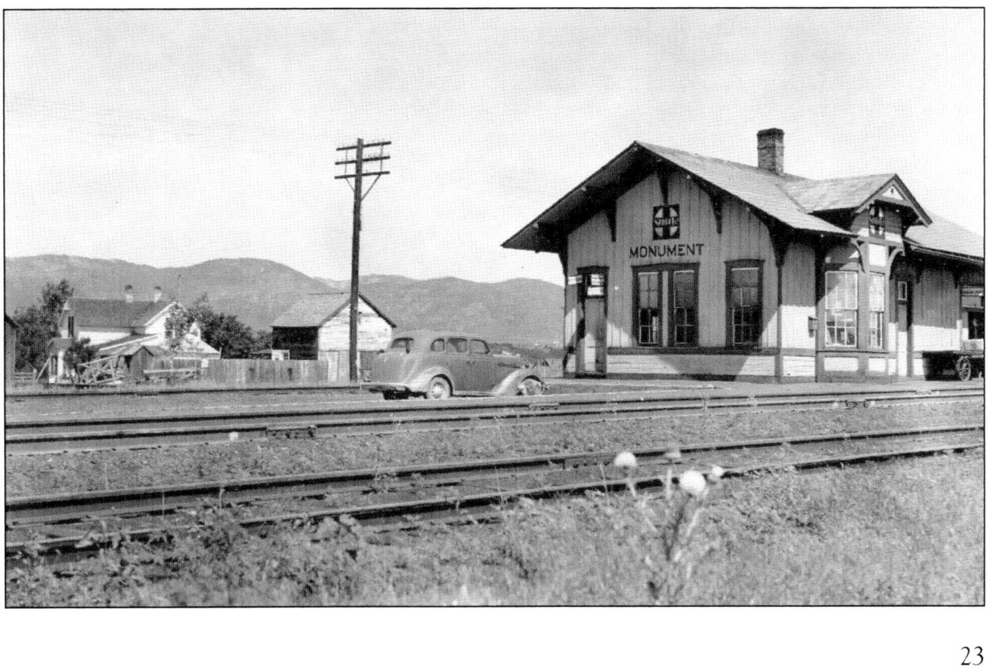

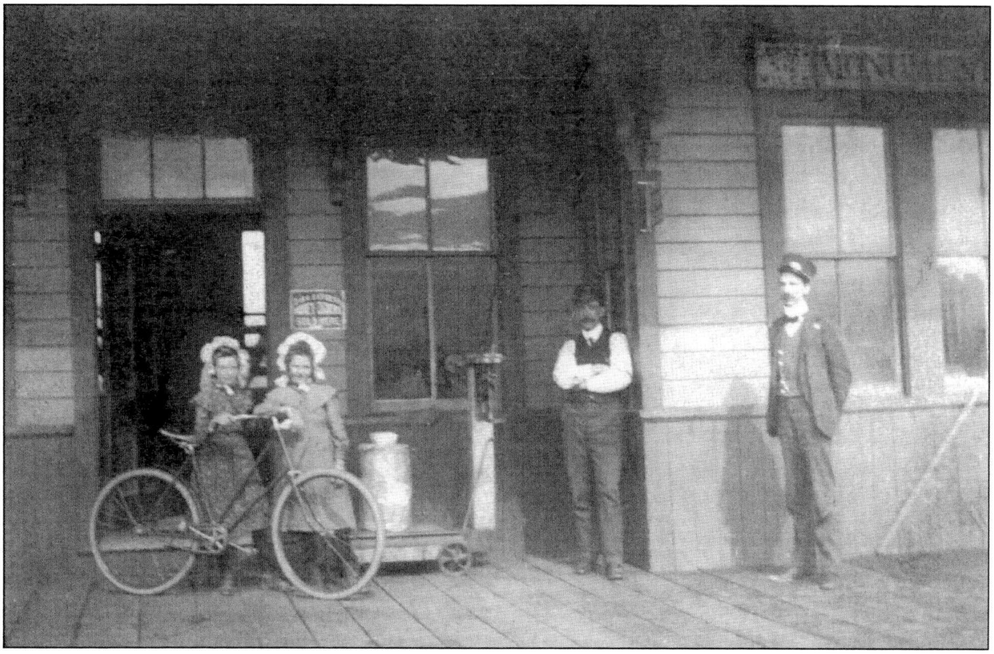

MADDOX, C. 1910, AND MONUMENT LAKE. The front of the Denver & Rio Grande Railroad Depot in Monument is seen above. Henry S. Maddox, the station agent, is shown in the center of the photograph. Maddox had also been the station agent in Palmer Lake. Almost everyone in the community conducted business transactions with the agent, who typically opened the depot around 7:00 a.m., except on Sunday. In 1891, the Colorado Assembly appropriated $30,000 to construct a lake on David McShane's property west of town on Monument Creek. Monument Lake was used for recreation, fishing, swimming, and to store water for irrigation. Pictured below are several individuals enjoying the lake. The four people in the boat are unidentified. The three people on the shore are, from left to right, Henry S. Maddox, his daughter Mate, and his wife Nettie.

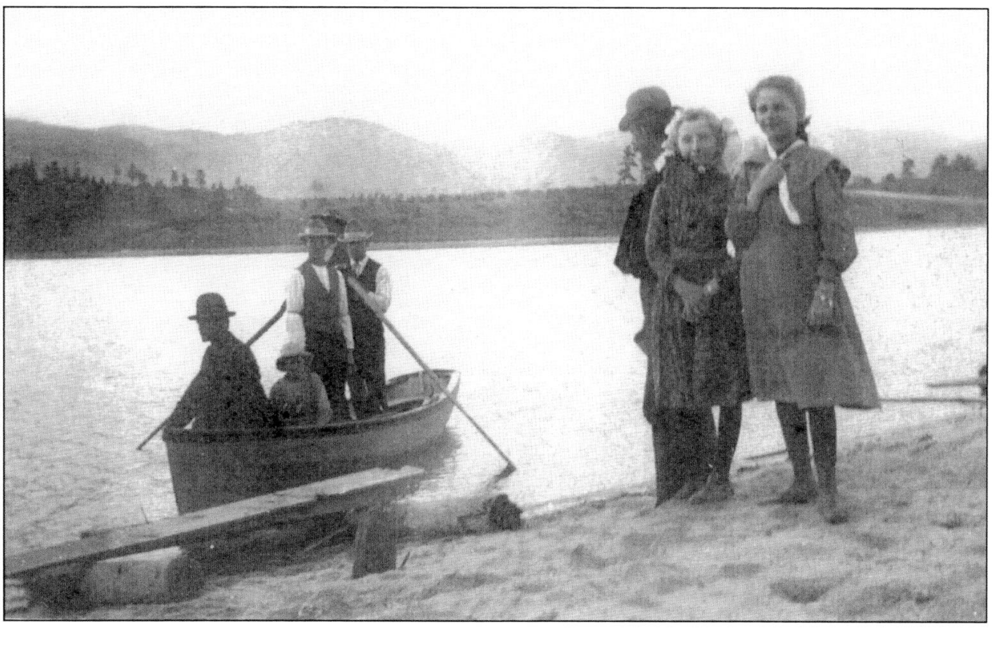

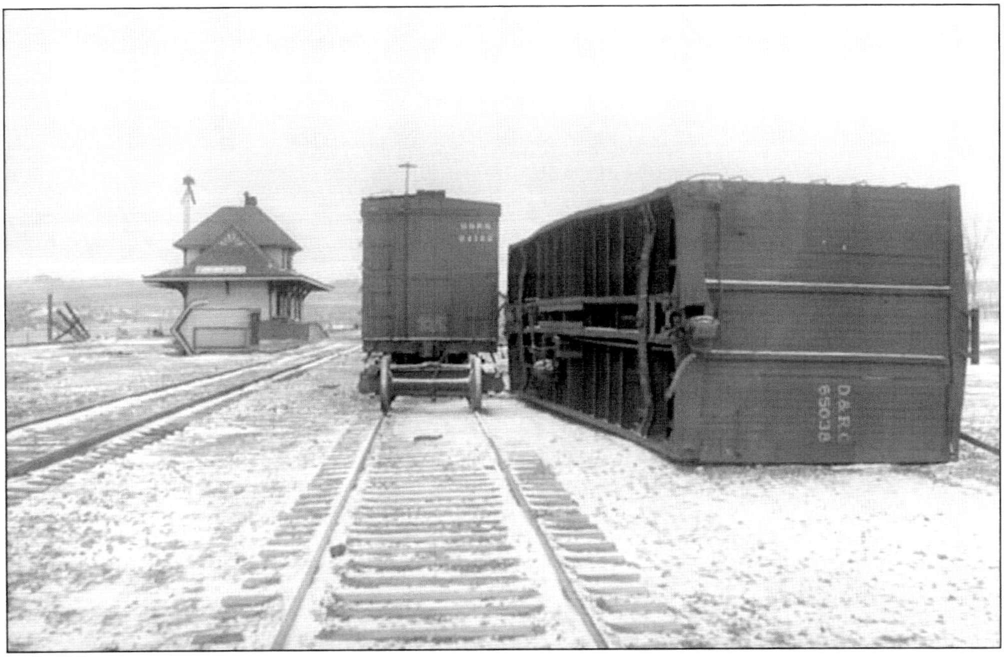

TRAIN MISHAPS. In the early years, train travel was perilous due to high winds, trains sharing the same track, human error, and equipment failures. A Denver & Rio Grande Railroad boxcar, pictured above, was blown over by high winds in about 1925. The Monument depot is on the left. Pictured below is the wreck of a Denver & Rio Grande Railroad train that occurred on July 17, 1895, in Monument, half a mile south of Second Street next to Beacon Light Road. The trestle, while being repaired, collapsed under the weight of the locomotive. Four people perished in the accident. (Both courtesy of the Younger Family.)

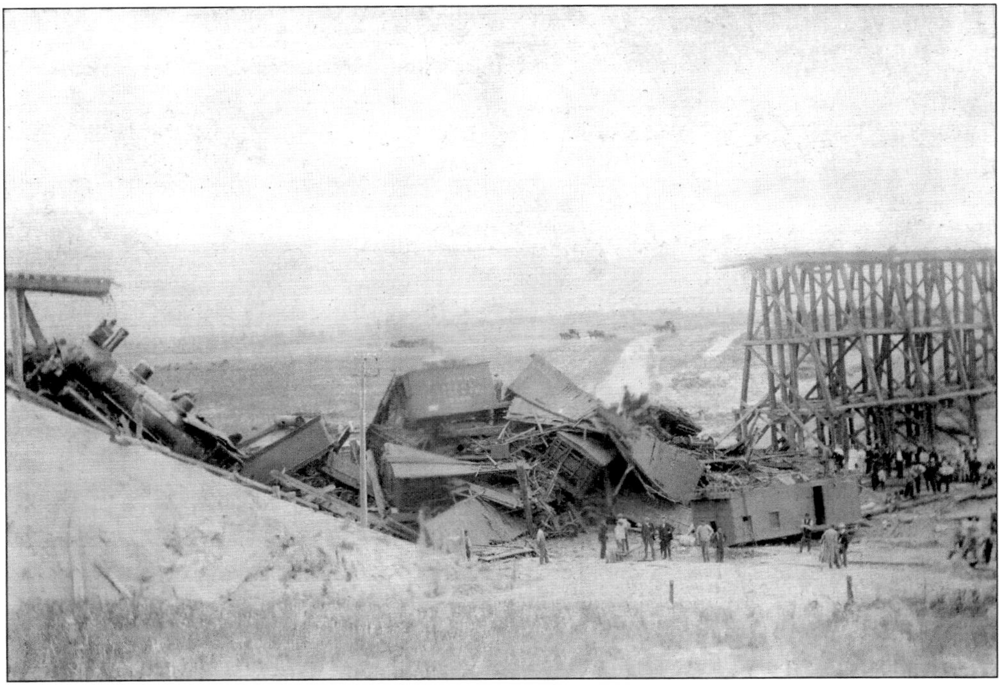

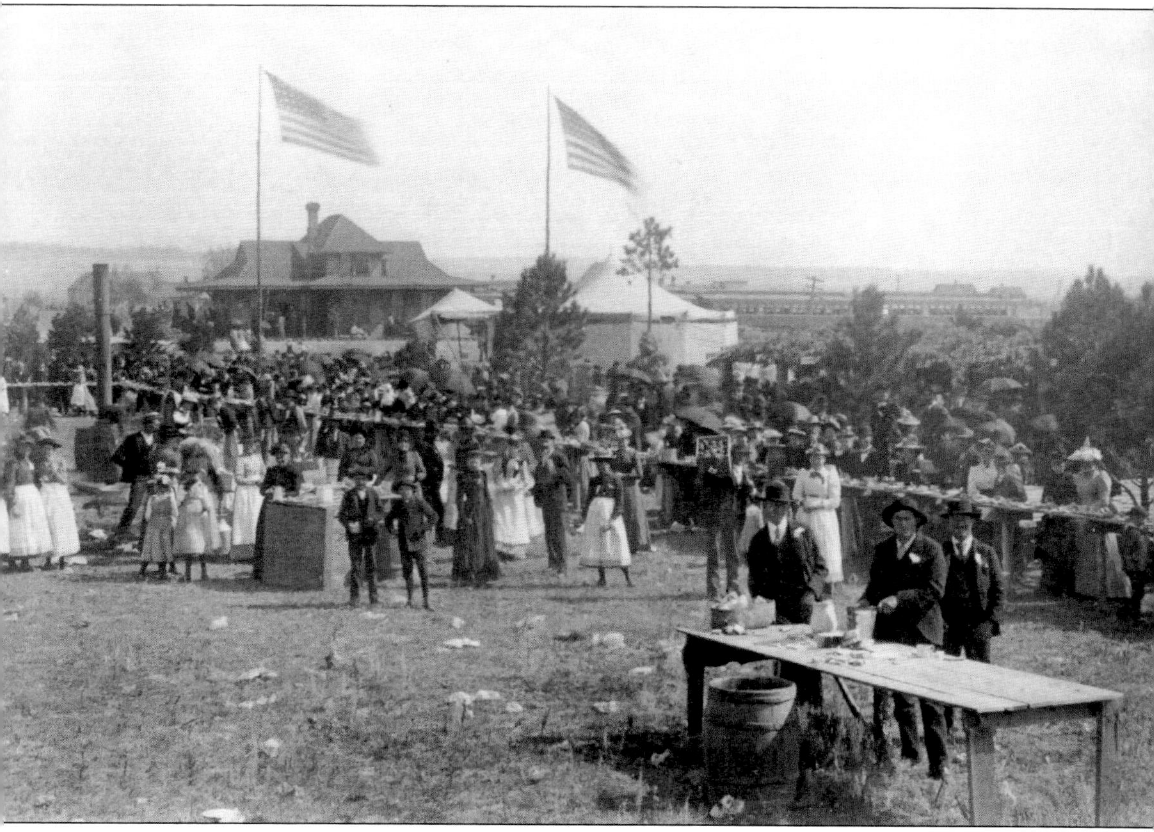

POTATO BAKE FESTIVAL, C. 1892. Potatoes were a major cash crop and the chief industry on the Palmer Divide for almost 20 years. Farmers took pride in the quality of their potatoes and the number they could produce per acre. In 1877, Paton Wilson produced 25,000 pounds to the acre, the average being 4,000 to 6,000 pounds per acre. It was estimated that Monument shipped 2,000 railroad cars of potatoes to destinations such as Denver, Colorado Springs, Kansas, Texas, New Mexico, and Arizona. Pictured above is the annual Potato Bake Festival held each October in Monument. This free festival drew 1,500 people who enjoyed two roasted beefs, four roasted sheep, two roasted hogs, 50 bushels of potatoes, homemade bread, and desserts. Beneath the two large American flags, a table formed in the shape of a large rectangle surrounded the fire pits used to bake the meat and potatoes. Diners ate standing at the board. The psyllid yellows, a blight caused by insects common on wild rose bushes, ended the commercial potato industry by 1900.

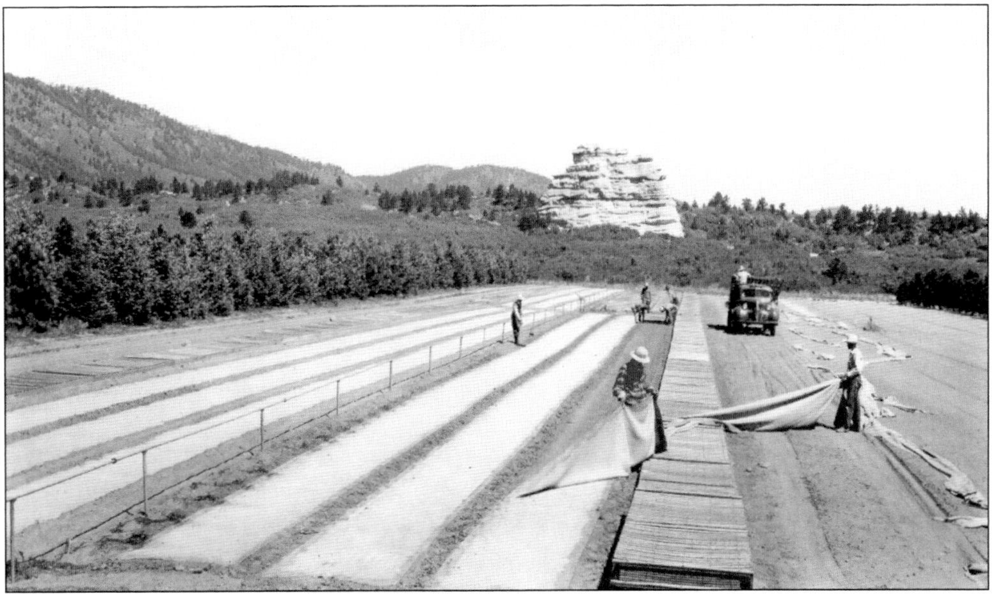

MONUMENT NURSERY, C. 1907. The Monument Nursery, pictured above, stretched below Monument Rock and Mount Herman. The nursery was established to provide trees to reforest 15,000 acres burned on Mount Herman in the 1880 forest fire. Seeds for the trees were extracted from pinecones. By 1926, the burned area was entirely reforested. The Civilian Conservation Corps (CCC) camp set up at the nursery during the Depression is seen below. The CCC camp provided work for men maintaining the environment. The men lived on the nursery, planted and harvested the trees, dug irrigation systems, and constructed Mount Herman Road. Two million trees were shipped annually from the nursery. The camp closed at the start of World War II. The nursery closed in 1965 when owners moved the business to Basalt, Colorado, where irrigation was available.

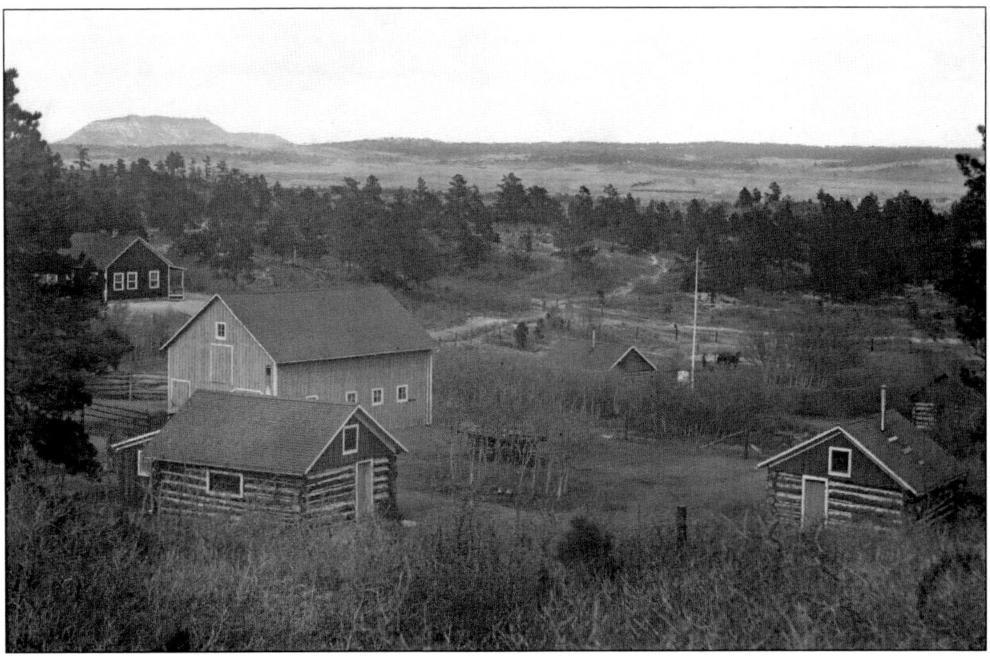

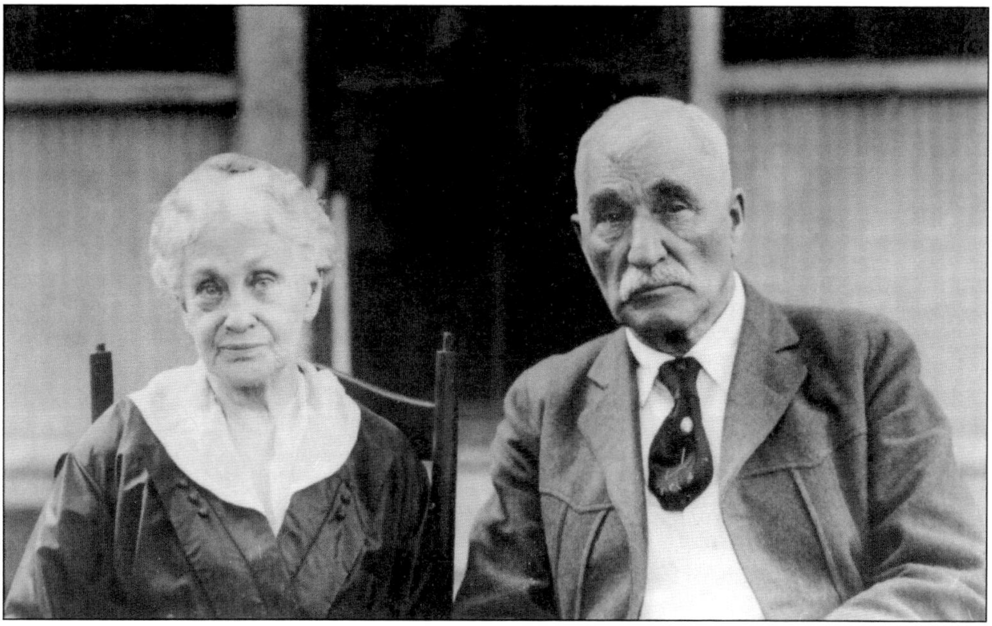

Colonel and Mrs. Ford. Colonel Ford and his wife are pictured above. The east side of the Monument Hotel, which Colonel Ford built in about 1870, is seen below. The hotel was located on Front Street. It had 19 large, well-ventilated rooms "furnished with the best of furniture and carpets, an elegant parlor," and "a cozy and comfortable reading room." A traveling journalist named "Tenderfoot" visited the Palmer Divide area in September 1878. He wrote that Col. Ford "is a born landlord . . . His hearty greeting makes one feel at home immediately. The dining room and culinary departments have the personal supervision of Mrs. Ford, whom we found to be a lady with rare qualities for the position she occupies." The hotel burned to the ground in March 1922.

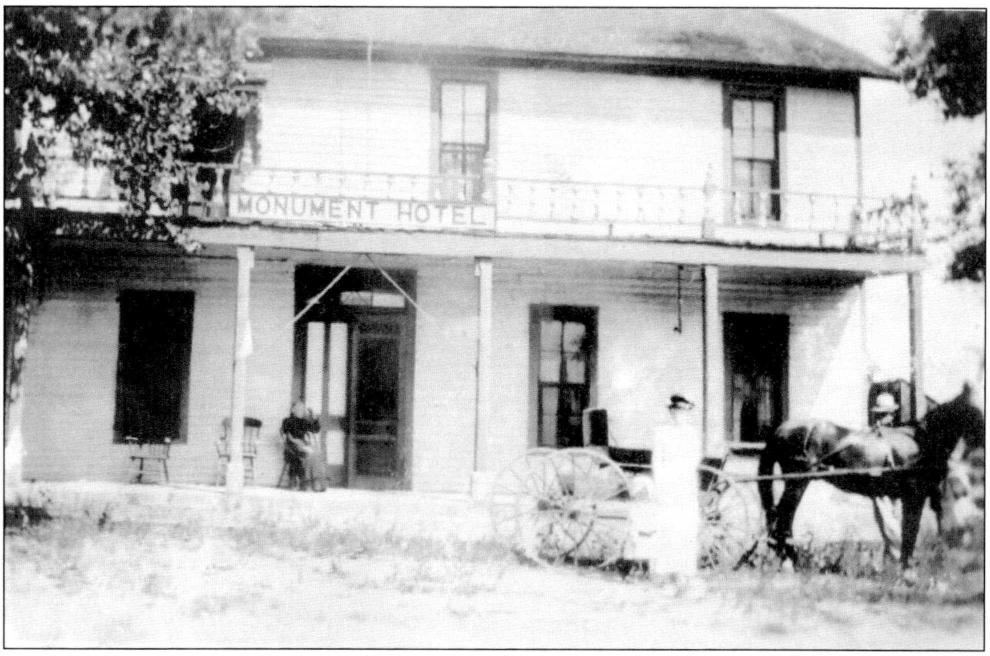

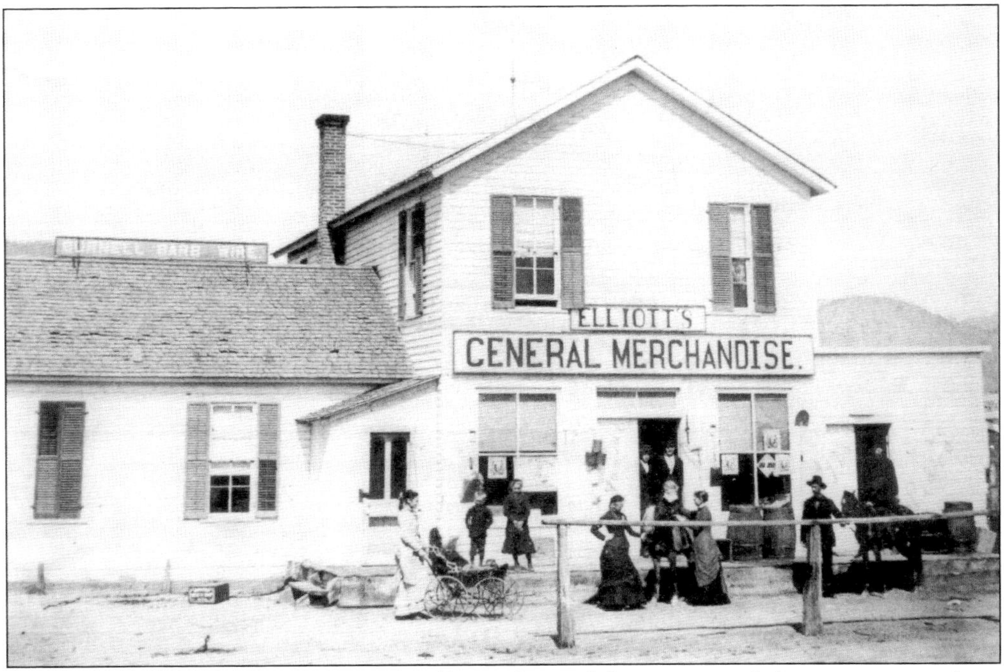

Merchandise Store and Repository. Elliott's General Store, pictured above, is seen in about 1886. The store was opened in 1879 on Front Street by Robert C. Elliott, a prominent man in Monument, and his partner, J. W. Mudge. Elliot married Mudge's daughter, Fanny. They were a hardworking couple who ran the store, a cheese factory, and the Carriage and Wagon Repository. Pictured below is the repository in about 1892. Just above the door is the advertisement for Studebaker Wagons, precursor of the Studebaker automobile. Until the advent of the automobile, liveries such as Elliott's were the full service transportation centers of the time. In 1889, Elliott was appointed as a town trustee. He also served as town clerk from May 1887 to April 1896. He and John Dickinson were on a committee that purchased Monument's three streetlights. The lights were coal oil lanterns on posts and cost $19.35.

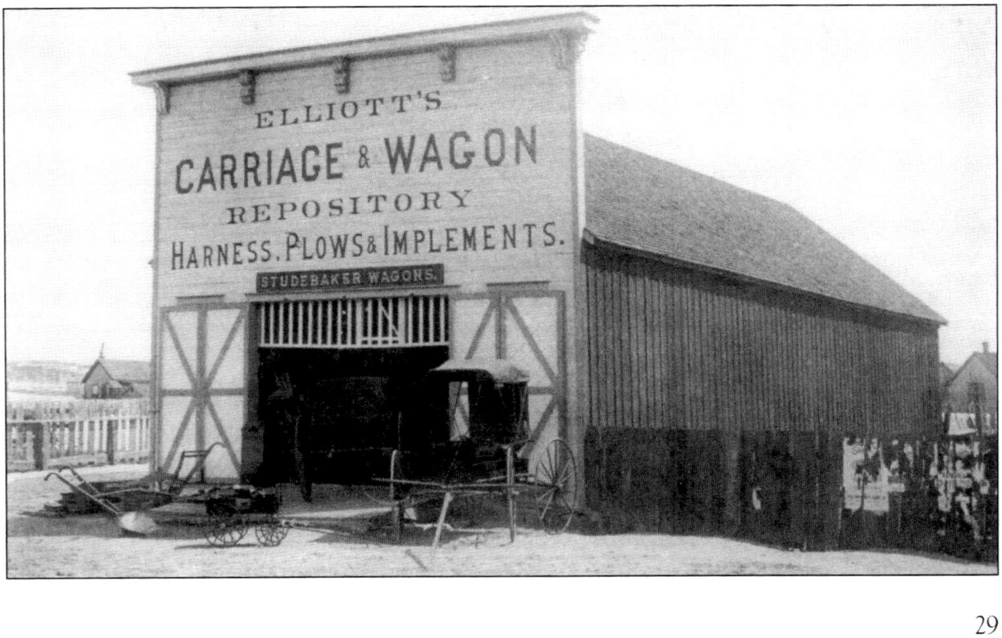

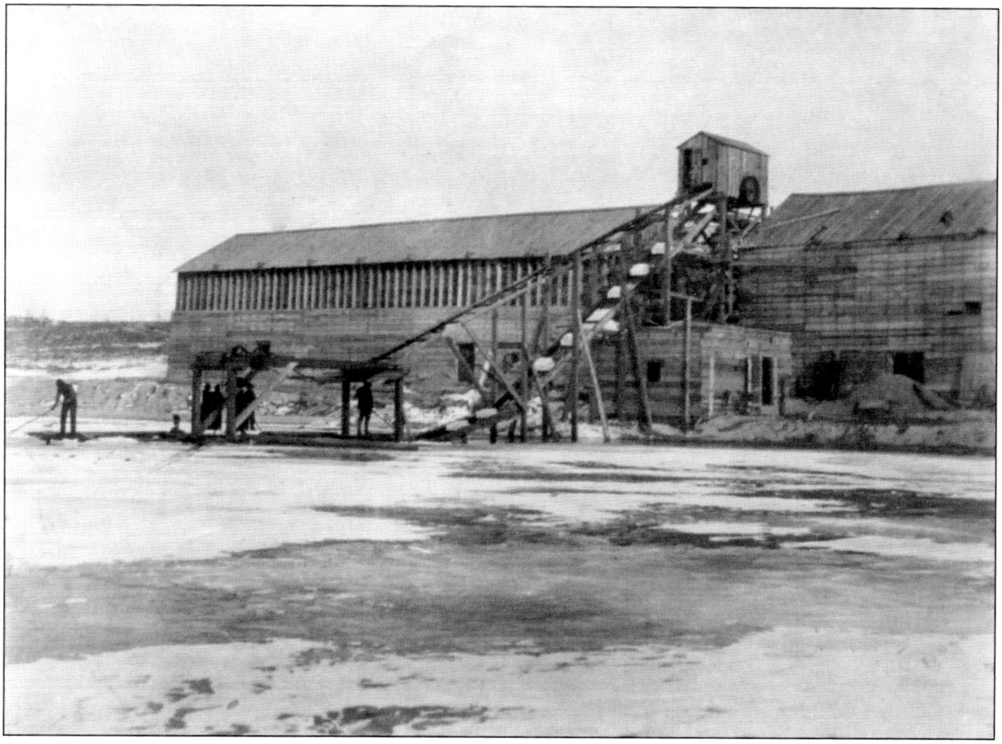

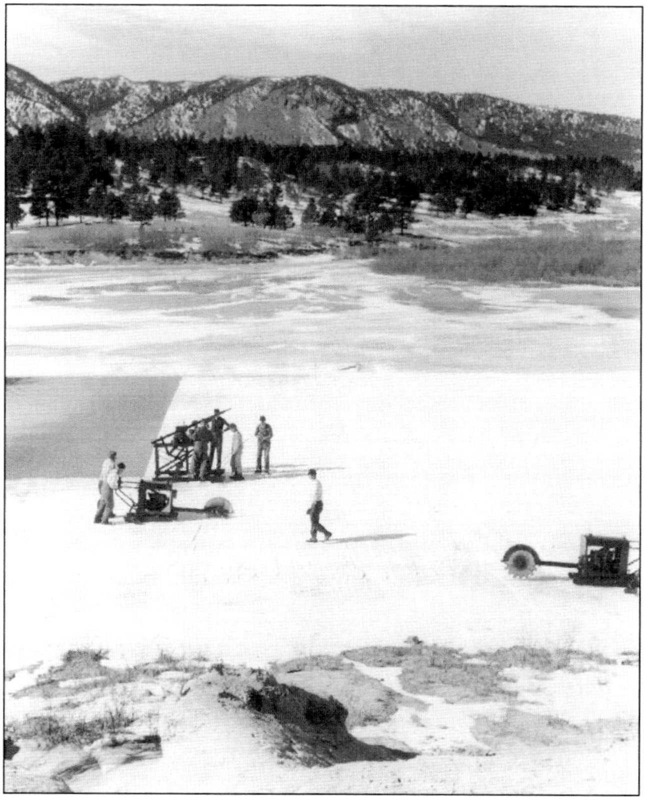

Monument Ice Harvest. Monument's first icehouse, which was built on Monument Lake in about 1901 by W. E. Doyle and Thomas Hanks, is pictured above. At left, several unidentified men use a saw powered by gasoline to cut the ice. Before the saw was available, ice was grooved by horse-drawn grooving knives that cut the ice into a parallel block pattern. Then a tool with prongs on one end was used to cut the ice into cakes. A pike pole pushed the cakes up the chute into the icehouse, where the cakes were covered in sawdust. In winter, a man could work 10-hour days for seven days a week and earn 40¢ per hour. A man with a team of eight horses earned $2 per day. In 1909, Doyle bought out Hanks and constructed five new icehouses.

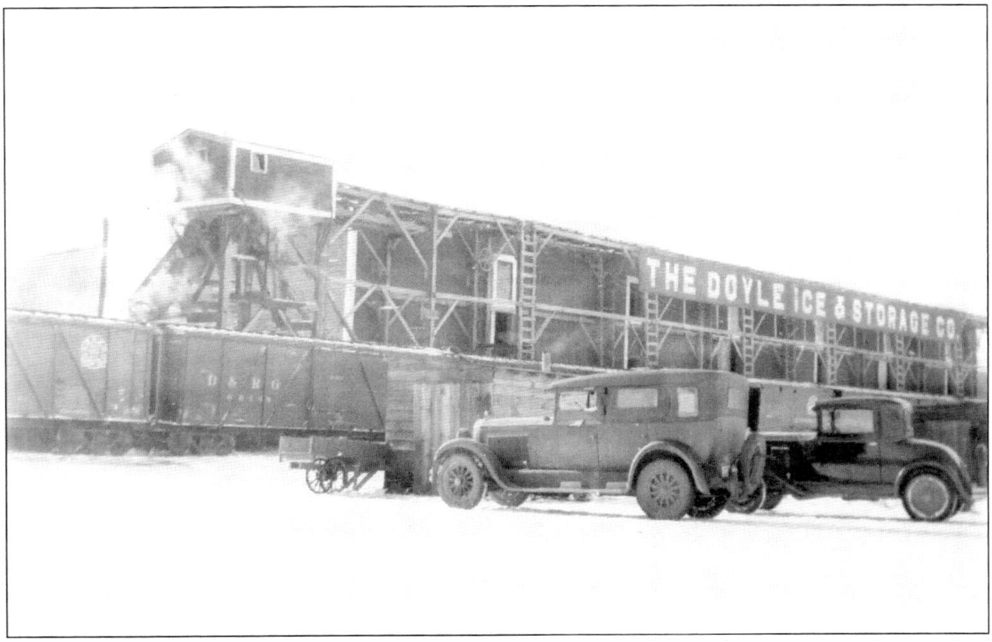

Loading the Ice for Shipment, c. 1923. Each of W. E. Doyle's ice houses or warehouses had a conveyor powered by a threshing machine steam engine owned and operated by Hugo and Charlie Schubarth. Ice was loaded directly into railroad cars that sat on a spur railroad track. During the summer, 20 men worked for 40 days to ship the ice to Colorado markets.

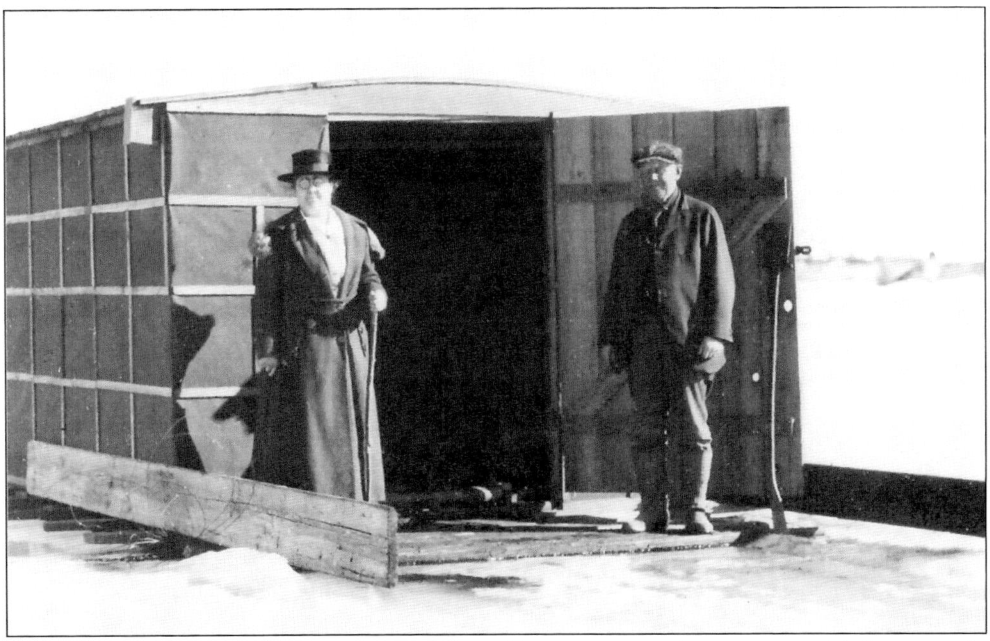

End of a Business. Until 1930, W. E. Doyle and his wife enjoyed a prosperous life because of a 20-year contract with American Refrigerated Transit. In 1930, the ice crop failed due to a warm winter. Because his contract had no escape clause, Doyle went from riches to rags and was forced to sell the business. Eventually, warmer winters and the introduction of refrigeration ended the ice harvest business.

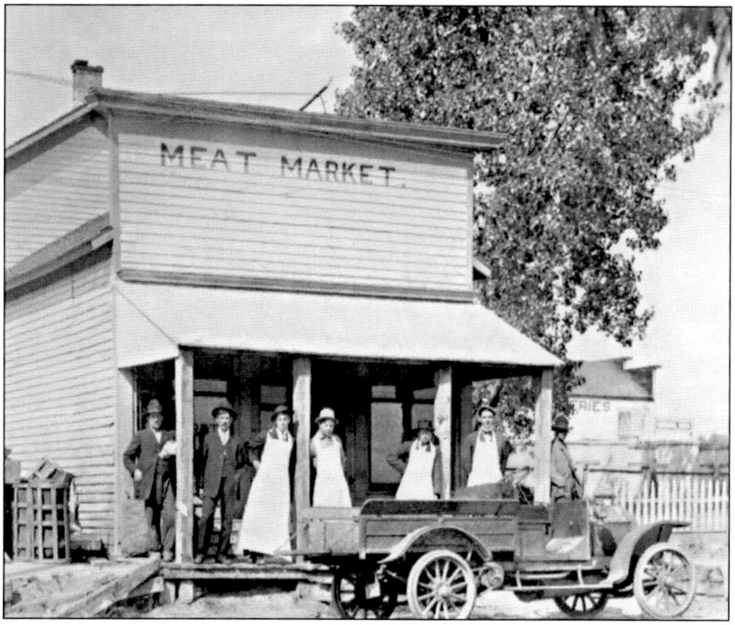

Meat Market, c. 1916. George Betz owned the meat market and operated the post office, which was located on 2nd Street, west of Washington Street. The butcher gave away the livers, kidneys, brains, and bones from the beef and cracklings after the lard was rendered from the pork. Sam Putman and Bail Simpson, boarders sleeping on the second floor, died when the building caught fire.

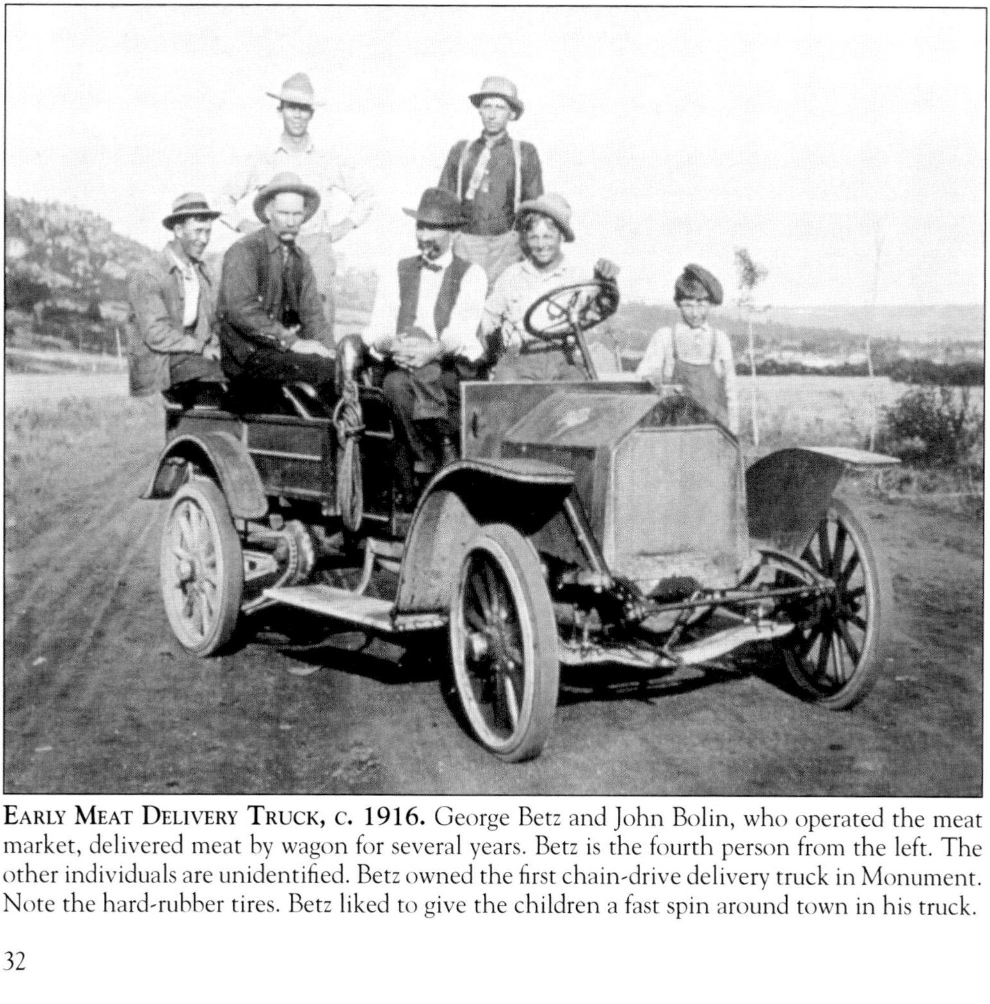

Early Meat Delivery Truck, c. 1916. George Betz and John Bolin, who operated the meat market, delivered meat by wagon for several years. Betz is the fourth person from the left. The other individuals are unidentified. Betz owned the first chain-drive delivery truck in Monument. Note the hard-rubber tires. Betz liked to give the children a fast spin around town in his truck.

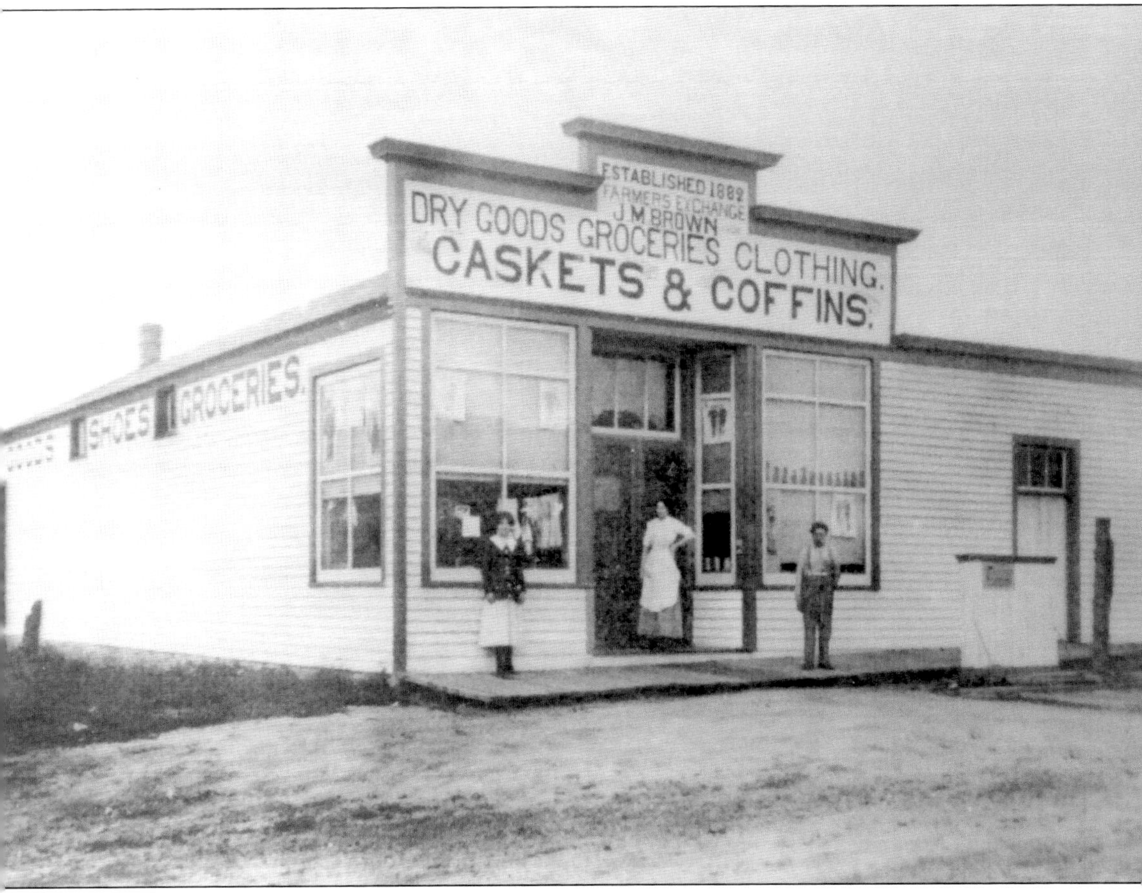

Caskets, Coffins, and Candy, c. 1889. Will Lierd's general merchandise store, later owned by J. M. Brown, opened for business in 1882. The store sold dry goods, shoes, and groceries, as well as caskets, coffins, and candy. Three pairs of men's socks cost 25¢. A special showcase displayed hard candy. A big seller was plug tobacco, and a special cutter on the counter was used to cut off a plug. A good coffin cost $50. Lierd threatened to sue one family for not paying for their $50 coffin. He earned the name "Penny Lierd" when the family paid what they owed in pennies and insisted that Lierd count them out one by one. Bertha Curry, Monument's last undertaker, laid the deceased's body out in a chosen bedroom where family members and friends sat up all night with the body. In the summer, tubs were filled with ice and set on the floor under the coffin to preserve the body until the funeral.

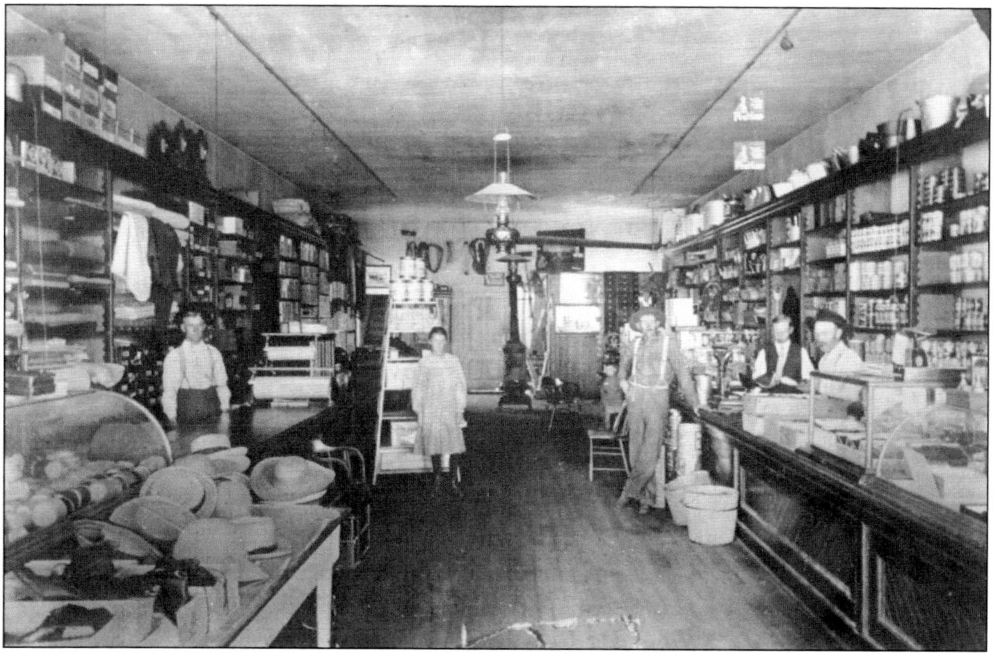

General Store. Seen above, the Higby Mercantile Company was opened in 1900 by J. W. Higby. The store was in continuous operation for 67 years. Higby's son, William, worked in the store after he graduated from East Denver High School in 1906 and later served as treasurer and mayor of Monument. He was elected state representative from El Paso County, state senator, and lieutenant governor. He also served on the Colorado Springs Board of Health. Below, several unidentified people stand on a 20-foot snowdrift in front of Higby's store after a 1913 storm that struck in early fall. Pearl Dutton, who lived 10 miles east of Monument, wrote, "After the storm my father and neighbors drove thirty head of horses to Monument to break the road to town. Everyone was out of groceries."

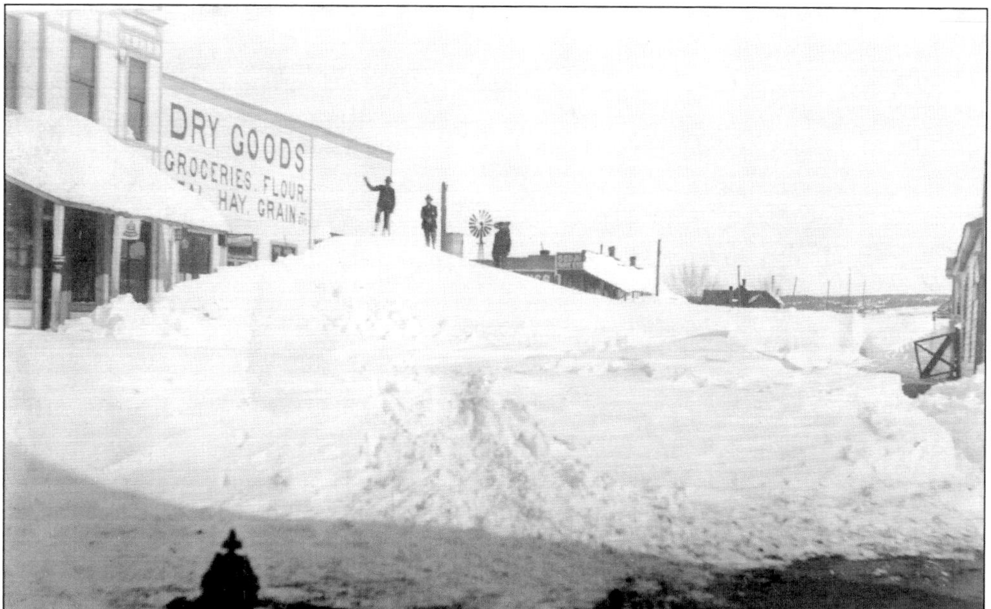

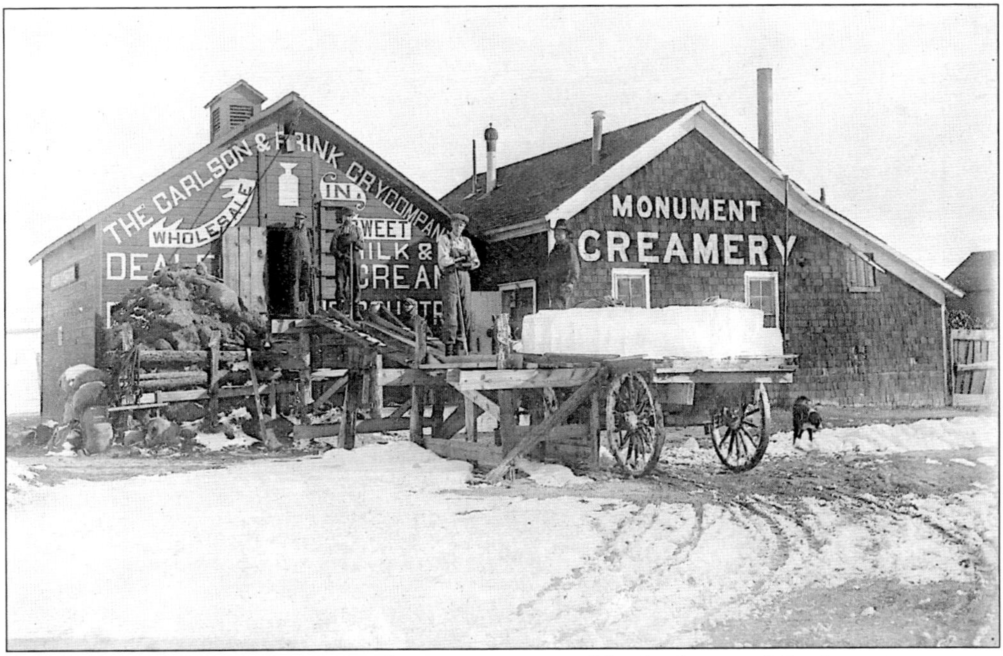

Monument Creamery, c. 1906. The creamery owned by Carlson and Frink receives an ice delivery, above. Each can of milk was placed in a canvas jacket filled with ice before delivery. The creamery shipped several loads of milk each day by rail. The creamery made thousands of pounds of Black Diamond cheese every year and shipped it all over the country. Andrew and Florence Cobel, operators of the creamery, were known for what was considered to be the best cheese in Colorado. A milk delivery to the creamery is depicted below. From left to right are Joe Pettigrew and Patrick Murphy hauling milk from Spring Valley. This provided their only cash income until harvest time. Milk sold for 10¢ a gallon.

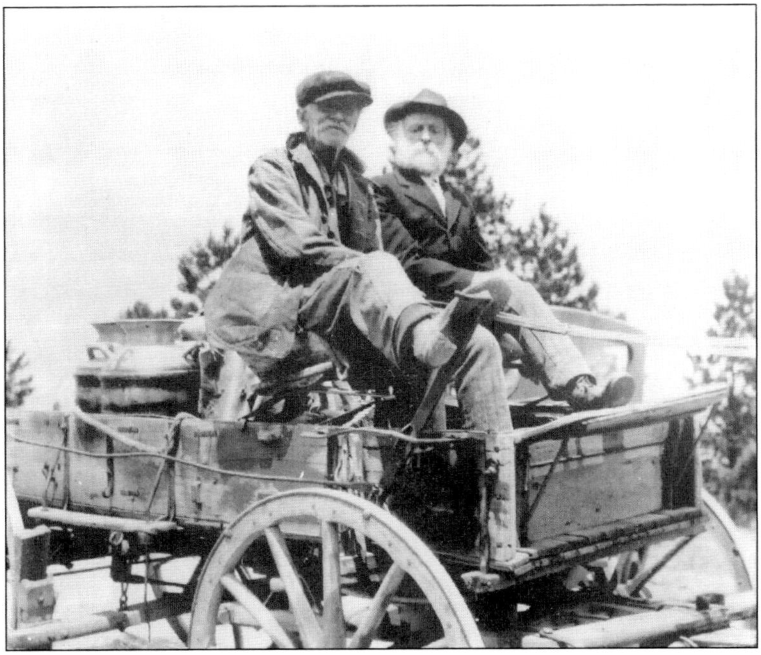

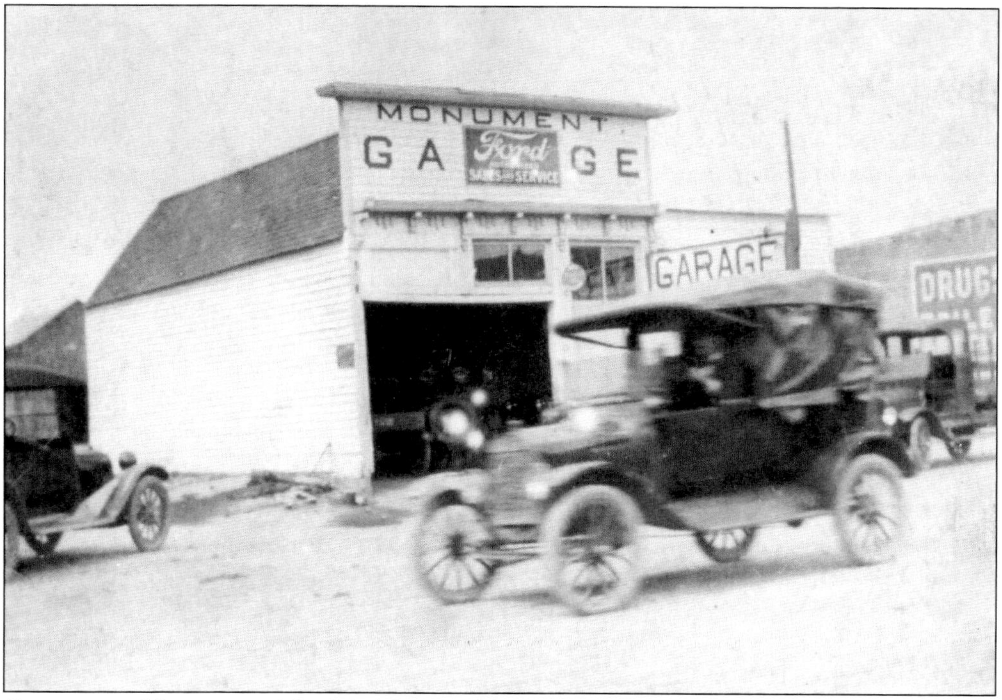

GARAGES IN MONUMENT. The Model T Ford became popular in the Monument area around 1912. The first auto service garage in Monument, above, was built by W. E. Higby about 1914. Pictured below is a second garage built by J. M. Umberger, who was Higby's first mechanic. Umberger built his garage in 1929 on the east side of Highway105 after the highway bypassed Monument's business district in 1928. The Greenland Lantern Cafe, next to the garage, was owned by Harry and Laura Stiefel. Laura was noted for her delicious homemade pies. Harry operated Harry's Barbershop, which occupied space in part of the building. There was a third garage on the east side of Front Street. The garages did a flourishing business, as the Model T had a "hard time pulling uphill from Denver to Monument."

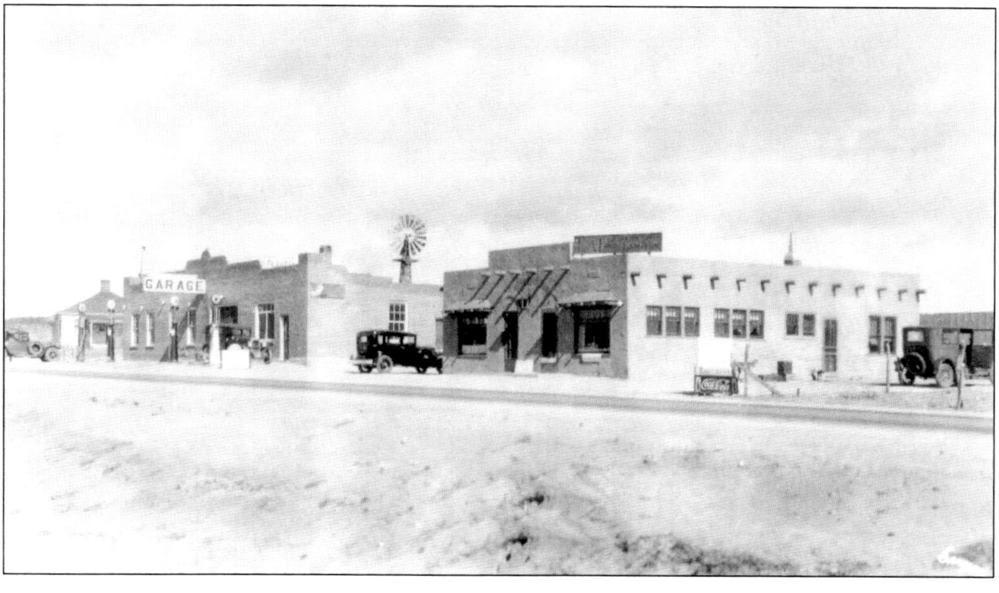

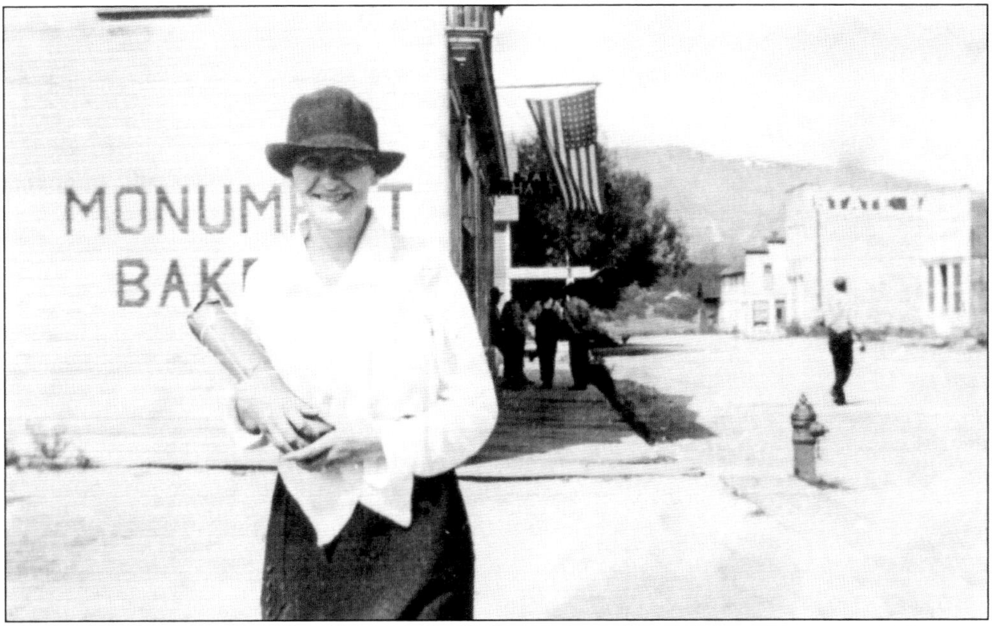

MONUMENT STORES. Maude Dolan-Willis is depicted in front of the Monument Bakery on Second Street about 1918. She and her best friend, Nellie McShane, had reputations as mischief makers. At an April Fools' community dance, the girls handed out Feenamint laxative chewing gum, treating the chaperones first. The chaperones, who watched the young people with eagle eyes, were the first to leave the building seeking the outhouse. After a while, "the dancers, instead of doing the two-step, were doing the Colorado quickstep!" Below is E. Vaiden Hunt standing in the doorway of his store, White Front Shoe and Harness Repair, in about 1922. An ad for the store, which was located on Front Street, stated that he had the only complete, modern shop between Denver and Colorado Springs. He received and delivered shoes by mail.

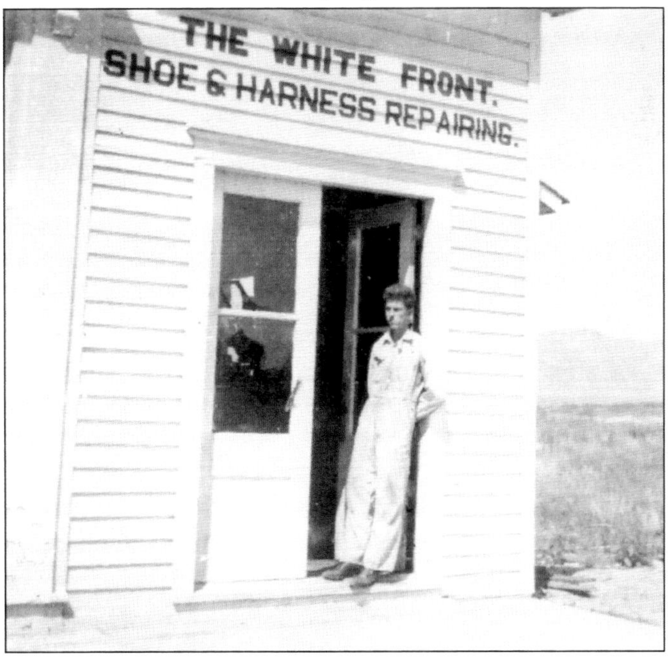

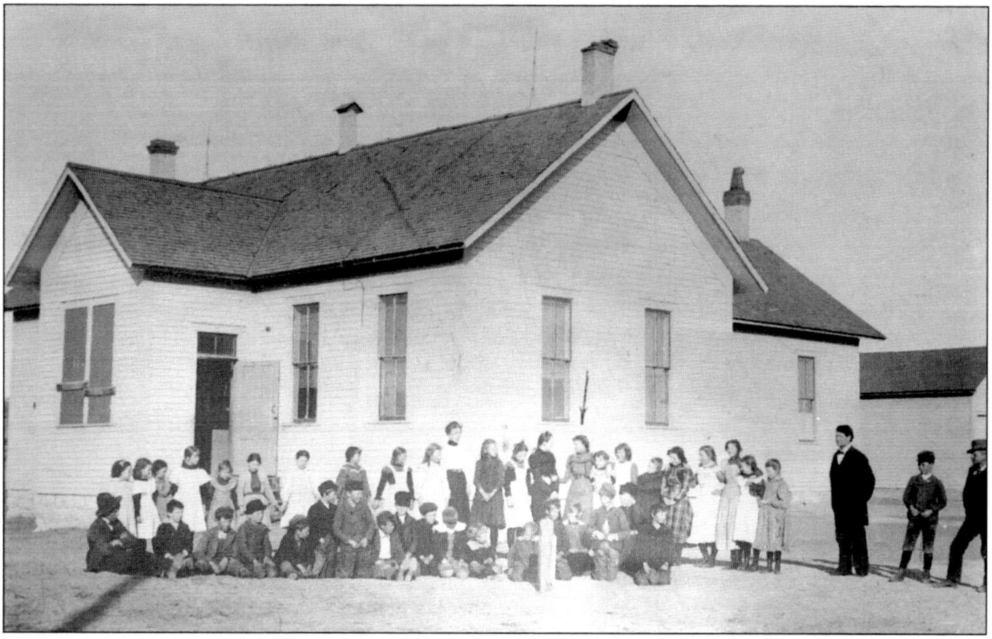

Early Monument School. The first Monument school was a one-room log building. In the 1880s, this three-room white frame building was built for grades one through eight. The third room served as a playroom in cold weather. After the building no longer functioned as a school, it was used as a garage and bus maintenance shop until it was torn down in 1970.

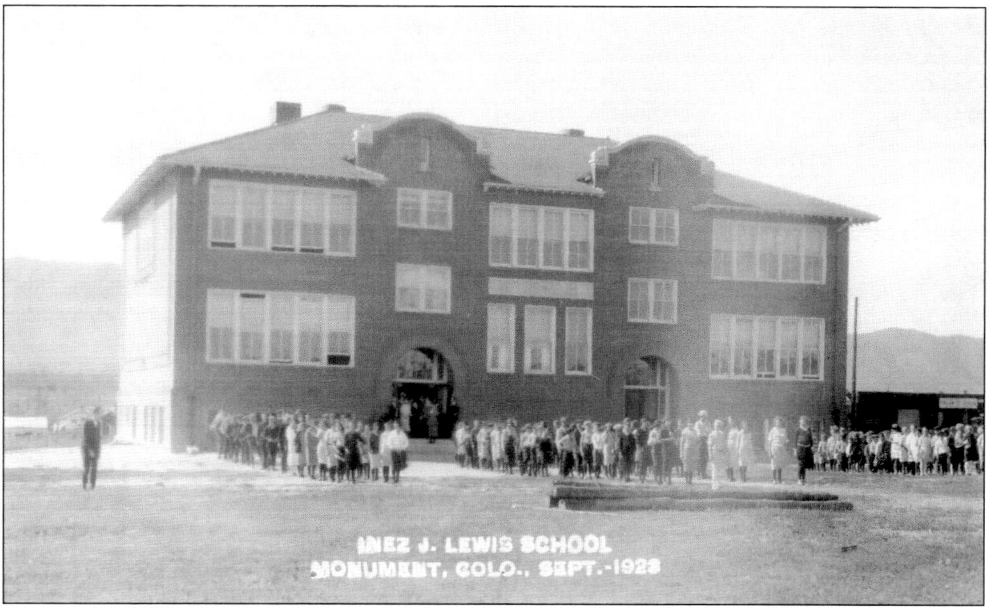

Lewis Consolidated School. In 1917, Inez Johnson Lewis, El Paso County's superintendent, began consolidating one-room schools. The new consolidated school opened in 1920 and was named the Lewis School in her honor. Today the school building is affectionately referred to as "Big Red" for its red bricks. In the 1930s, Palmer Lake School, District Number 33, consolidated with Lewis Consolidated School, District Number 5, to create Lewis Palmer School District 38.

MONUMENT GIRLS' BASKETBALL TEAM, 1926. Although all the rural schools were small, they all had sports teams. Pictured is the girls' basketball team of Lewis Consolidated High School. The only player identified is Mildred Hagedorn, who is second from the left.

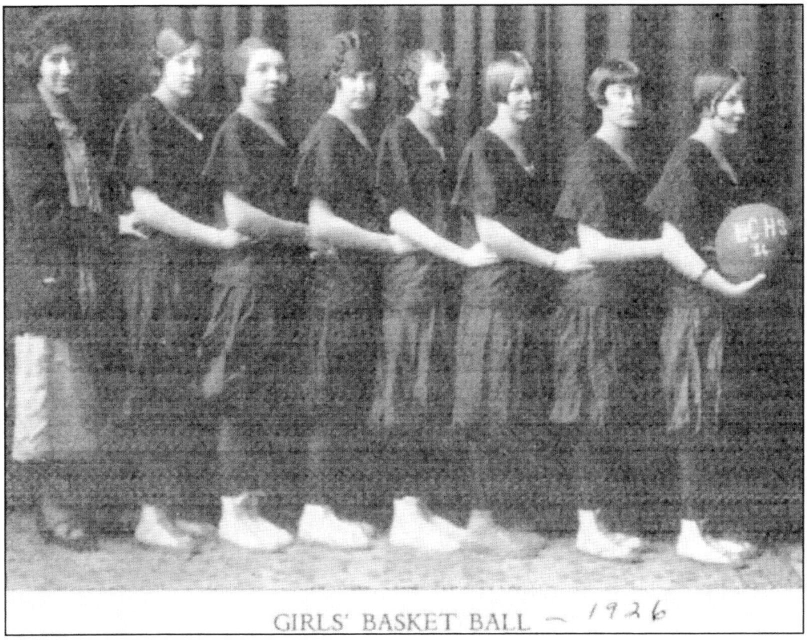

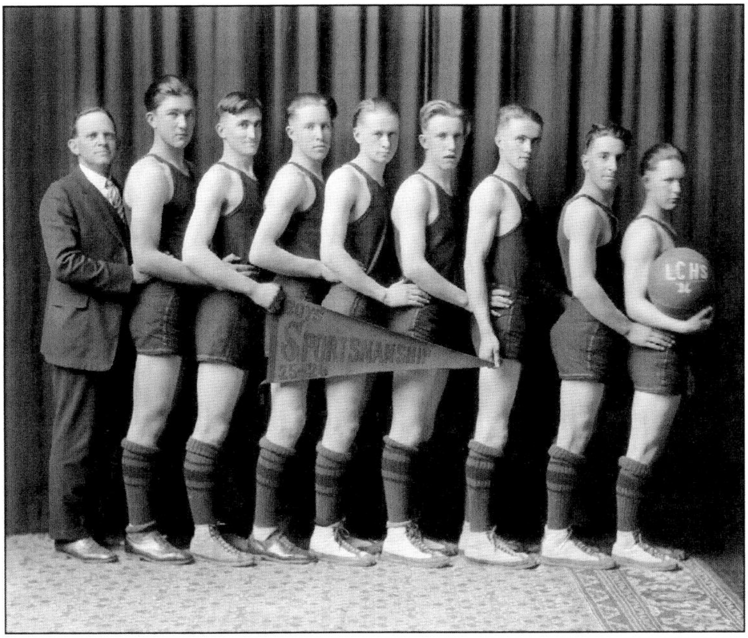

MONUMENT BOYS' BASKETBALL TEAM, 1926. Pictured is the boys' basketball team of Lewis Consolidated High School. From left to right are N. J. Rice, Frank Barnhart, Russell Hagen, Gregory Dwyer, Byron Medlock, Wilbur Emery Bovard, Bert Gossage, Paul Losey, and John Burnhart. Medlock later became mayor of Palmer Lake and Bovard the mayor of Monument.

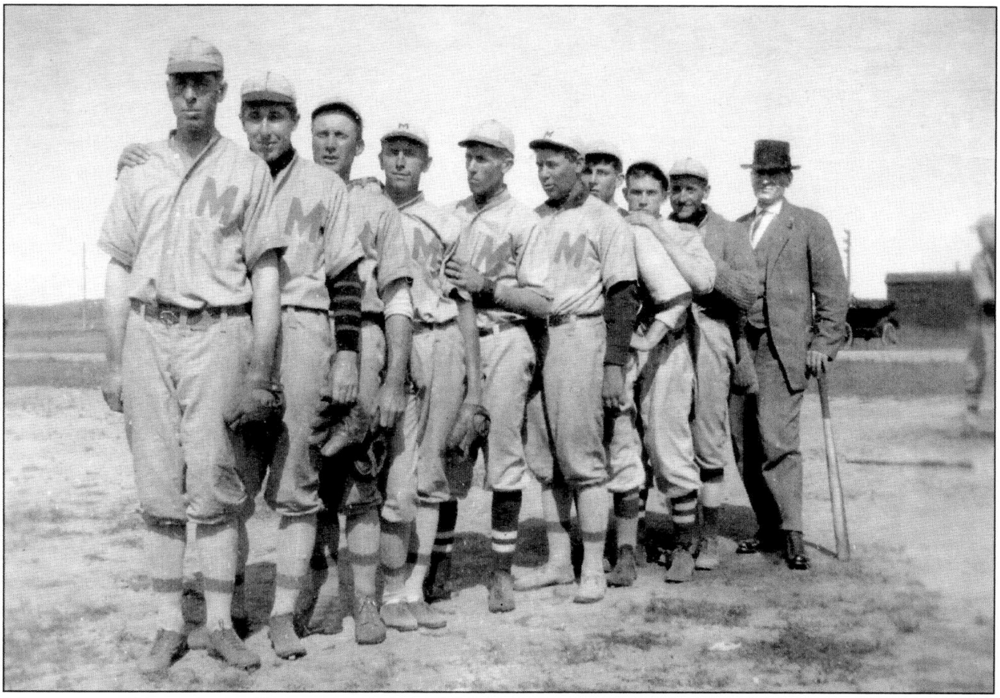

Monument Baseball Team. Pictured above is Monument's baseball team. The team won the El Paso County Baseball Championship in 1916. The team sponsored dances and sought sponsors to help buy uniforms and meet expenses. After the games, everyone went to Ed Hunter's lunchroom to enjoy hand-churned ice cream in a cone for 5¢.

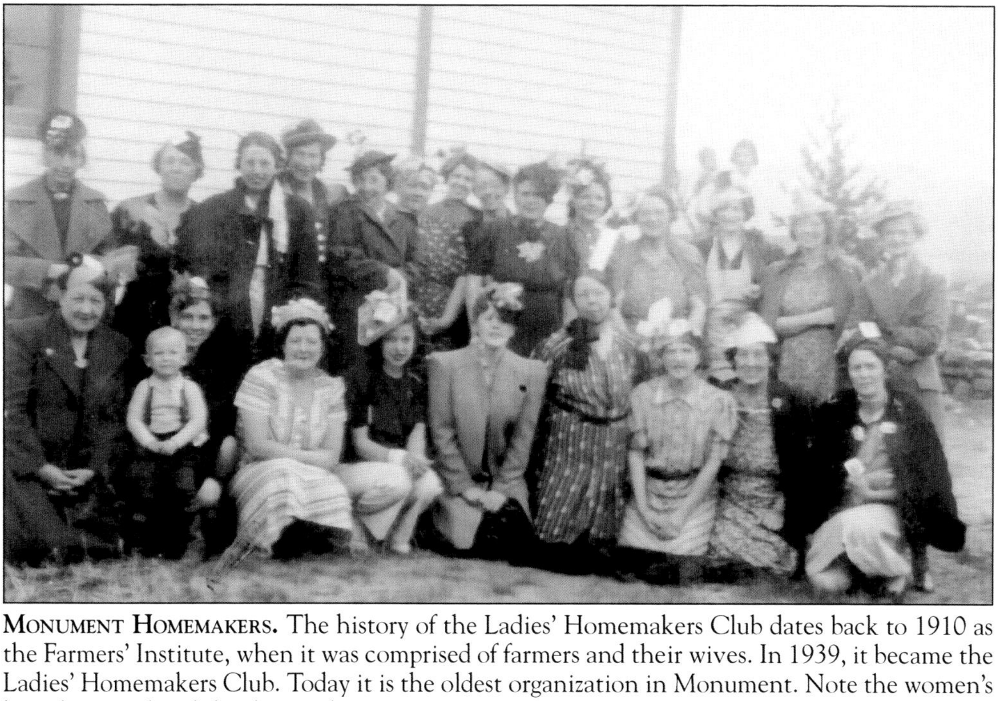

Monument Homemakers. The history of the Ladies' Homemakers Club dates back to 1910 as the Farmers' Institute, when it was comprised of farmers and their wives. In 1939, it became the Ladies' Homemakers Club. Today it is the oldest organization in Monument. Note the women's hats decorated with kitchen gadgets.

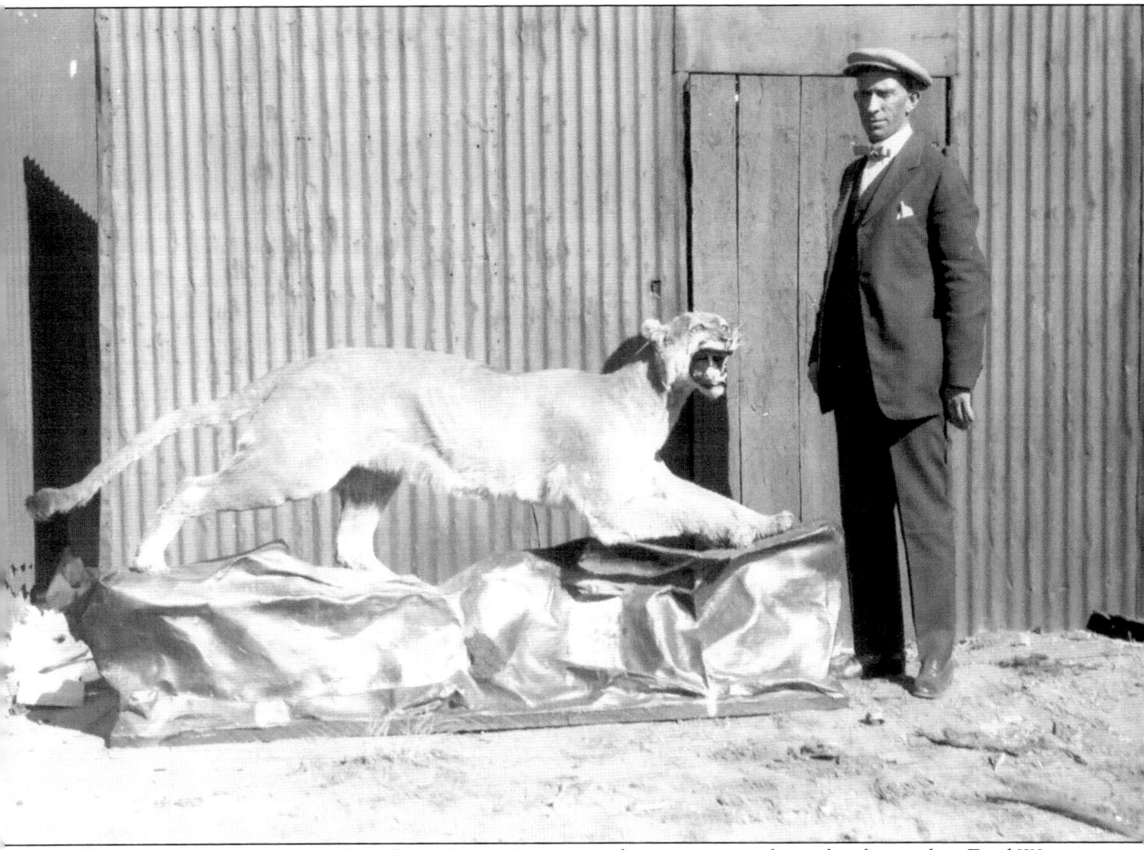

"Old Disappearance." In October 1922, Monument farmers were relieved to learn that Fred W. Simpson had killed a huge mountain lion that had been killing calves and young stock for years. With the aid of his dog, Rover, Simpson tracked the lion for three hours over the snow before it was treed and brought down by a .22 caliber bullet through its brain. "Old Disappearance," as the lion was named by the ranchers, had killed more than 30 calves. Wilbur Doughty had suffered more losses than neighboring ranchers. The lion weighed 160 pounds and measured 8 feet and 2 inches tip to tip, with paws 5 inches across. Based on the number of broken teeth and scars on its skin, the lion was estimated to be 15 years old. For his effort, Simpson was awarded a bounty of $25 by the *Denver Post*. Old Disappearance now resides on permanent display at the Lucretia Vaile Museum in Palmer Lake.

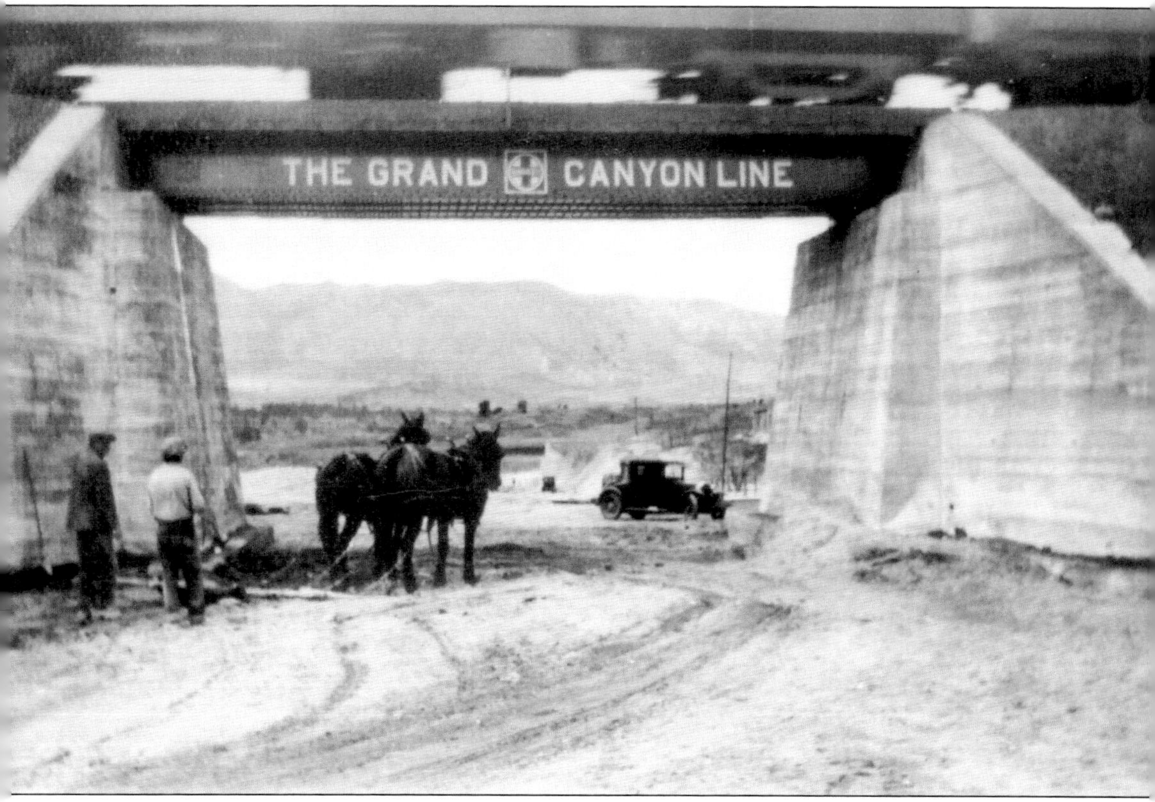

GATEWAY TO PALMER LAKE AND POINTS NORTH, C. 1927. The Santa Fe Railroad underpass on Highway 105 was once located just east of Washington Street. From left to right are John Bovard and Clarence Lavelett. With their horses and scrapers, they prepared the new roadbed for the highway that opened in 1928. The new paved road improved "the ribbon of death," as the road between Monument and Larkspur was sometimes called. When this new road bypassed Monument's business district, some merchants shifted their businesses to the new highway. This first paved road between Colorado Springs and Denver opened up travel connecting Monument, Palmer Lake, Greenland, Larkspur, and Sedalia.

Three

Town of Palmer Lake

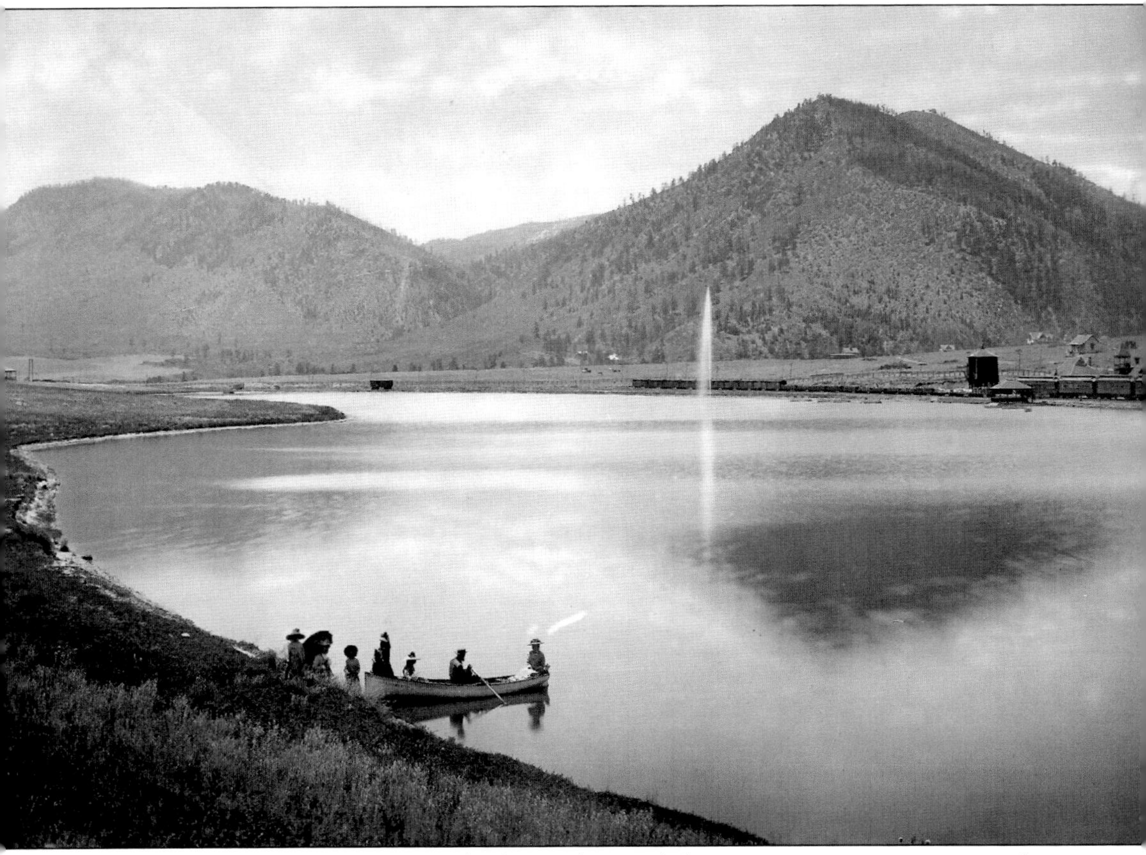

Palmer Lake. The picturesque town of Palmer Lake, nestled against majestic mountains on the Palmer Divide, began as a small settlement situated near the lakeshore. It included a crude log depot and a section house that supported the Denver & Rio Grande Railroad. In the late 1800s and early 1900s, the town flourished as a tourist attraction. (Jackson Print from the Palmer Lake Historical Society.)

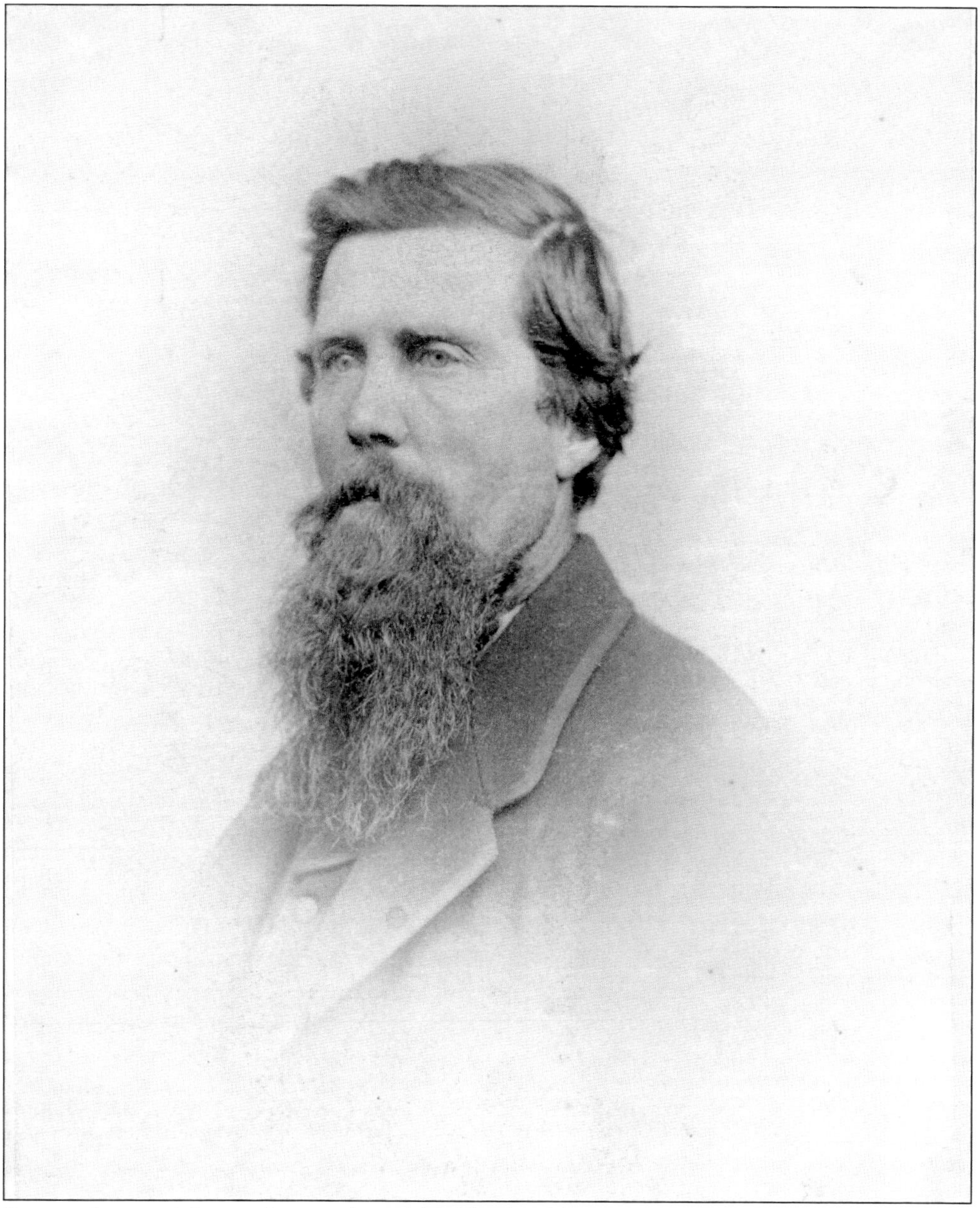

DANIEL OAKES. After working in the gold fields of California, young Daniel Oakes and his wife, Olive, settled in a tent on their homestead near the Douglas and El Paso County line. In 1859, while visiting back home in Iowa, Oakes published a guidebook to the Colorado gold fields. This publication contributed to the "Pikes Peak or Bust" gold rush. However, extracting gold in the Rocky Mountain region proved harder than prospective miners expected. Burial effigies of Oakes sprang up throughout the territory. They read, "Here lies D. C. Oakes, who was the starter of this damned hoax." Unfazed by the backlash, Oakes would become Douglas County's first postmaster of the town of Huntsville, one of the earliest established towns in Colorado Territory, and later one of the region's earliest Indian agents. Oakes was a partner in one of the first large ranches on the Palmer Divide, located at the base of an outcropping now known as Ben Lomond.

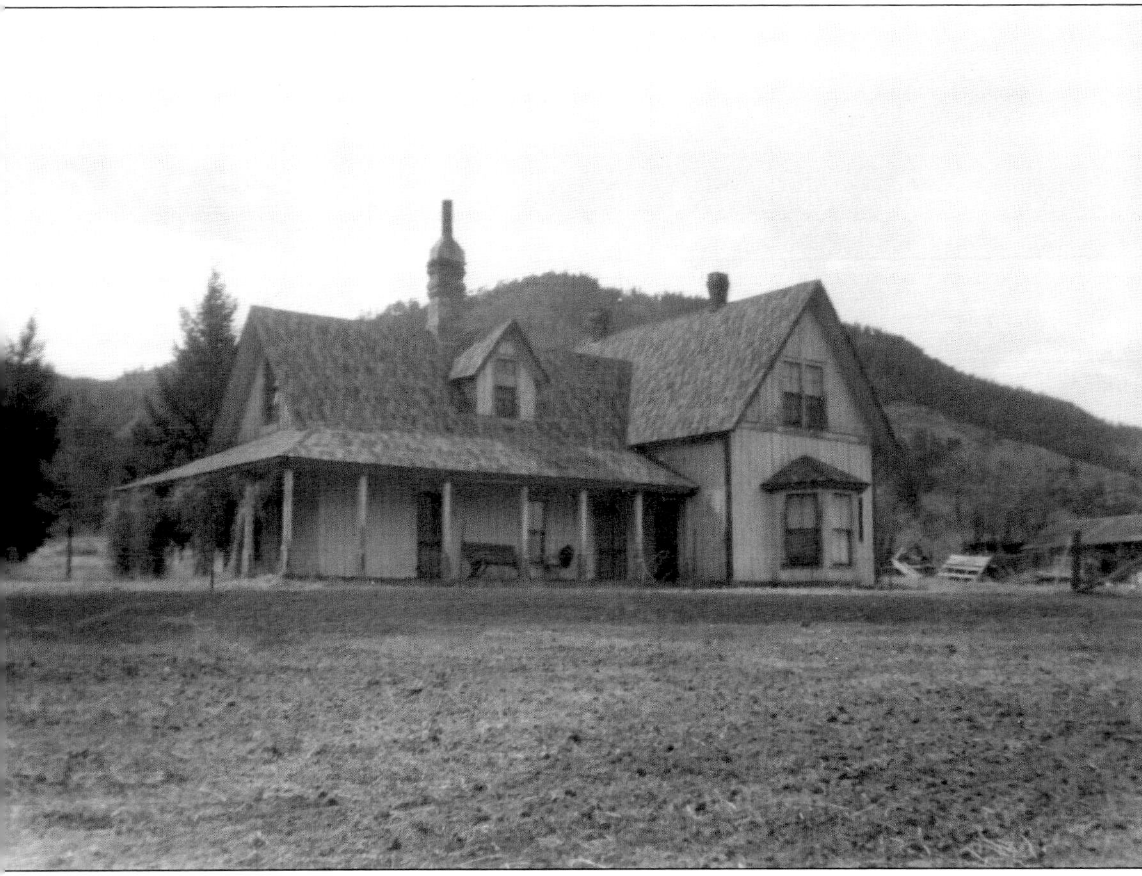

Ben Lomond Ranch House. In the early 1800s, the Ben Lomond Ranch was named for Ben Lomond Mountain. The buildings of the ranch were mainly in El Paso County, near the town of Palmer Lake. However, the vast acreage of the ranch was in nearby Douglas County. In 1871, the ranch was jointly owned by Daniel Oakes, Alvin Daniels, Judge Hiram Bennet, his eldest son Hiram P. Bennet Jr., and Joseph F. Bennet, the judge's brother. In 1885, the ranch was known as the Famous Daniels Ranch. Reportedly, it consisted of thousands of acres of land, some of which was cultivated in oats, millet, and hay. Dairy cows were also kept, and the ranch was considered an excellent dairy farm. The partnership sold the ranch in 1885 to Frank McClure. Thomas Hanks, who owned Hanks Livery, raised and sold horses on the ranch until 1894.

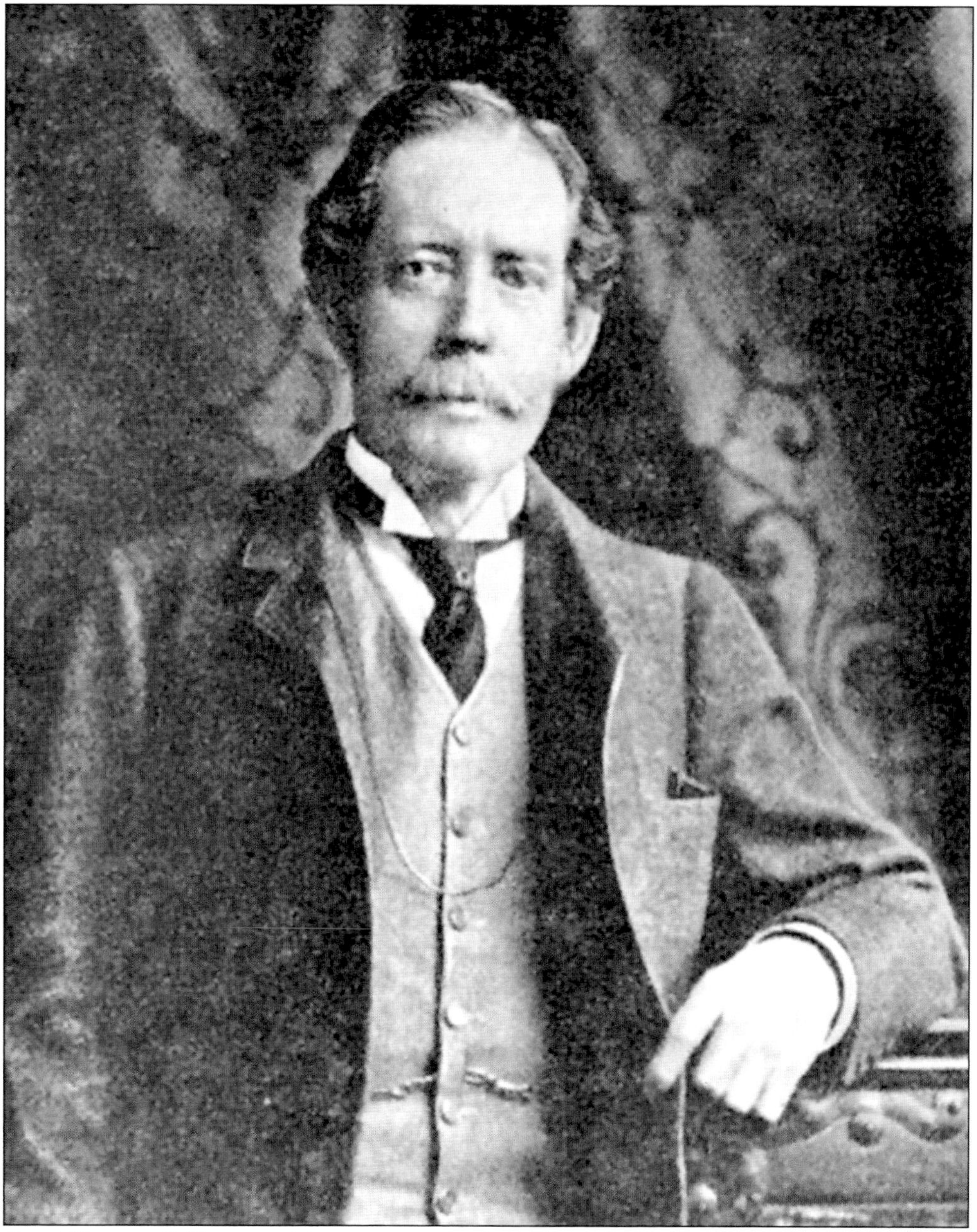

GEN. WILLIAM J. PALMER. Like many towns throughout the Colorado Territory, the town of Palmer Lake owed its beginning to Palmer's dream of building a railroad from Denver to Colorado Springs and beyond. As a 33-year-old engineer, Palmer proposed his idea to the Kansas and Pacific Railroad, but it was rejected. Disappointed, he organized his own railroad. Mountainous terrain determined the decision to use the 3-foot gauge rail bed. Hundreds of men and teams of horses and oxen worked in outlying forests, especially in the pineries of the Palmer Divide, to cut and haul ties to the railroad line. In the fall of 1871, Palmer's railroad made its debut run through the town of Palmer Lake. According to an 1870s map, the town of Palmer Lake was once called Weissport, named for the reclusive postmaster and railroad man, Camillus Weiss. Eventually, it became the only Colorado town to carry Palmer's name.

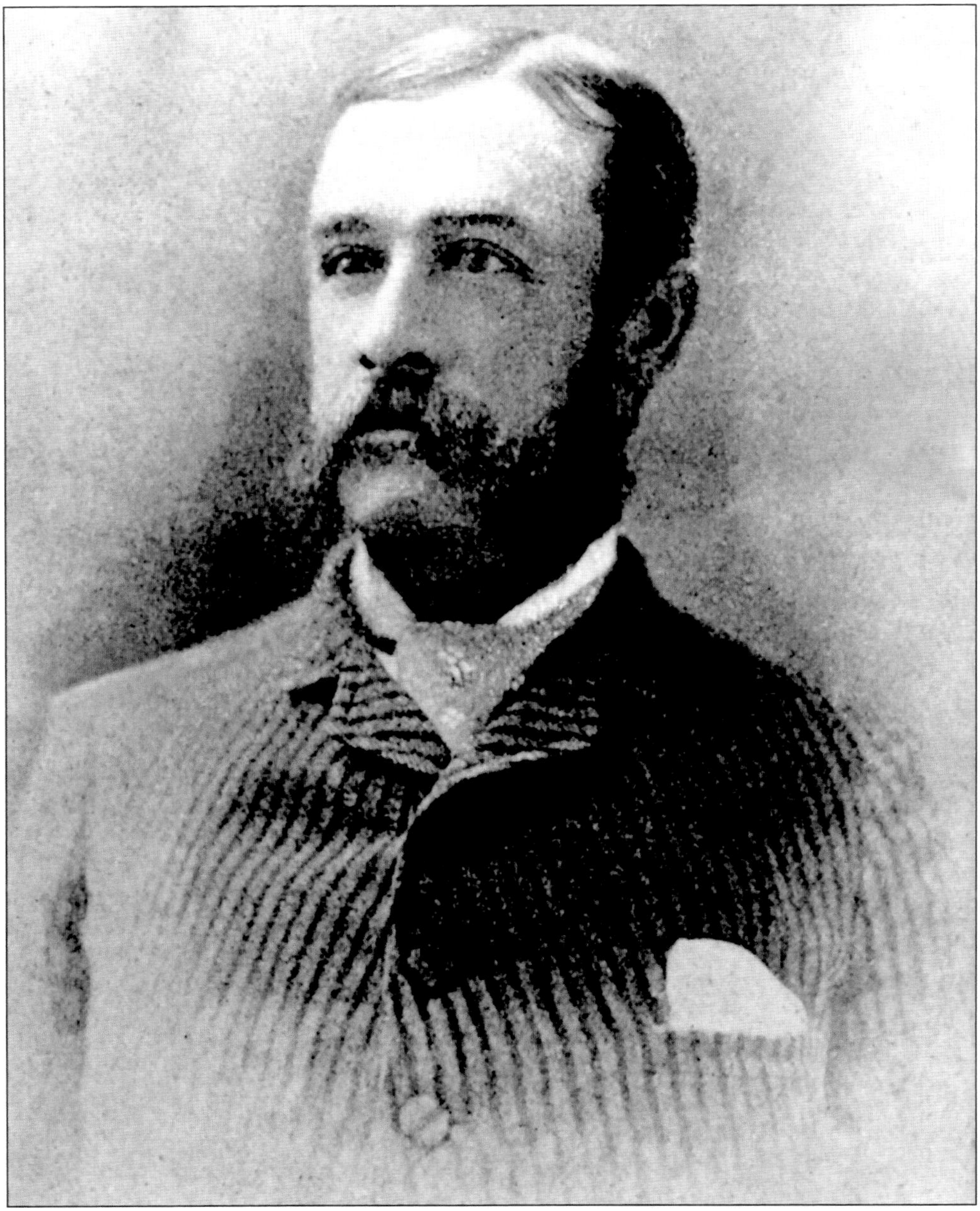

Founder of Palmer Lake. Dr. William F. Thompson, a wealthy dental surgeon, thought the land around the lake was ideally suited to be a summer resort aimed toward health, luxury, and cultural enrichment. Thompson was a visionary as well as a persuasive, enthusiastic man. In 1882, he and his dentist colleague, D. A. B. Visick, jointly and individually purchased land around the lake. Thompson subsequently moved his wife, Ada, and his three daughters to the area. He built a beautiful home, Estemere, possibly named for his daughter, Estelle, and began his efforts to develop Palmer Lake. People were drawn to the mild-mannered Thompson, who dressed well, loved sports, and hosted lavish parties. In 1889, he was elected mayor of the newly incorporated town of Palmer Lake. Thompson had borrowed large sums of money, and by 1890, he was unable to meet his financial obligations. In August 1890, he and his family left Palmer Lake and moved to New York City. Thompson died in Mexico in 1892 of typhoid fever.

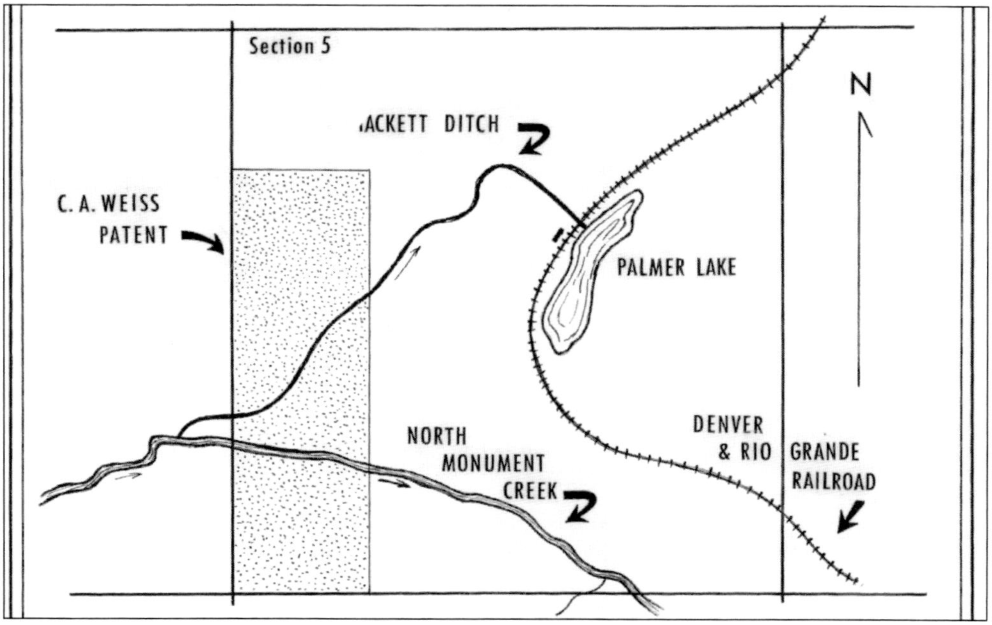

Hackett's Ditch, c. 1882. Samuel Hackett was a railroad employee tasked with pumping water by hand from Palmer Lake into a holding tank that fed the steam engines. To deal with drought conditions, Hackett dug a ditch to divert water from Monument Creek into the lake. The railroad abandoned the ditch in 1882. Hackett subsequently secured the water rights to Hackett's Ditch for domestic, mechanical, and irrigation purposes.

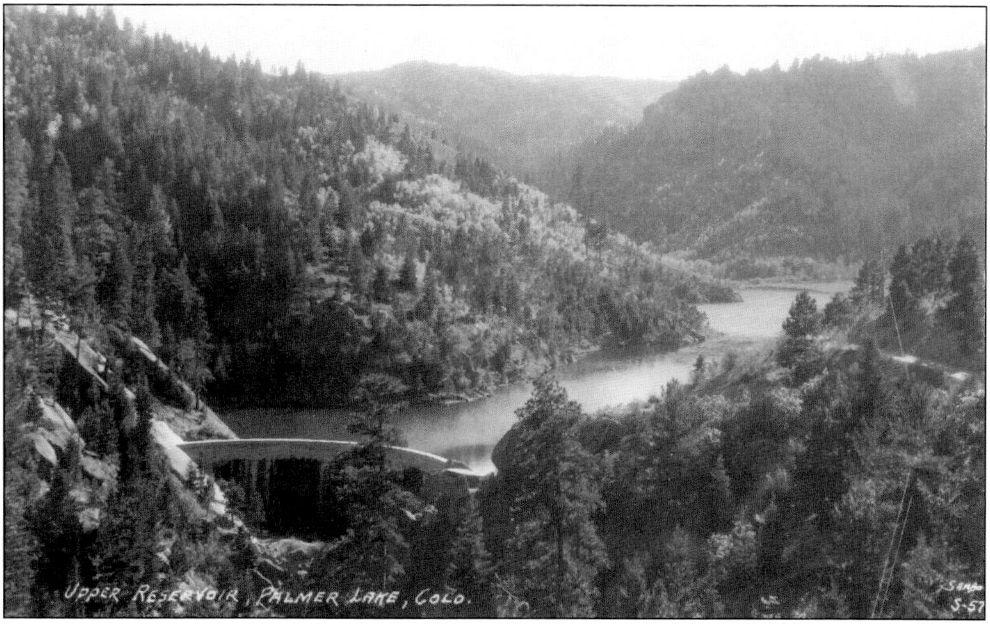

Upper Reservoir, c. 1905. By 1905, the railroad had built the lower and upper reservoirs in North Monument canyon to provide water storage. The reservoirs contributed to the later development of Palmer Lake, Glen Park, and Pine Crest. They became favorite swimming holes of town locals. Young William Vaile wrote in his diary, "Didn't have to take a bath today because I'd been in the reservoir so much this week." Today swimming is illegal in both reservoirs.

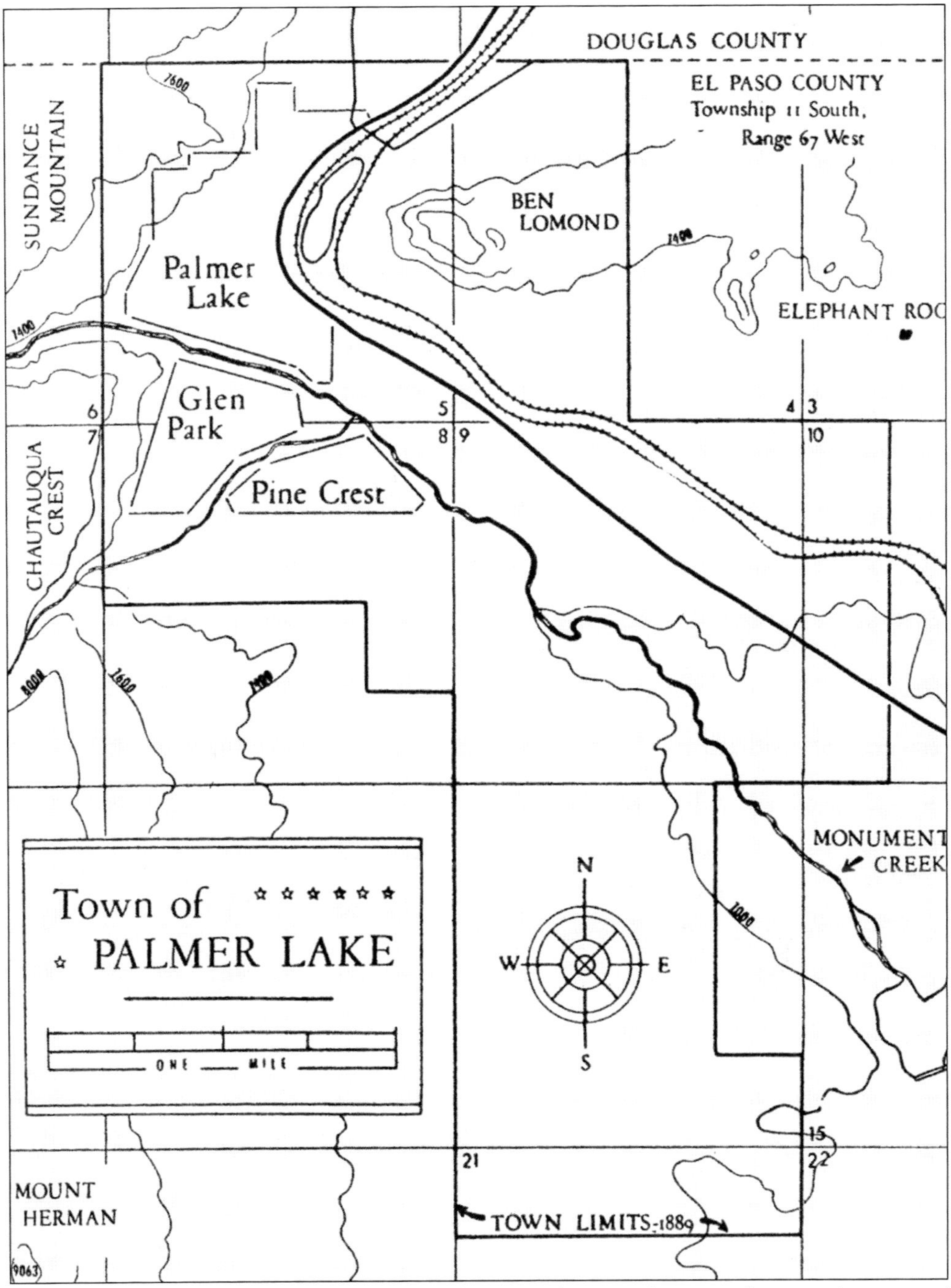

Map of Palmer Lake, c. 1889. This map illustrates the town limits at the time the town of Palmer Lake was incorporated in 1889. At that time, the name "Palmer Lake" could mean the lake itself, the town platted just west of the lake in 1883, or the incorporated town of Palmer Lake. The lake is a natural body of fresh, spring-fed water. It sits directly at the top of the Palmer Divide and is unique for having flows in wet years going both north and south. The Palmer Lake Historical Society was originally formed in 1956 to publish Marian Sabin's manuscript, *Palmer Lake, A Historical Narrative*, which contains this map.

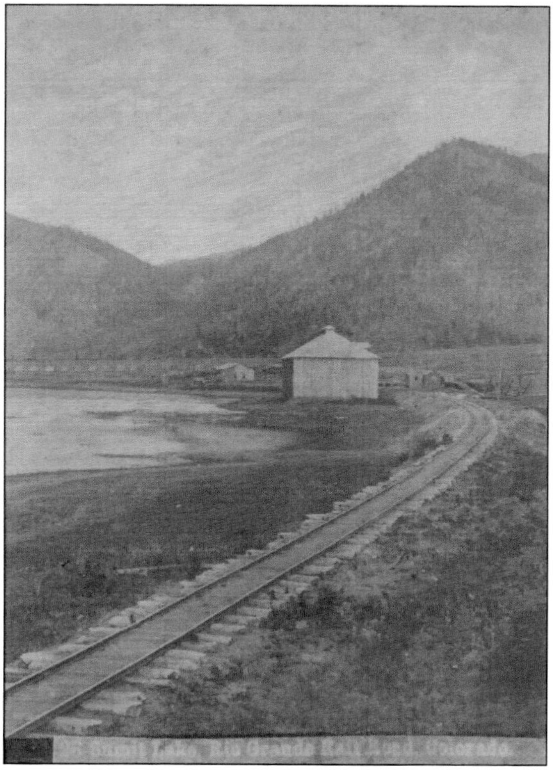

Summit Lake and Icehouse, c. 1873. In 1835, an expedition led by Col. Henry Dodge mapped a body of water on the Palmer Divide that they named Summit Lake. The lake was later known as Divide Lake, Loch Lomond, Lake Palmer, and finally Palmer Lake. Reportedly, in March 1882, 900,000 tons of ice was harvested from the lake. Ice harvesting on the lake ended in 1926.

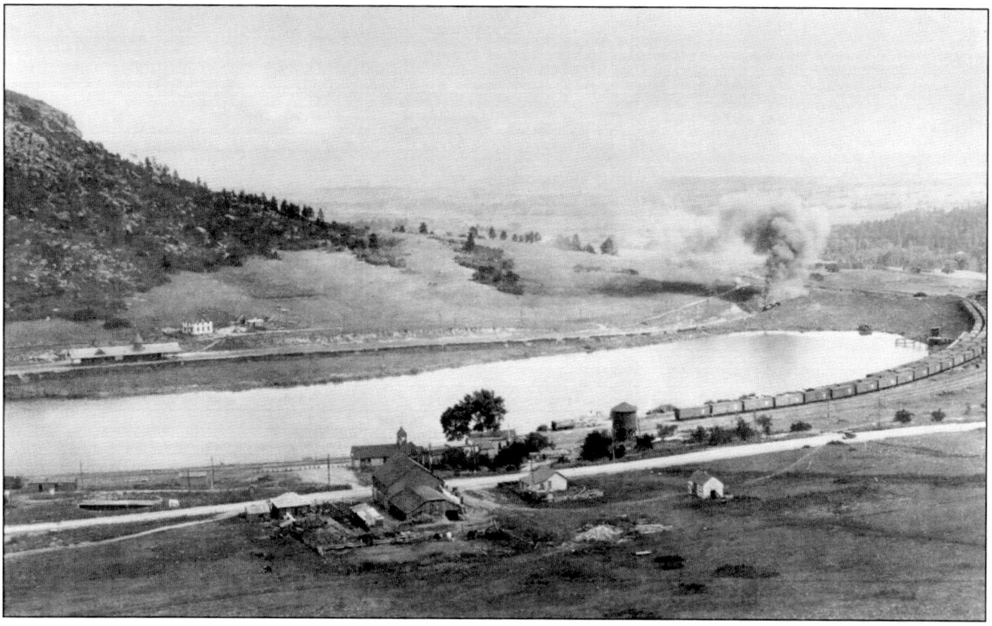

Railroads in Palmer Lake. The Santa Fe Railroad tracks and depot can be seen across the lake on the eastern shore, with the Denver & Rio Grande Railroad tracks and depot in the foreground. This scene sparked a childhood memory recorded by Alice Guire Dolan in her memoirs. She recalled the "iron monster belching clouds of steam" and thought it would explode. Instead, "it rushed away down the valley."

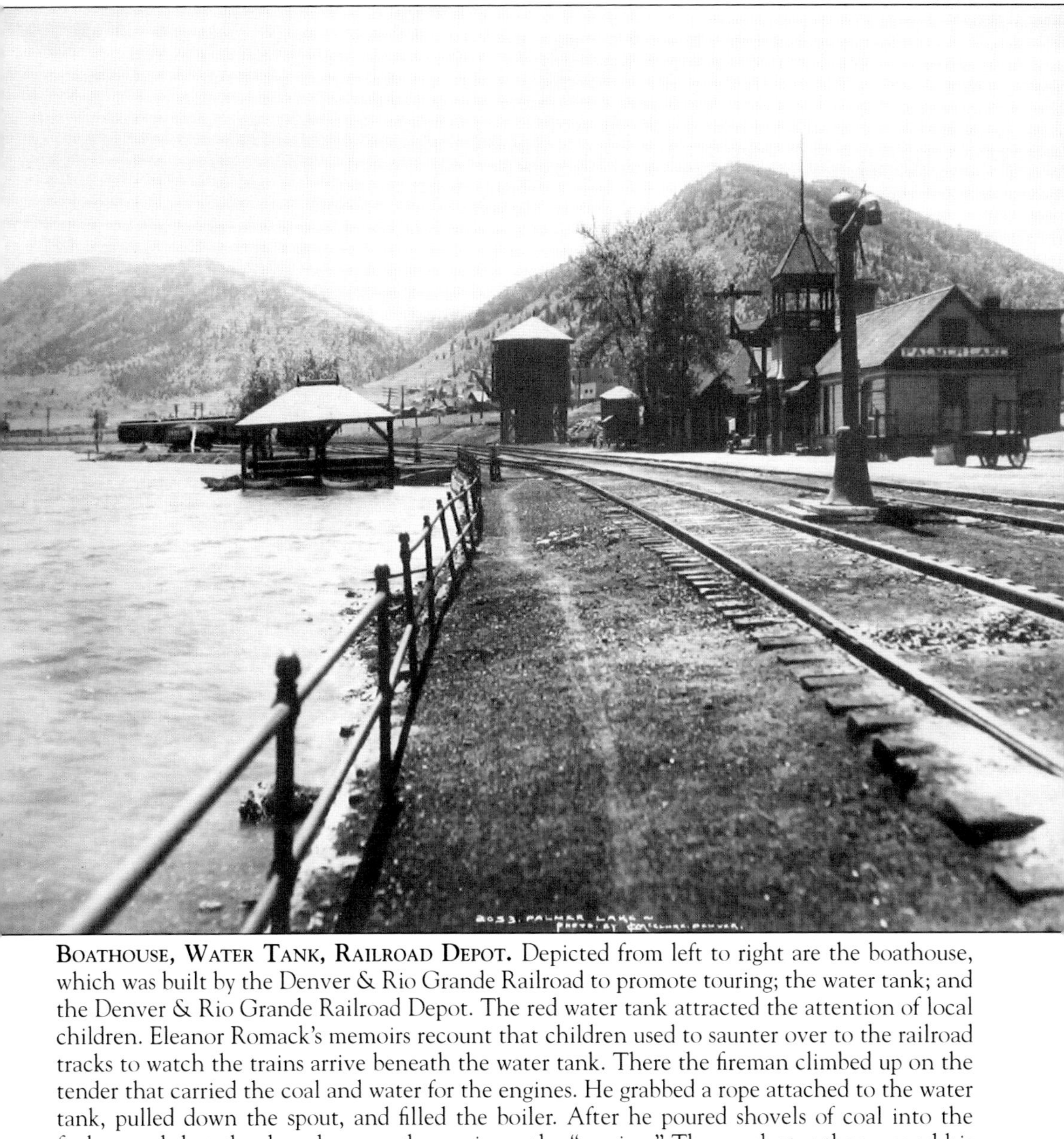

Boathouse, Water Tank, Railroad Depot. Depicted from left to right are the boathouse, which was built by the Denver & Rio Grande Railroad to promote touring; the water tank; and the Denver & Rio Grande Railroad Depot. The red water tank attracted the attention of local children. Eleanor Romack's memoirs recount that children used to saunter over to the railroad tracks to watch the trains arrive beneath the water tank. There the fireman climbed up on the tender that carried the coal and water for the engines. He grabbed a rope attached to the water tank, pulled down the spout, and filled the boiler. After he poured shovels of coal into the firebox and shut the door, he gave the engineer the "go sign." The conductor then waved his hand and called "all aboard!" Eleanor writes, "The whistle blew, a bell rang, the wheels turned, and the train chugged on down the tracks out of sight."

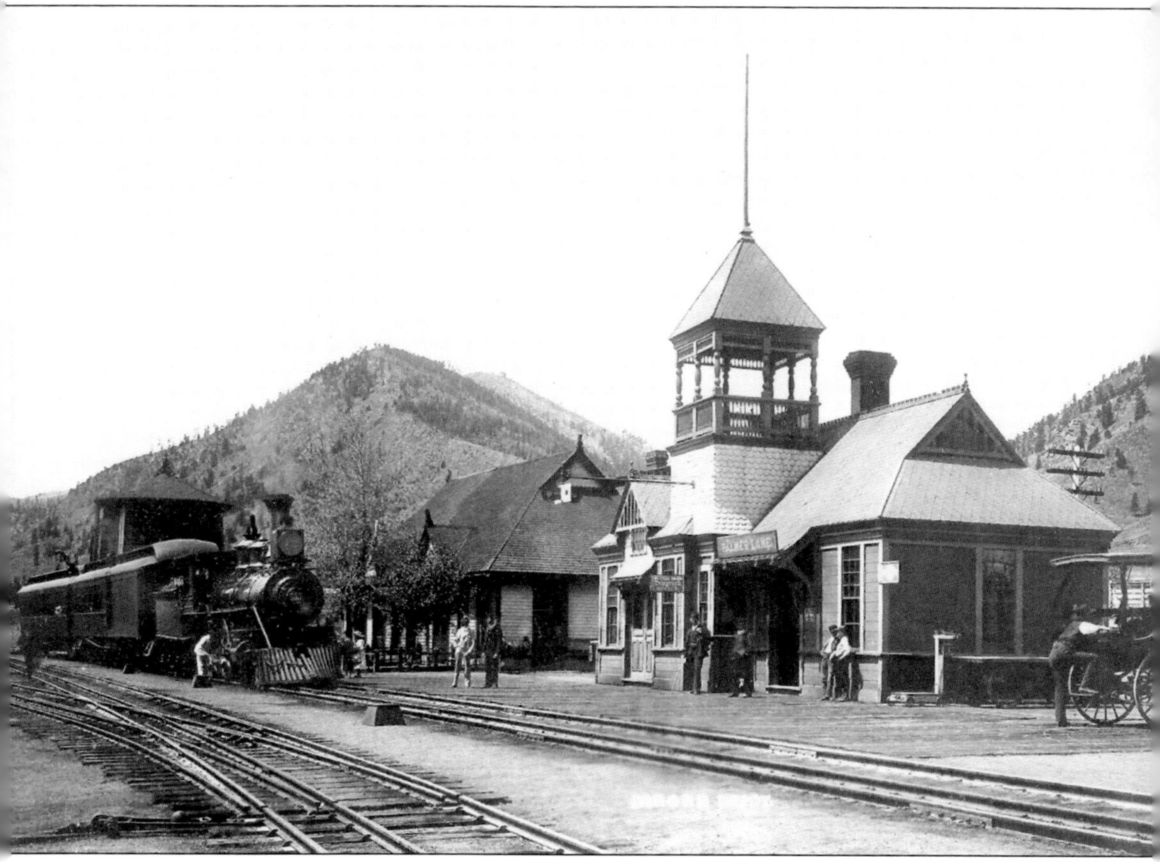

Denver & Rio Grande Railroad Depot. Built in Denver for an 1882 National Mining and Industrial Exposition, the depot, with its unusually elaborate belfry cupola, was painted mustard yellow and trimmed in white. It was moved to Palmer Lake after the exposition closed and replaced the original, much simpler depot. In summer, the women had their own waiting room, as did the men so they could smoke. In winter, women and men used the same waiting room and shared the warmth of a big, round-bellied stove. To the north of the depot was parking space for red plush hacks, shiny carriages and buggies, wagons, and later automobiles. Since all trains stopped at the depot to have their brakes tested and take on water, the crew usually took time to get a cup of coffee and a bite to eat at Judd's Eating House, located south of the depot.

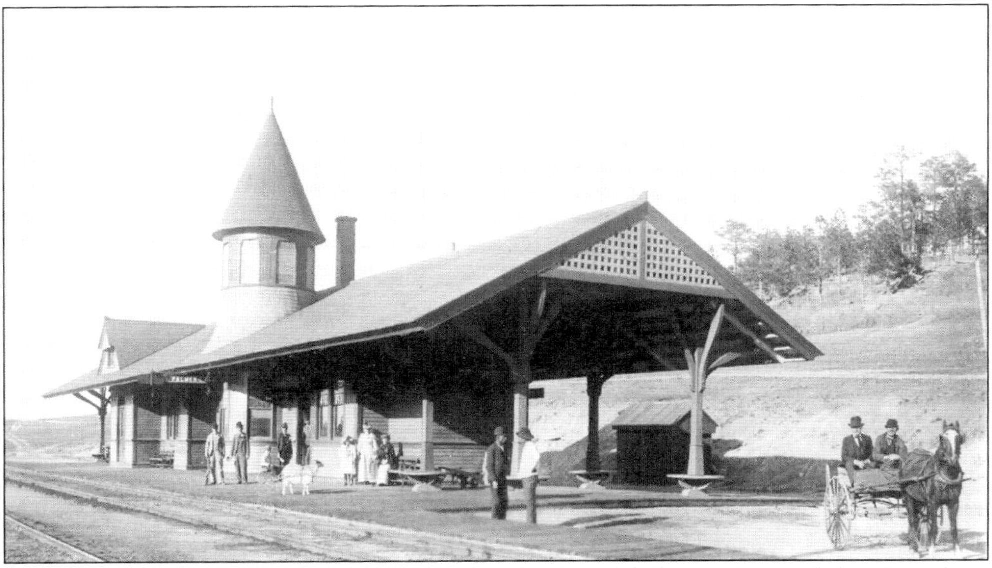

Santa Fe Railroad Depot, c. 1887. In 1887, the Santa Fe Railroad extended its lines from Pueblo to Denver. Pictured are two views of the small, buff, and red-roofed depot located on the east side of the lake. The depot had an enclosed tower and windows at one end to protect travelers from stormy weather. William Fonash, manager of Harvey's Lunchroom in the depot, was fondly remembered for his meats, cakes, and pies that were tucked into boxes. They were elaborately decorated by ladies and auctioned at the town's box socials. Love-struck young men bought them for as much as $12 each. When Harvey's Lunchroom closed, the space became quarters for the station agent. The Denver & Rio Grande Railroad Depot across the lake is visible in the picture below.

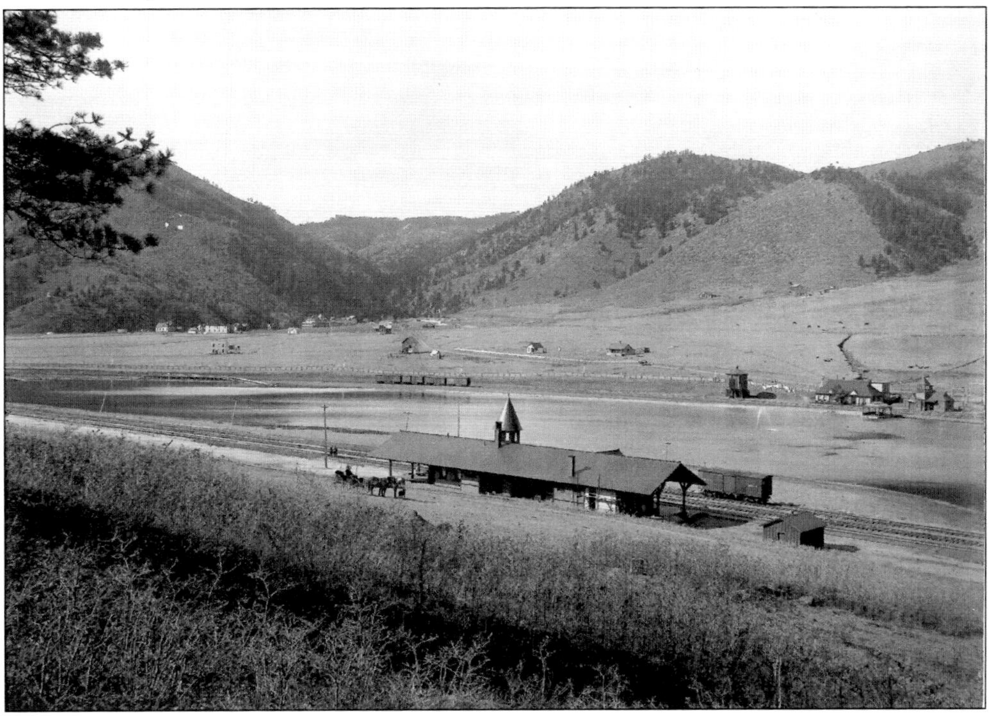

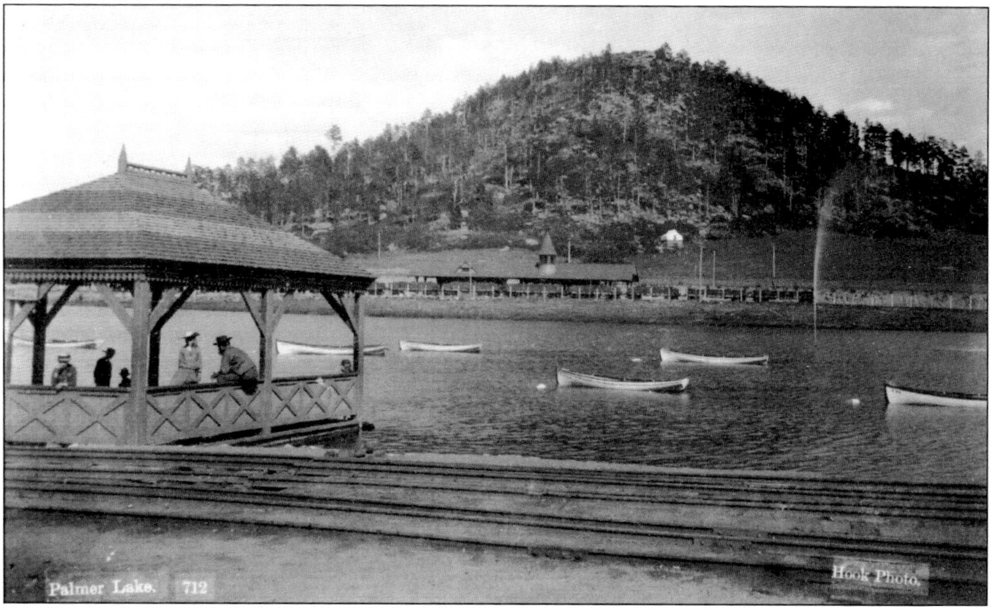

BOATHOUSE AND PAVILION. The boathouse, picnic grounds, and pavilion were a popular social center of the town. Pictured above is the boathouse where boats were for hire. One could row on the lake or fish from the piers. Eleanor Romack's memoirs describe the day a young girl walked to the edge of the boathouse, threw her arms over her head, cried "goodbye cruel world," and jumped into the lake. Romack's father jumped into the water and saved the girl. Pictured below is the Denver & Rio Grande Railroad open-air pavilion where dances and lectures were held. It had drop shutters for protection during inclement weather and a raised platform centered on one wall for the band or lecturer. The pavilion was later moved to Pine Crest. (Both courtesy of the Idleman Collection.)

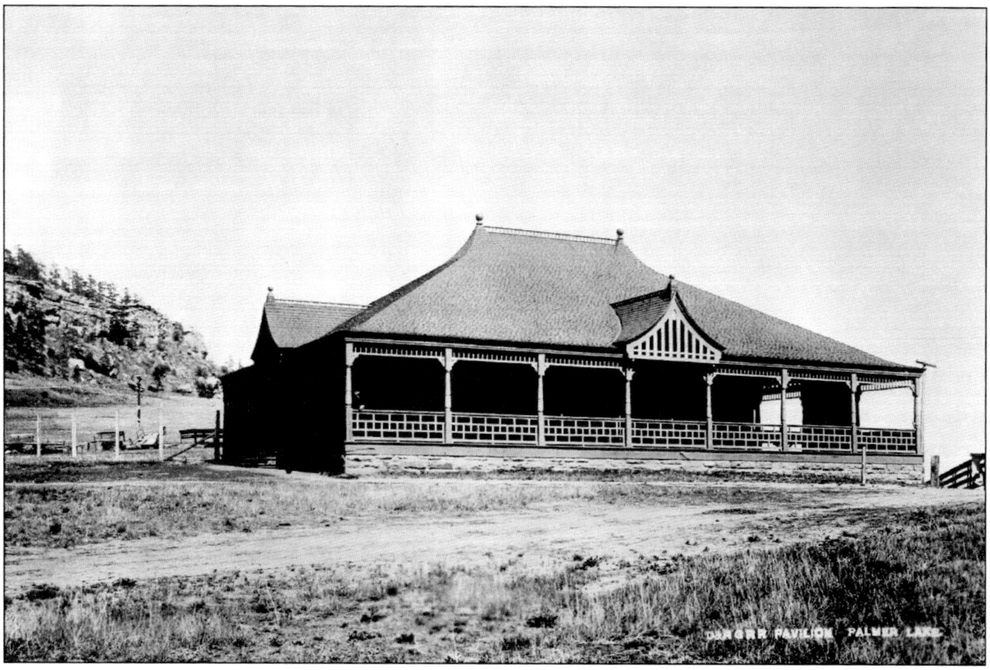

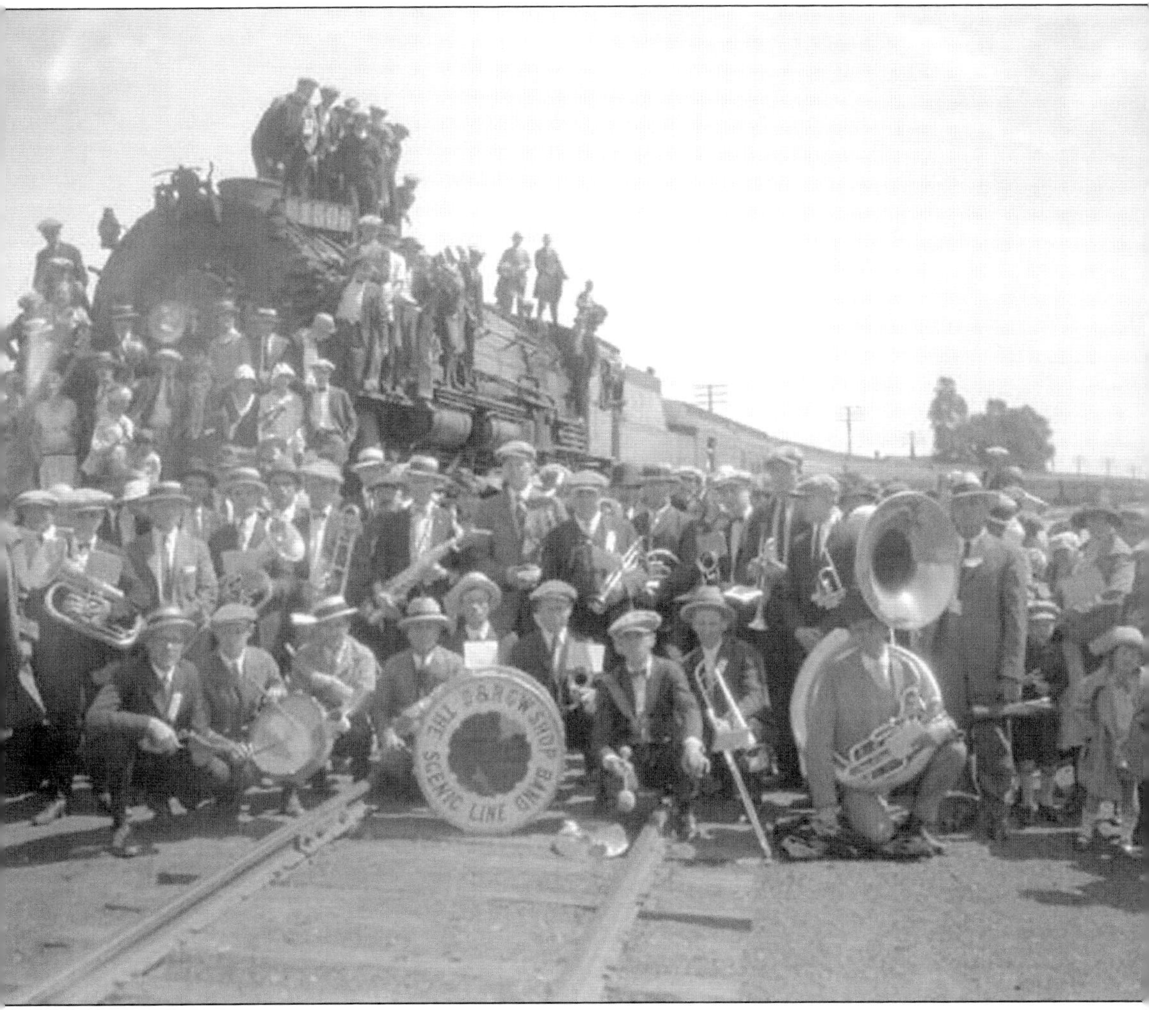

Denver & Rio Grande Railroad Excursion. Dr. William F. Thompson's small booklets contained illustrations advertising the attractions of Palmer Lake and brought excursionists, such as the Scenic Line Band pictured above, who are ready to play at the pavilion. In his memoirs of Palmer Lake, William Gillett wrote, "On Sunday, there were as many as four excursion trains on the sidetracks that went around the southwest corner of the lake. Large companies chartered trains for annual employee picnics and the different departments engaged in several athletic events, which made an exciting day for everyone." Round trip from Denver to Palmer Lake cost about $1, which made an affordable trip for fraternal groups, schools, and naturalists. In the late 1890s, when bicycle riding became fashionable, special trains that allowed passengers to bring their bikes along operated between Denver and Palmer Lake.

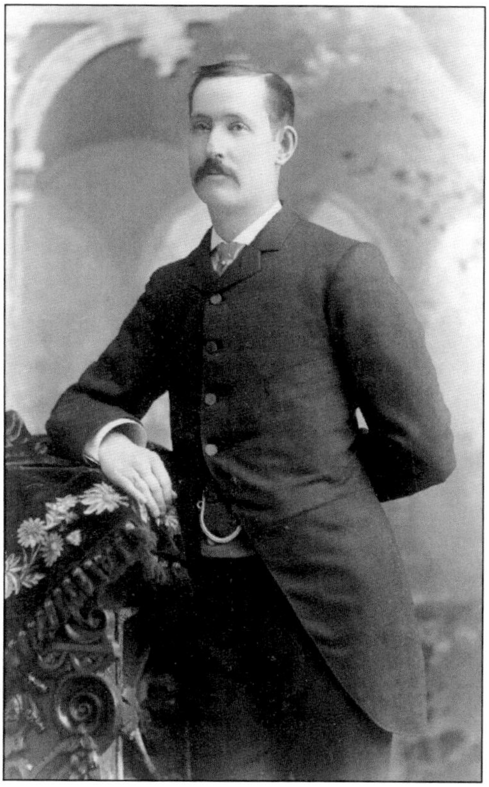

John and Annie Reed Judd. John Judd, pictured at left, was a former car conductor on a Chicago railroad. He moved to Colorado with his wife, Annie, on the advice of her doctor. Annie, pictured below, suffered from chronic anemia. Judd's uncle, Irish Haddock, who owned the Cliff House in Manitou Springs, suggested that the couple settle in Palmer Lake. In 1890, Judd was elected mayor and in 1898, he became the new proprietor of the Palmer Lake Lunch Counter, which became known as Judd's Eating House. Also plagued by ill health, Judd unsuccessfully sought a diagnosis from California and Oklahoma doctors. He died in 1914 and left Annie to manage the restaurant. In 1929, the restaurant was sold. Annie kept only the dishes marked "Palmer Lake" and those that had been reserved for General Palmer and Teddy Roosevelt.

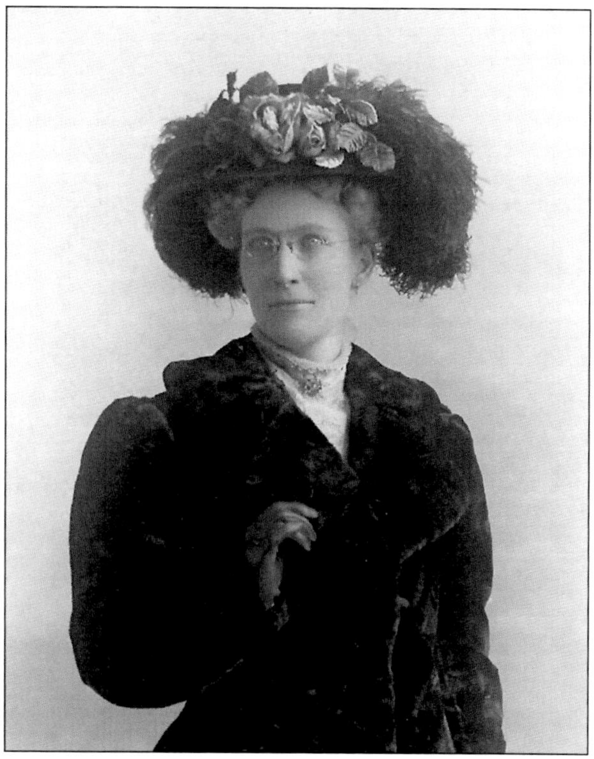

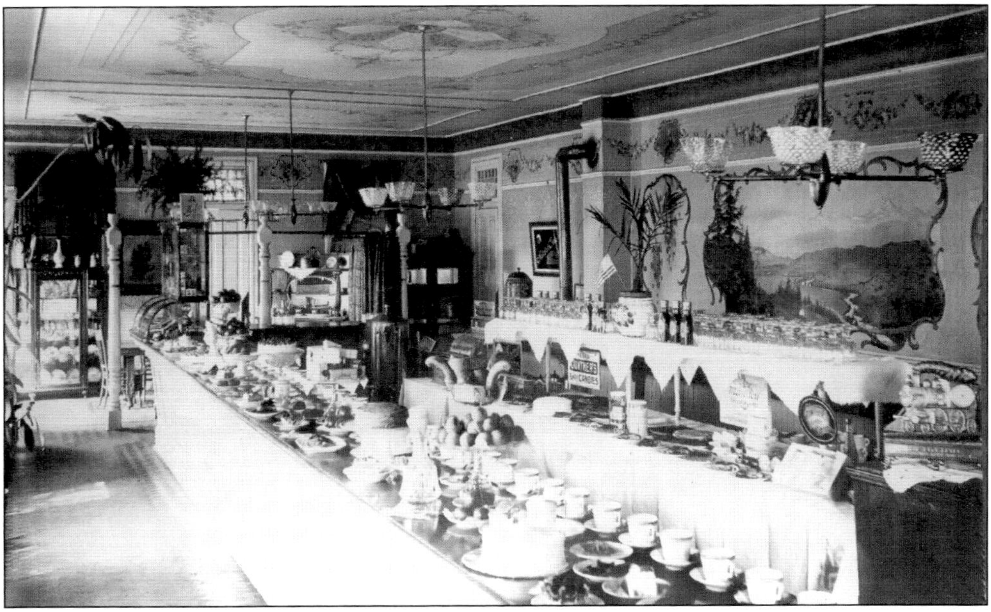

JUDD'S EATING HOUSE, C. 1889. The elegant interior of Judd's Eating House, depicted above, was open 24 hours a day to service train passengers. The establishment soon earned a distinguished reputation for excellence and glamour. As a train approached, a huge Chinese brass gong was sounded, inviting all to eat at the establishment. Unfortunately, the train stopped for only 10 minutes, which gave little time for relaxed dining. Eleanor Romack recalled the wonderful aroma of food, and the clear glass compotes and wedding bowls filled with fresh fruit that were placed on the horseshoe-shaped counter every so often. She also recalled mounted animal heads such as deer, elk, an eagle, and a "wise old owl" that hung on the walls. Pictured below is a Denver & Rio Grande Railroad train pass issued to Annie Judd. The Judds received lifetime railroad passes in appreciation for the gracious, speedy hospitality their establishment offered to railroad passengers, management, and staff.

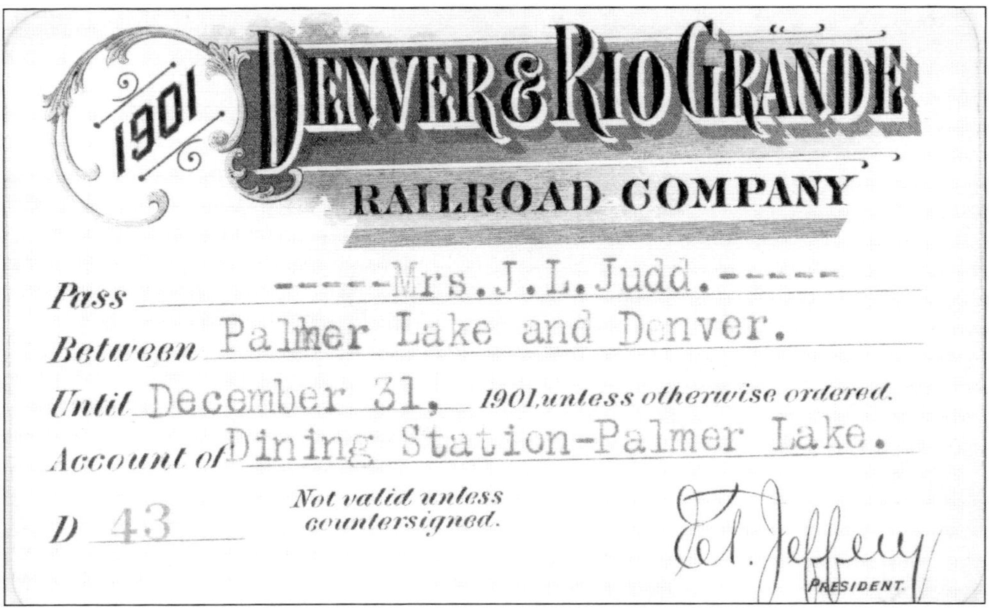

1901

DENVER & RIO GRANDE

RAILROAD COMPANY

Pass -----Mrs. J. L. Judd.-----

Between Palmer Lake and Denver.

Until December 31, *1901, unless otherwise ordered.*

Account of Dining Station-Palmer Lake.

D 43

Not valid unless countersigned.

E. T. Jeffery

PRESIDENT.

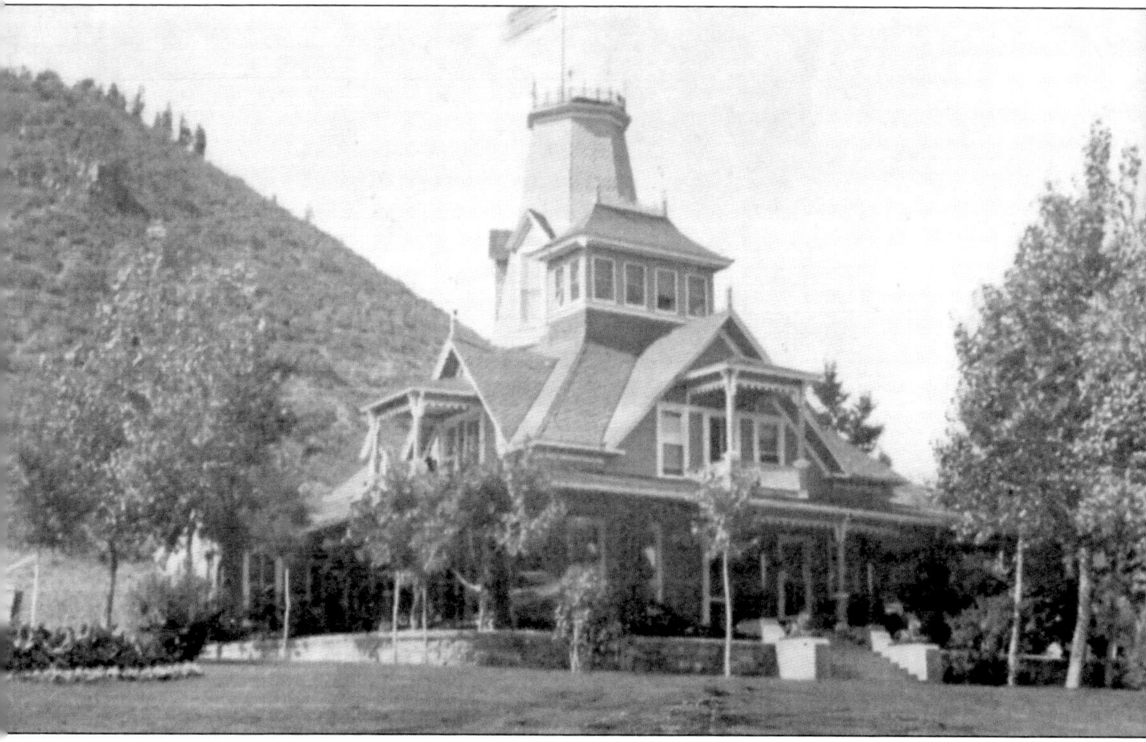

ESTEMERE MANSION, C. 1900. Chapin Gard described Estemere, the Victorian mansion built by Dr. William F. Thompson during 1887 to 1890, as "the Gem of the Rockies." Gard wrote, "the rooms bespeak rare skill and taste. The billiard room has rich stained glass that softens and subdues the light which makes the room grand and inviting." From the observatory, one viewed a "scene of loveliness unexcelled on the face of the globe." The mansion, still standing in grand style, contains 18 rooms, exclusive of the cellar, closets, pantries, and hallways. Through the years, Estemere has been the private residence of several owners, a summer camp, rental apartments, and a lodge. The current owners completely restored the mansion and generously invited the Palmer Lake Historical Society to sponsor fund-raising tours every other year.

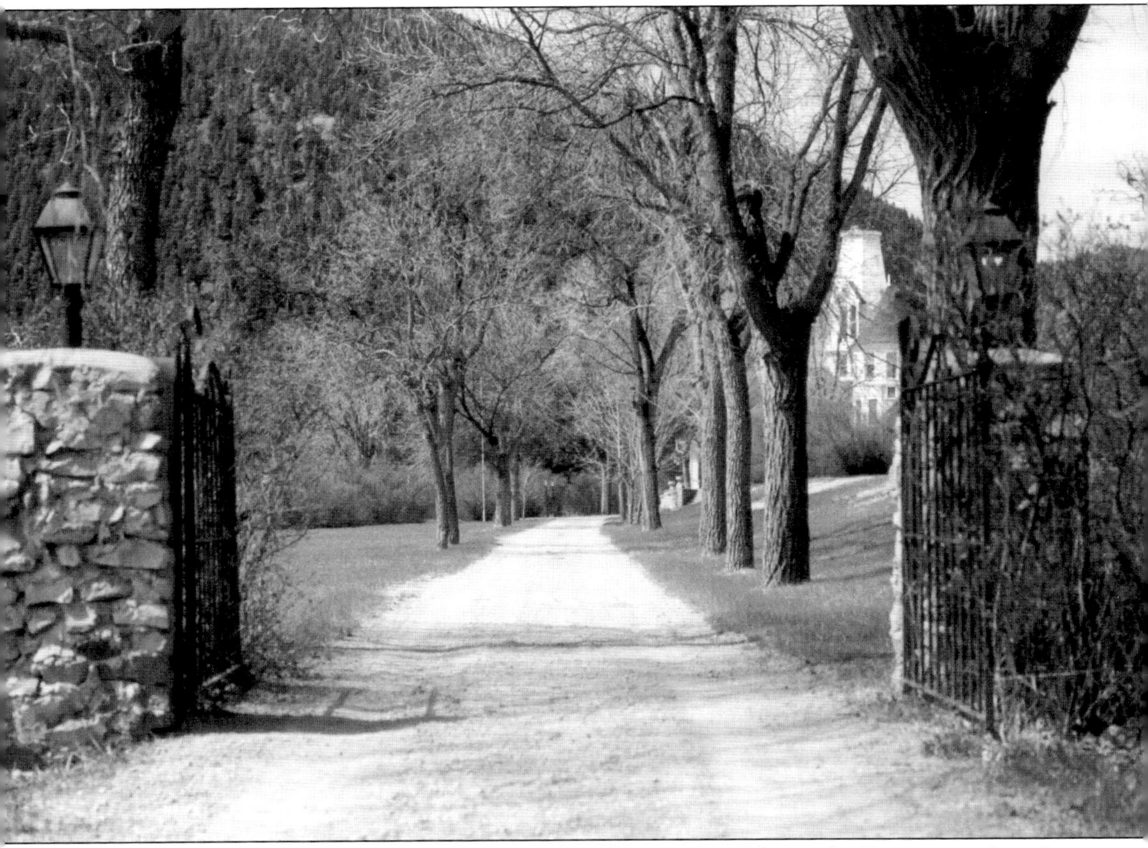

ESTEMERE LANE. In 1898, Eben Smith, a multimillionaire, and his wife, Emma, purchased Estemere from the Rollins Investment Company, which had received the property by deed from Dr. William F. Thompson's wife in 1891. Once again, the estate received "singing praises." It was described as "a happy valley where the keynote is peace and the harmony with nature is perfect." One article boasted, "It is a city mansion. Behind it are fine stables in which 12 fine horses are kept, and there are fine dogs in the kennels." Roberta Graham Clark, who spent two summers as a teenager at Estemere in the 1930s, remembered the mansion as a party house. She said that the young crowd always ended up there. They had lots of dances and ate lots of peanut butter. The lane that leads to Estemere is located on the northeast side of the mansion.

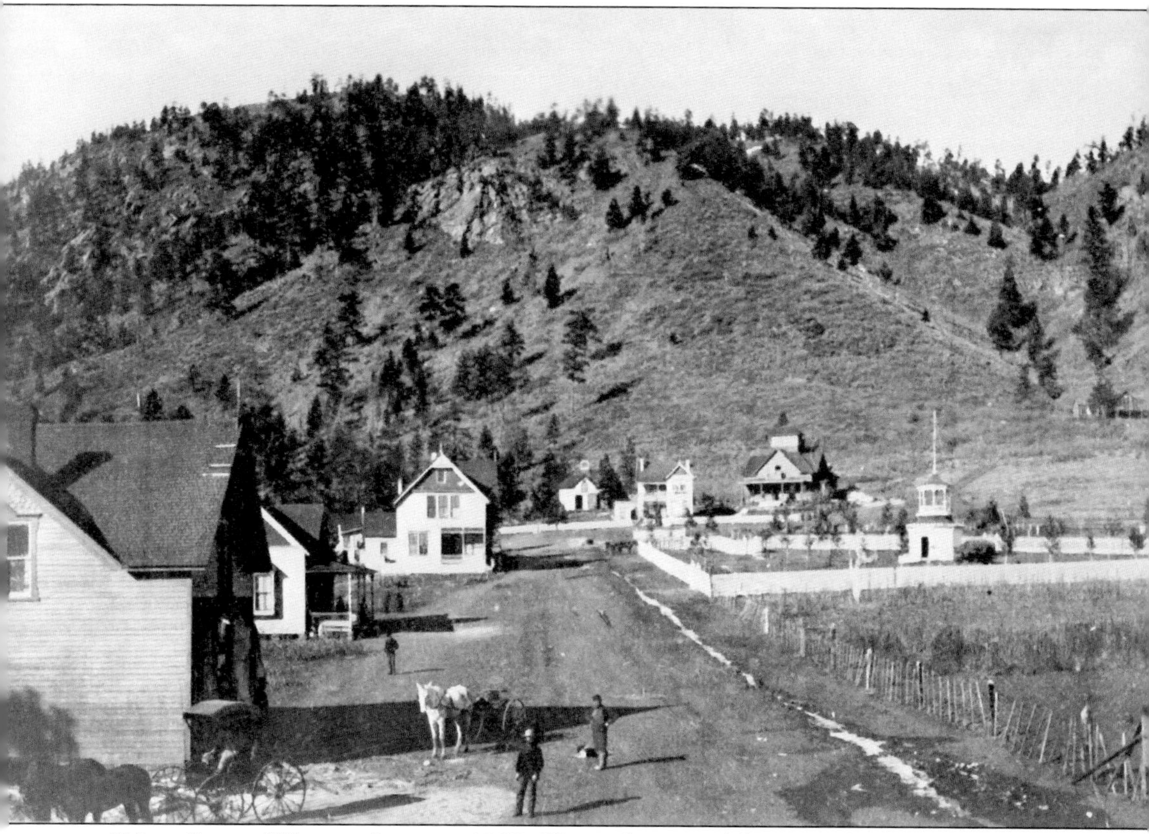

"Main Street" Palmer Lake, c. 1887. This early view of the town shows, from left to right, the Pillsbury Store, McIntrye Cottage, Glen House, Deer Park, and the first Estemere house before the mansion of the same name was built. Small villas were planned as guesthouses or to be used as rentals. Dr. William F. Thompson remarked that from the verandas of Glen House and through the "elegant bay windows," visitors could gaze upon Deer Park, which was a small preserve shaded by large evergreens. Visitors and residents of Palmer Lake found Deer Park "a delightful after-dinner retreat." People strolled along the walkways enjoying flowerbeds and fountains, and were entertained by local musicians. Deer that grazed in the park were tame and ate out of people's hands. Descendents of those deer wander nonchalantly through the yards and gardens of today's residents.

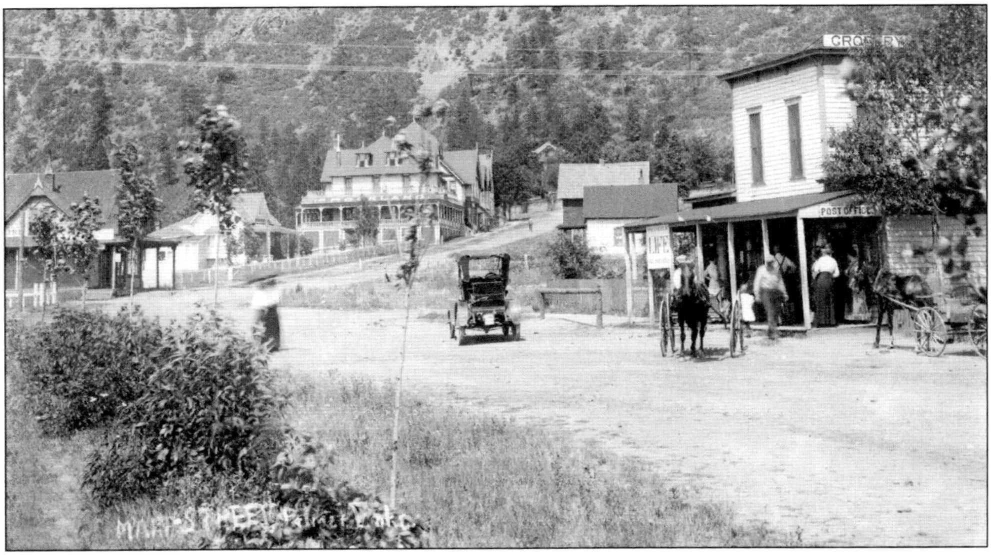

Palmer Lake Business District, c. 1912. Pictured is the Rockland Hotel in the background and the Wilson store on the right. The store, which was built in 1900, was owned by Fred Wilson. Wilson served two terms as mayor of Palmer Lake. His wife, Harriet, with Mrs. H. E. Nickerson and her son, started a paper called the *Palmer Lake Life*, subtitled *Echoes from the Glen and Crest.*

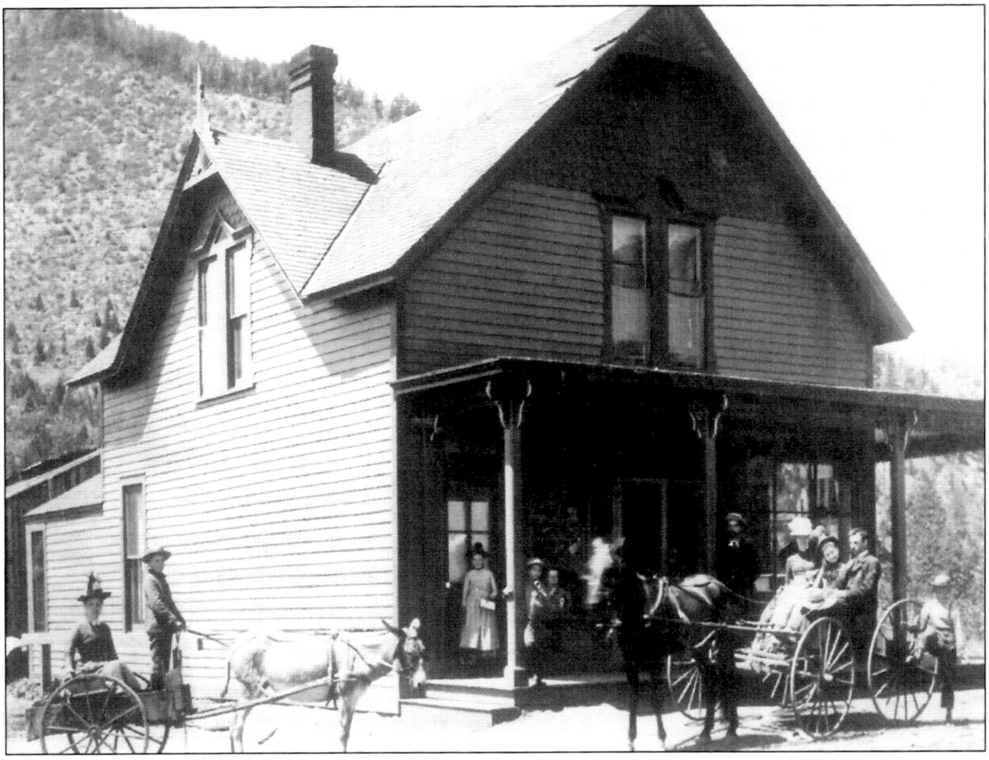

Pillsbury Store, c. 1888. Charles H. Pillsbury and Charles C. Pillsbury, unrelated, arrived in Palmer Lake in June 1886 as guests of Dr. William F. Thompson. Thompson told them that if they built a grocery store, he would provide the land for free. The building housed a meat market on the first floor and rented rooms on the second floor. It is a private residence today.

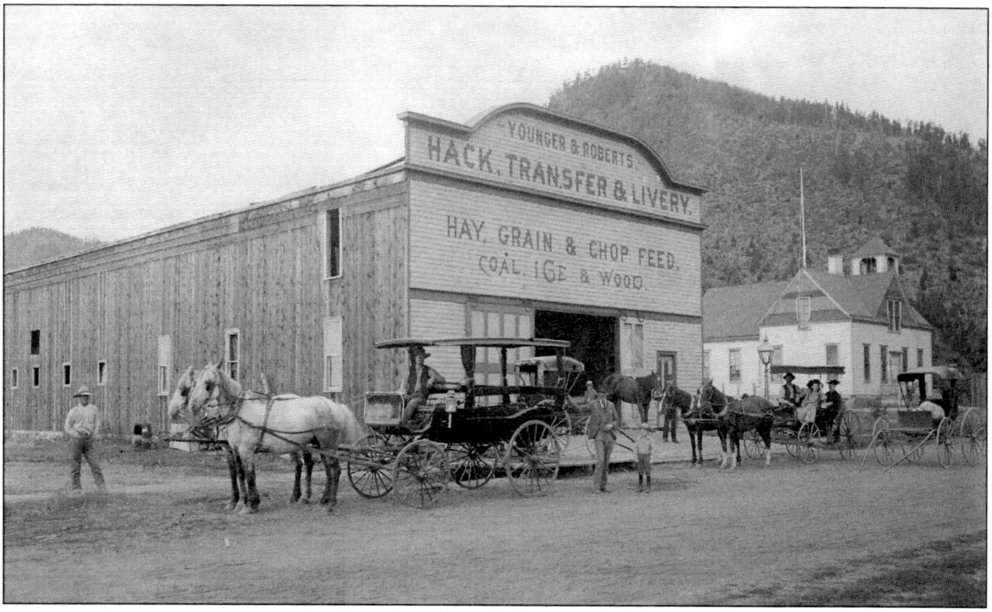

Younger's Livery. In 1890, William Younger and Bernie Roberts built a livery stable on South Valley Road. They had a bitter rivalry with Thomas A. Hanks, who also owned a livery stable. To limit competition, they arranged a business deal with the local railroad superintendent for exclusive rights for their carriages to occupy spaces nearest the railroad depot. The town council intervened, which stopped the attempted monopoly.

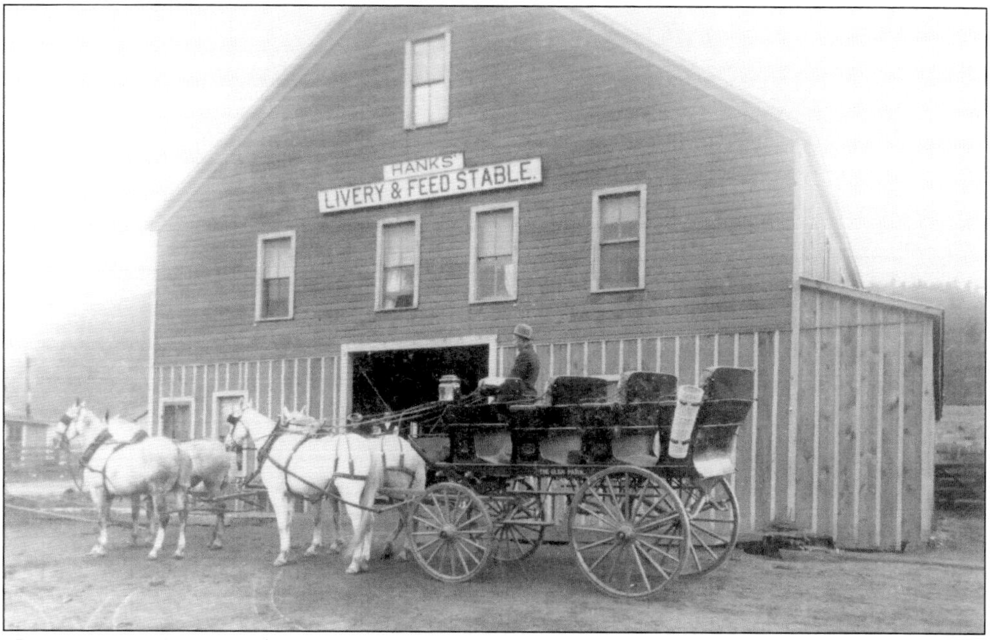

Hanks Livery Stable. Thomas Hanks drove a mountain stagecoach from one summer resort in the Palmer Divide area to another before he established his livery stable. He was famous for his "tally-ho" parties, in which a three-seated surrey pulled by his favorite team of four white horses carried 12 people at a time for tours of Palmer Lake and surrounding areas. In 1899, Hanks was elected mayor of Palmer Lake.

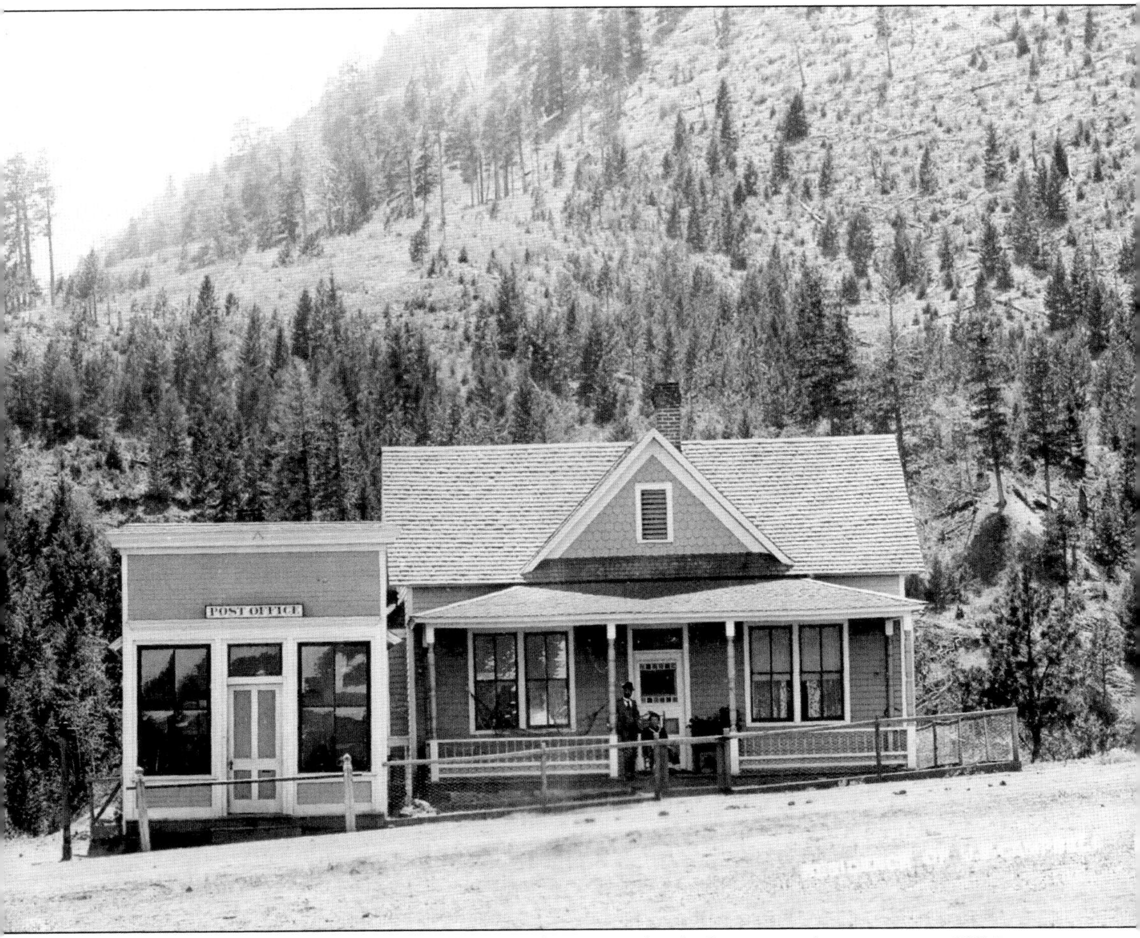

Campbell/McIntyre House. Dr. William F. Thompson built the original structure in 1884 as a clubhouse for the Glen House hotel. In 1888, Thompson donated the cottage to the community to serve as a one-room schoolhouse. It also functioned as a church whenever a minister could be secured to conduct services. From 1891 to 1893, Mr. Campbell, the Denver & Rio Grande Railroad agent, and his wife, Della, the postmistress, lived in the house. Attached to the side of the house was a small enclosure that served as the post office with a pass-through window to the main house. The Henry McIntyre family purchased the house for a summer retreat in 1898. Today McIntyre's grandson, Rogers Davis, who is the Lucretia Vaile museum director, and his wife, Susan, live in the house.

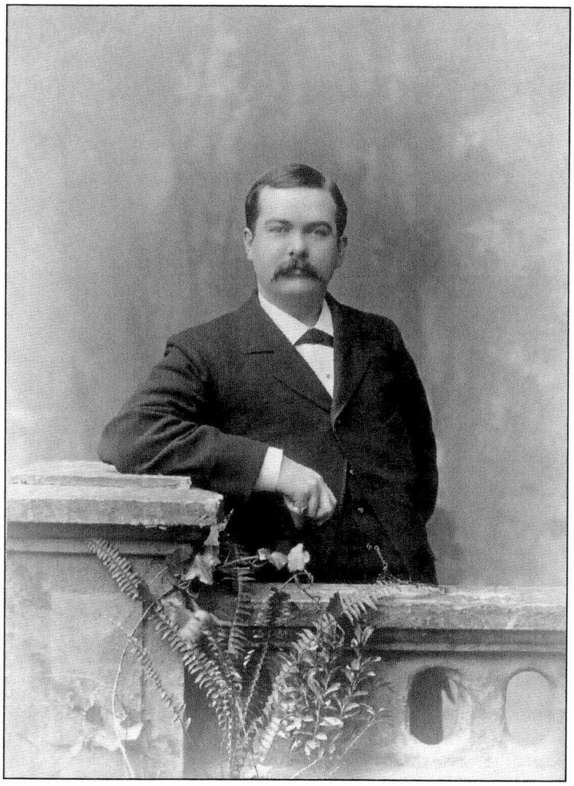

Henry A. McIntyre, c. 1869, and Marian W. Young, c. 1895. Pictured at left is Henry Azile McIntyre. Before he and Marian W. Young married, he worked as a surveyor and rear flagman for the railroad. During that time, he wrote about his experiences in *Diary of a Tenderfoot, Denver and Rio Grande Survey of 1871*, which provides valuable insight into life on the Palmer Divide. Gen. William J. Palmer appointed McIntyre the proprietor of the first Colorado Springs hotel. One day, McIntyre saw Young, pictured below, when her family was checking in at the reception desk. The 14-year-old girl captured his heart, but she was too young to court. They became friends and eventually married on May 13, 1877. The couple had two children, Newell and Marian Dorothy. In 1898, McIntyre purchased the former Campbell house in Palmer Lake. (Both courtesy of Rogers Davis.)

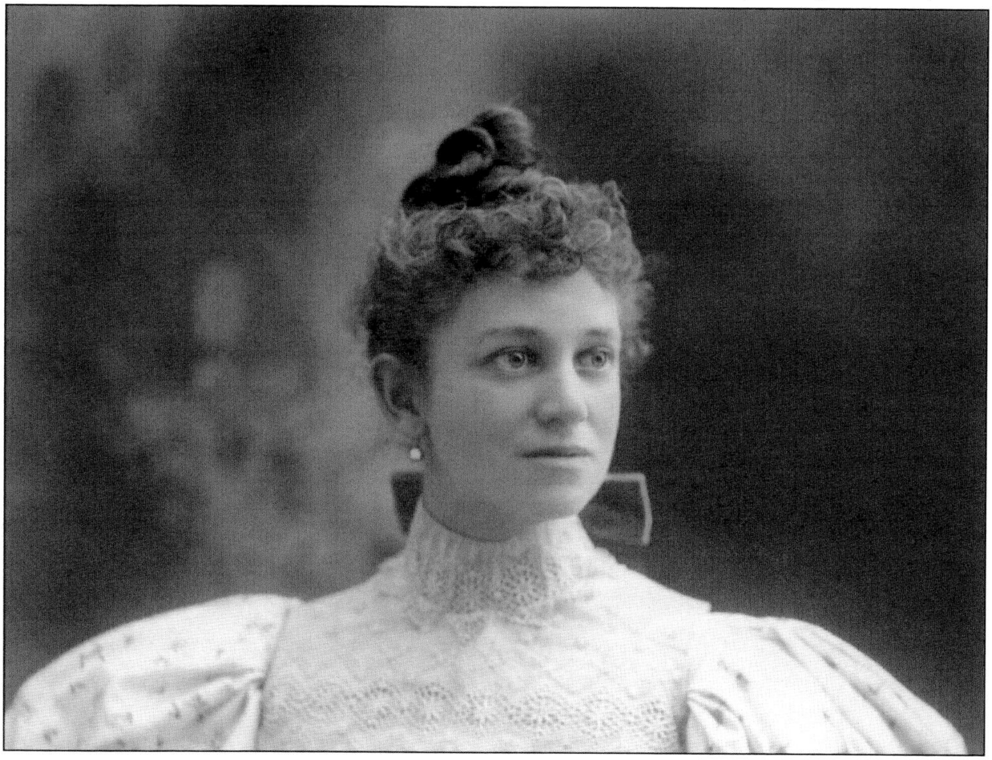

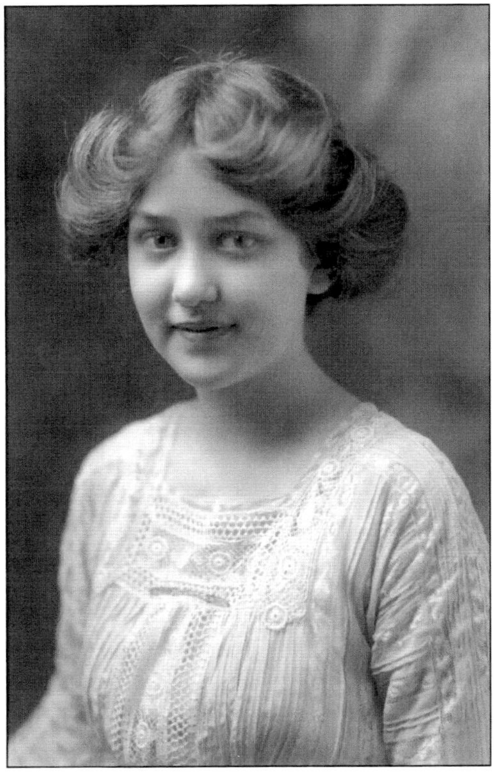

Marian D. McIntyre and Rogers Maxwell McDonough. For many years, the McIntyre family summered in Palmer Lake. They traveled on the train, followed by a coachman in a carriage bringing the family dog and a crate of chickens. Marian D. McIntyre, pictured at right at age 16, made pets of the chickens. When they became Sunday's dinner, she couldn't eat them. Described as beautiful, with gorgeous hair piled high, she presented a picture of "regal elegance" that captured the fancy of Rogers Maxwell McDonough, pictured below. Eleanor Romack remembered the young McDonough as "rampageous, the hub of the wheel, neat in appearance . . . handsome . . . a young blade." The "dashing blade" and the "beautiful girl," wearing her galoshes, eloped to Golden, Colorado. After returning to Palmer Lake, McDonough went on to become mayor of the town. (Both courtesy of Rogers Davis.)

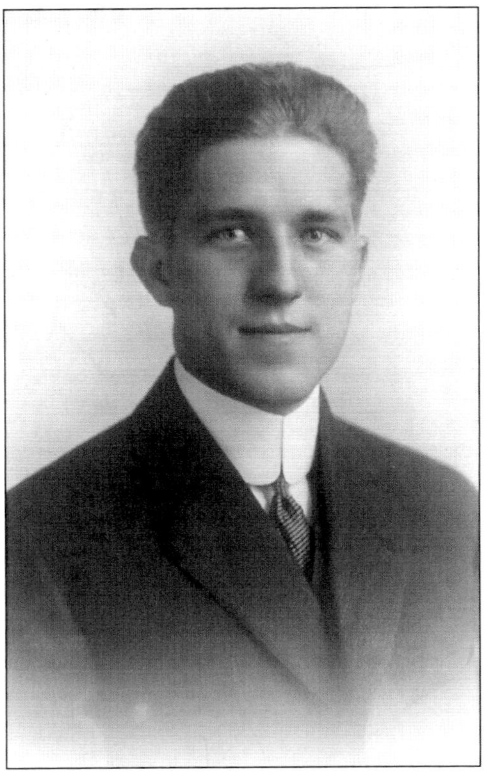

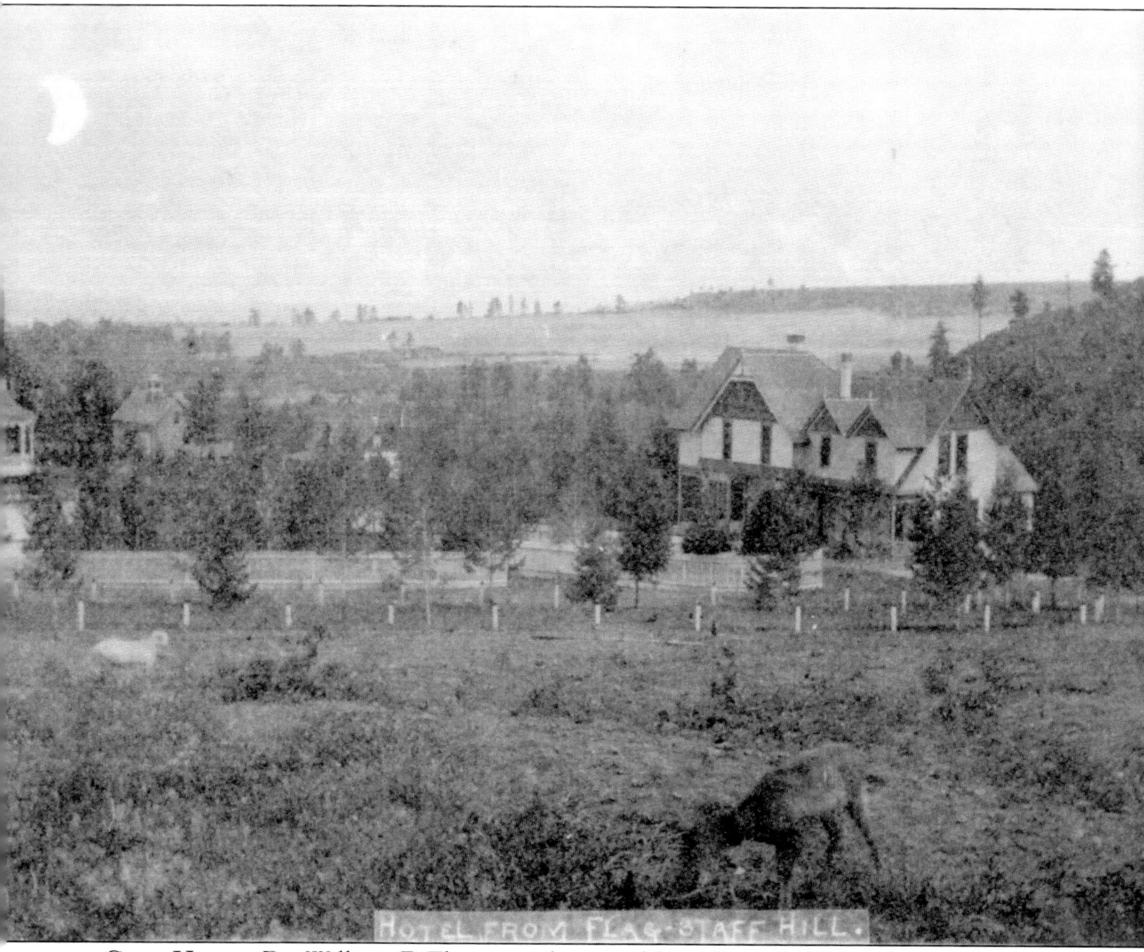

GLEN HOUSE. Dr. William F. Thompson borrowed heavily to fulfill his dream of a summer retreat. The Glen House, considered "a very good little hotel," later became a part of the famous Rockland Hotel. Thompson was determined that the hotel was not to be advertised as a family pension (boarding house) and not to be advertised as a sanitarium. He designed and printed a 3-by-5 inch card, stating "The Glen House. New Hotel, open June 1, 1884. Palmer Lake, Colorado. Offers to the Public and Tourists Superior Accommodations. Elegantly Furnished Rooms, with Bath Rooms and Closets on each Floor. H. N. Smith, Manager." Small print at the bottom of the card disclosed that the "Dairy and farm owned by the proprietors of this House will supply the Hotel."

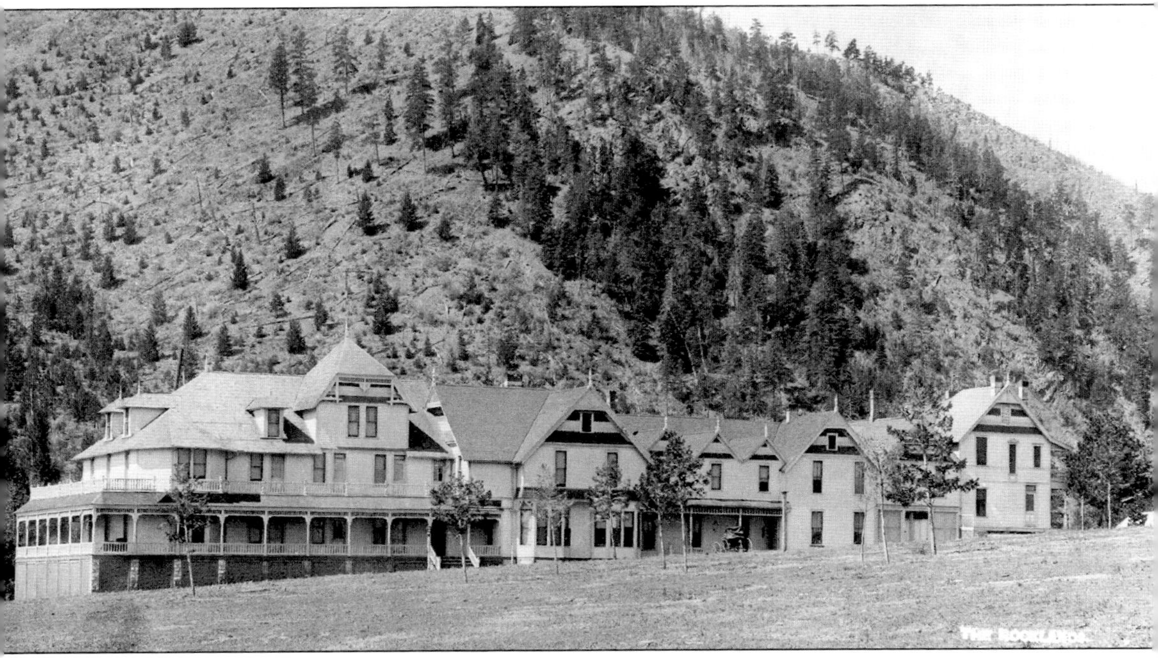

Rockland Hotel, c. 1893. In 1889, the Rockland Hotel was built by the Colorado Hotel and Sanitarium Company. The company was established by Dr. William F. Thompson and his Denver partners, realtor Jacob Murphey and attorney William Malone, specifically for resort and health spa development in Palmer Lake. The hotel was connected to the Glen House hotel and further enhanced by the addition of Dr. Thompson's first Estemere house, which was moved to form the west wing of the building. The imposing hotel structure was 260 feet long and featured 60 rooms. For more than 30 years, it stood as a grand showcase of luxury and enjoyed success as the best summer getaway in the Rocky Mountains. In 1920, a gas explosion tore through the building and set it afire. The towns' people watched heartbroken and helpless as the grand hotel burned to the ground. They mourned the loss of the hotel as a "great calamity" in the town's history.

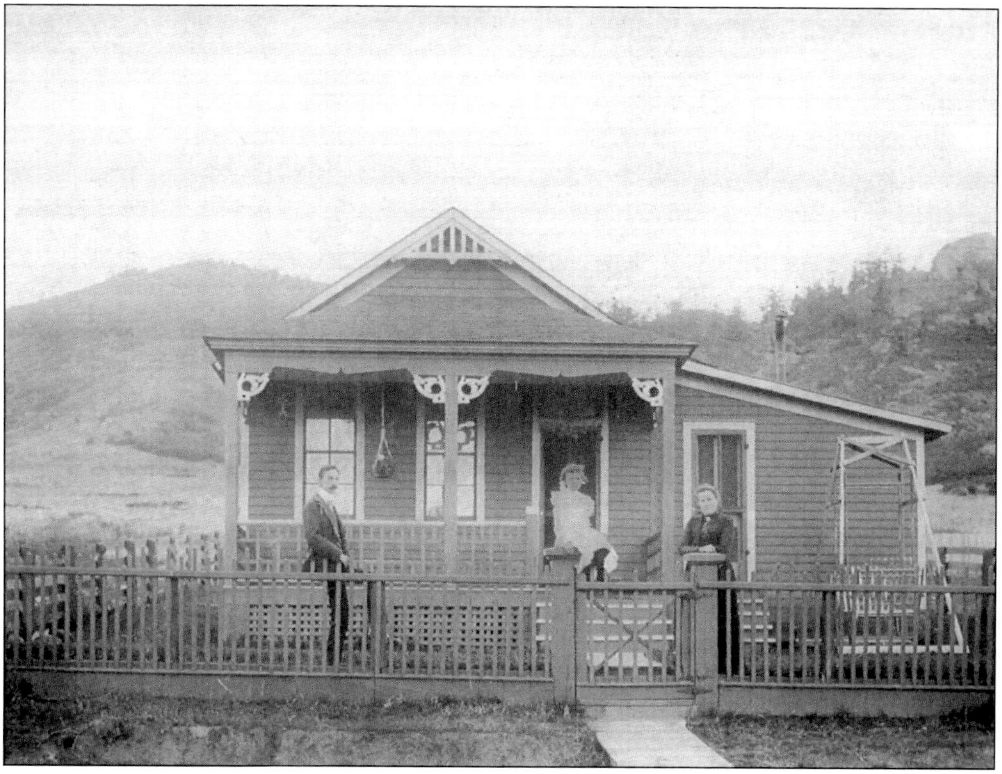

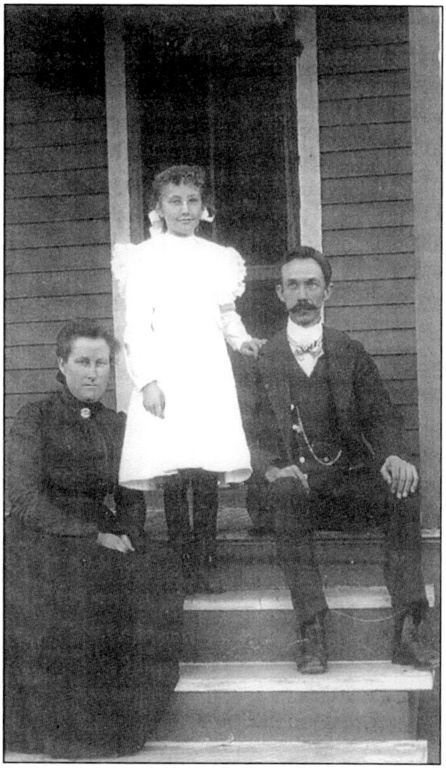

The Maddox Family, c. 1902. Henry S. Maddox served as the Denver & Rio Grande Railroad stationmaster in Palmer Lake in about 1899, before being transferred to Monument. A stationmaster had to be at least 18 years of age with a high school diploma, able to telegraph at least 15 words per minute, and know the operating rules. Responsibilities included tickets, telegrams, express shipments, and shipping and receiving. Maddox checked trains for trouble such as hot boxes, defective equipment, or sticking brakes and would flag the train's caboose as it passed if something was amiss. Maddox was also a councilman and mayor of Palmer Lake. Pictured above is the Maddox family in front of their Palmer Lake home, which was built in 1883, and still stands today. Pictured at left, from left to right, are Maddox's wife Nettie, his daughter Mate, and Maddox.

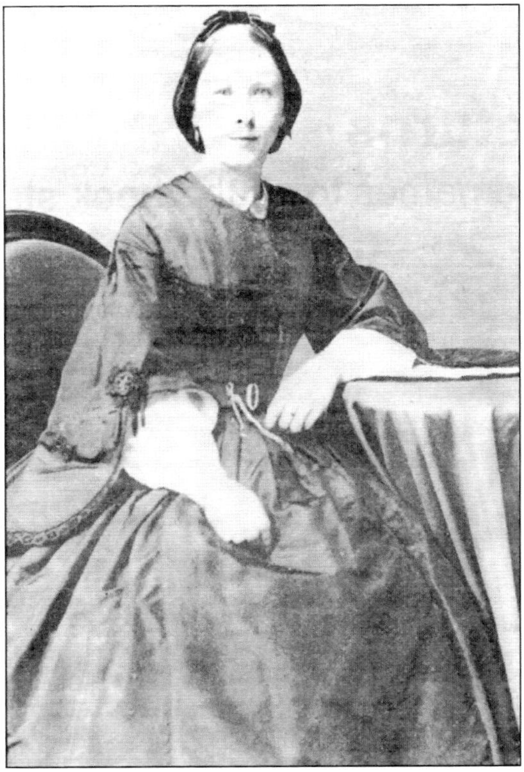

A Countess in Palmer Lake. Young Countess Katrina Wolf Murat is depicted at right around 1860. She was thought to be the first white woman to settle in Denver when she arrived in 1858 with her husband, Count Henri Murat of French aristocracy. She was known as the Betsy Ross of the Colorado Territory for making a flag considered the first American flag raised in Colorado. In 1887 at age 63, Murat moved to Palmer Lake. The Pioneer Society of Colorado helped finance her retirement years by paying the town of Palmer Lake to pipe water to her door free of charge for as long as she lived. Pictured below is Murat in about 1908. She was a recluse for 23 years and died in 1910. Her grave marker states, "In Memory of the Maker of the First U.S. Flag in Colorado."

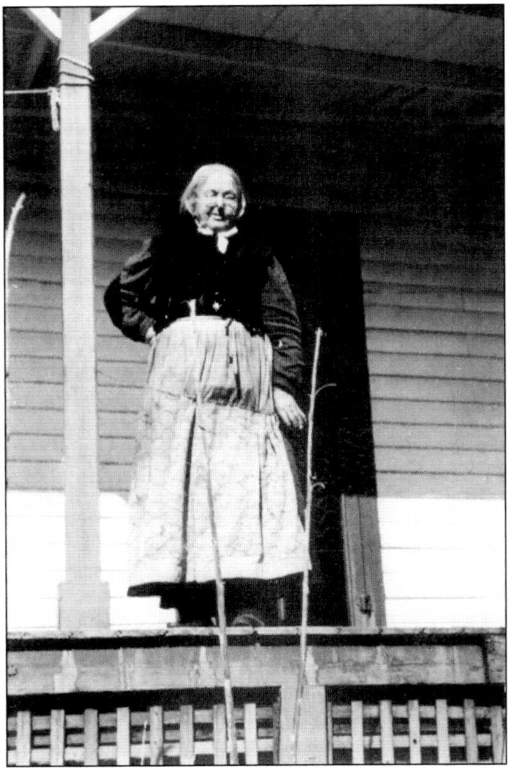

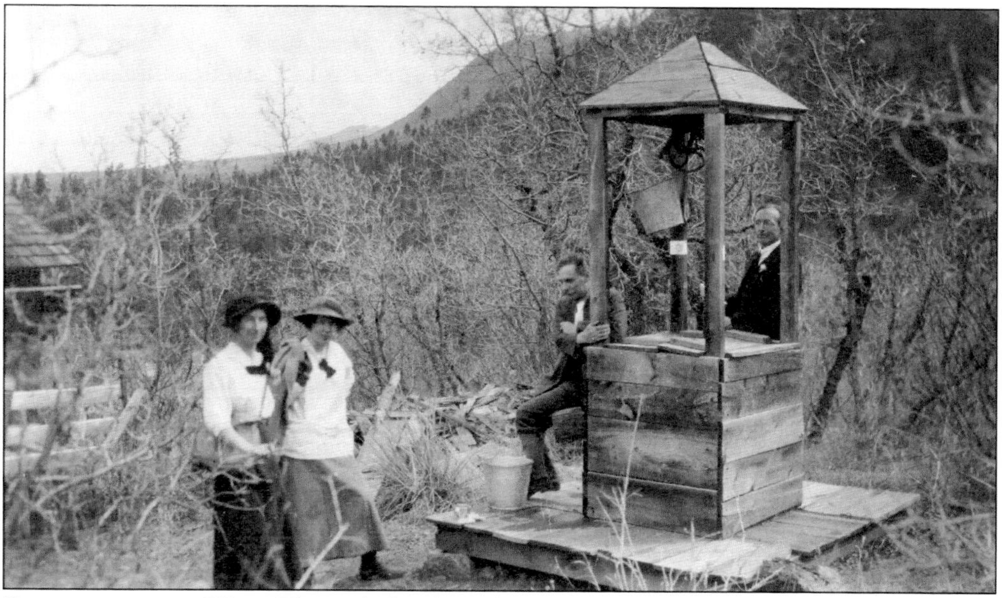

GATHERING AT THE WELL. The Vaile family, Joel Frederick, a prominent attorney, and Charlotte Marion, an author of children's books, built their summer cottage on a mountain slope above Estemere mansion. Pictured from left to right are Lucretia Vaile, unidentified woman and man, and William Vaile, who later became a U.S. congressman from Colorado. All four Vaile children spent much of their time tramping through the local mountains. (Courtesy of Victor Vaile.)

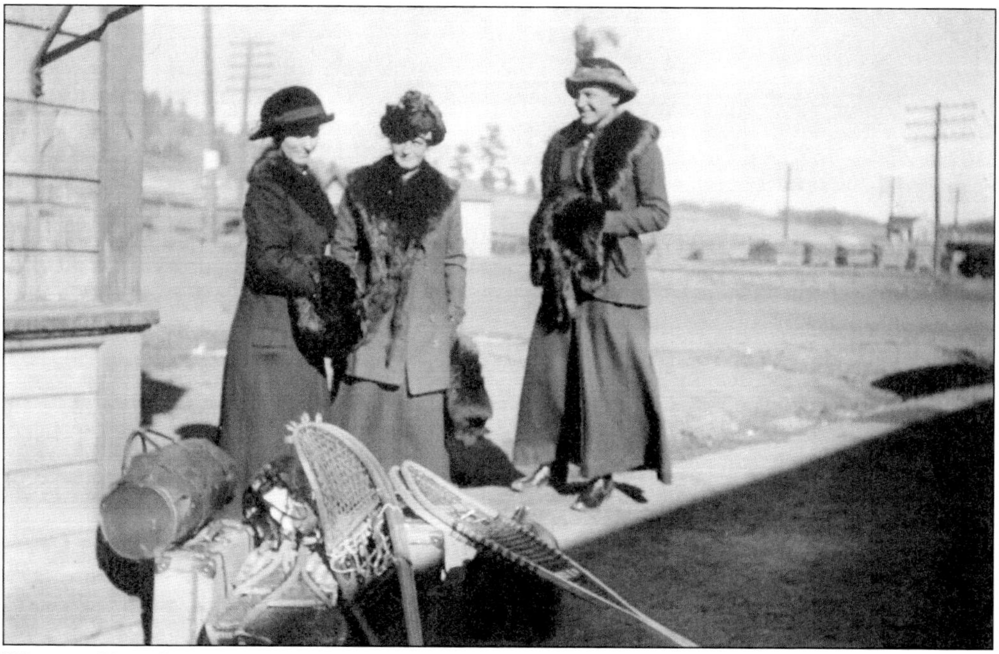

WOMEN WITH SNOWSHOES. Lucretia Vaile, on the right, and two unidentified women await the arrival of the train. An outdoors woman, Vaile and 24 hiking enthusiasts organized the Colorado Mountain Club in 1912. Vaile was a librarian in New York and Denver before retiring to Palmer Lake. She was active with the Historical Society and bequeathed funds for the Lucretia Vaile Museum in Palmer Lake. (Courtesy of Victor Vaile.)

An Afternoon Outing, c. 1912. Summer thunderstorms on the Palmer Divide can erupt with fury, leaving dirt roads muddy, washed out, and deeply rutted. Following such a storm, it took three unidentified individuals to push and one to steer this Ford over the rugged terrain on County Line Road.

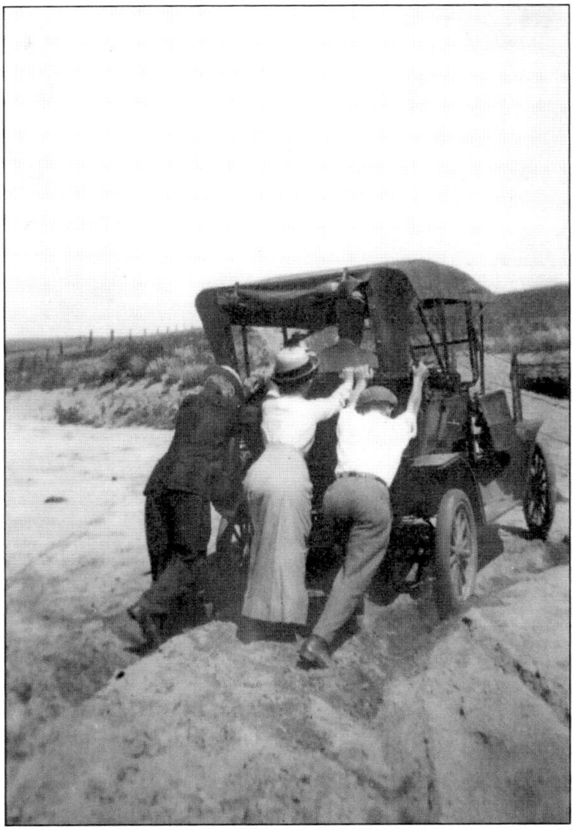

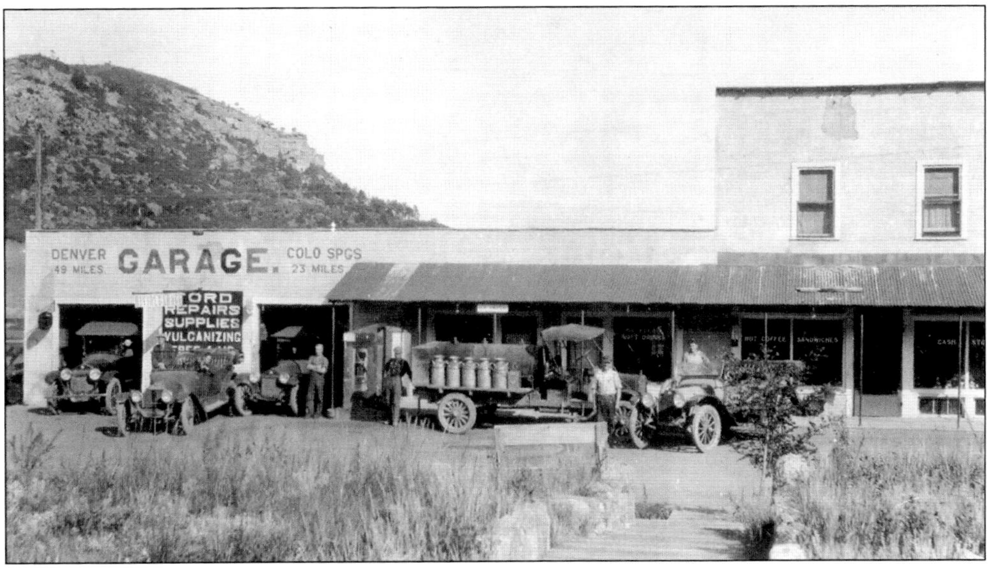

Carl's Garage, c. 1917. This garage was a thriving business on the old Denver Highway. Note the creamery truck loaded with milk cans in the foreground. In addition to performing repairs on Fords and selling supplies, employees treated tires with sulfur to increase their elasticity and strength. The first automobile to reach Palmer Lake was in 1899. Reportedly, George Giem was the first citizen to own a car.

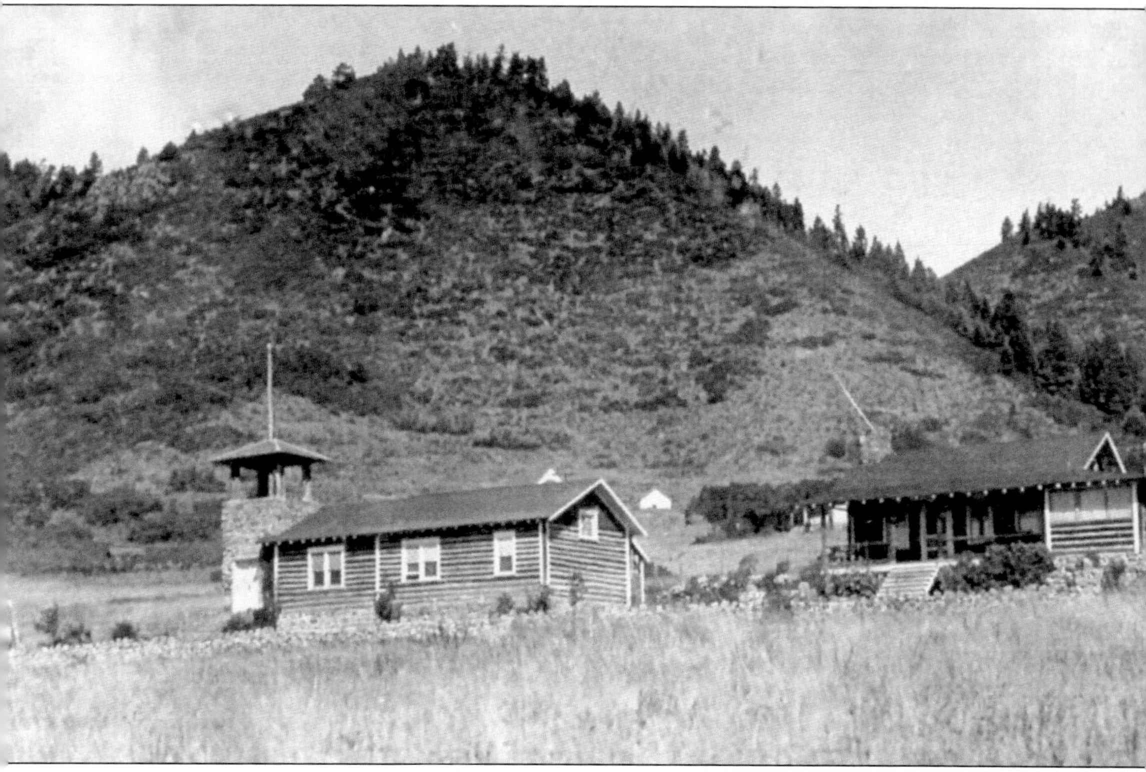

Little Log Church. Palmer Lake's first community church has been in continuous service since 1924. The Little Log Church was originally organized as the Palmer Lake Friends. Services were first held in the Palmer Lake Town Hall until the 41 charter members accepted a proposal by Huldah Nichols in 1925 to purchase two log houses for $2,700 and convert them into a sanctuary and parsonage. Until 1933, gas and coal oil lamps were used in the parsonage and church. The original bell from the first Palmer Lake schoolhouse is now in the belfry of the church. Orville Bender served as first pastor and moved into the new parsonage with his wife, Myrtle, and their three children. Pastor Bender's ill health forced him to resign in 1930.

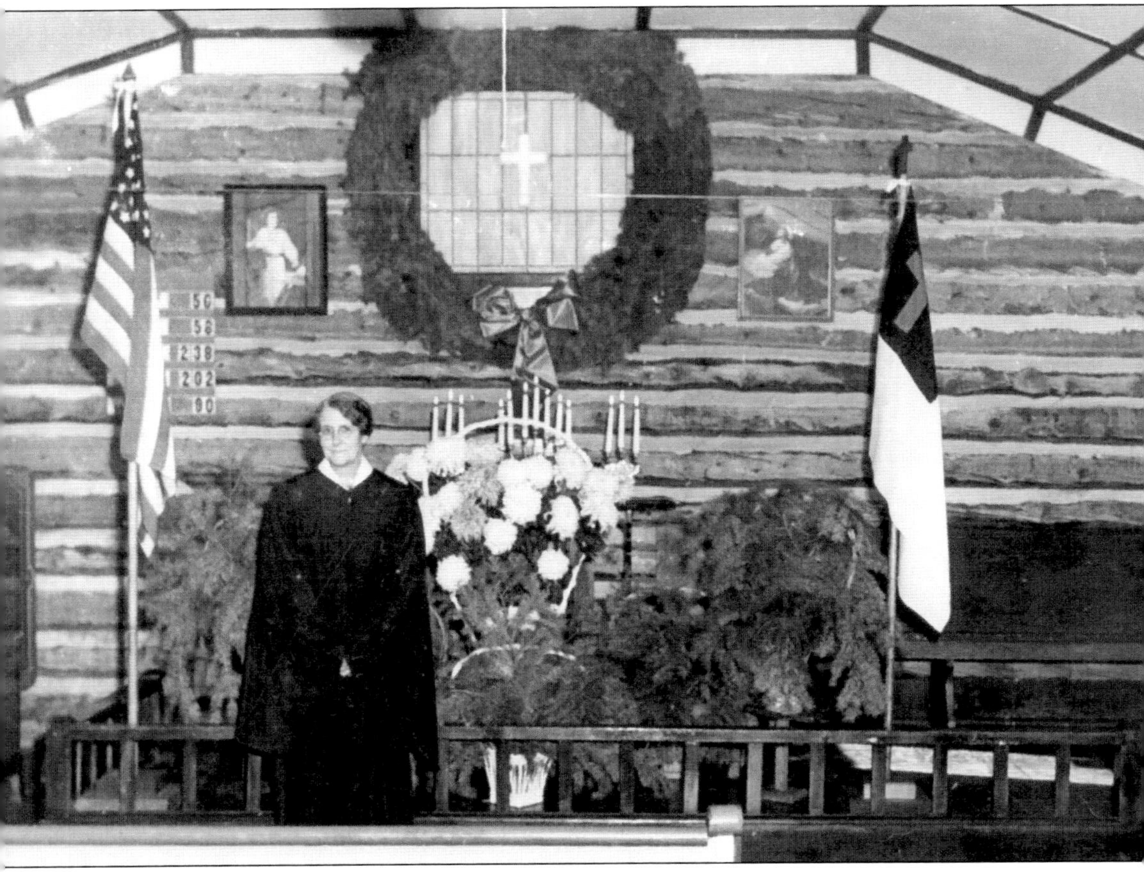

MISS MACY INSIDE THE LITTLE LOG CHURCH. Dr. Evalena Macy replaced Orville Bender as pastor of the Little Log Church in 1930 and served until her retirement in 1959. She was born of Quaker parentage near Emporia, Kansas. A member of the Society of Friends, she received her Bachelor of Arts degree from Friends University in Wichita and her Masters degree from Columbia University in New York. She served as a missionary and teacher in Cuba from 1920 to 1923. Poor health brought her to the drier climate of Colorado, where she entered treatment for tuberculosis in a private sanatorium. She wrote that to be without friends and family in a faraway place, perhaps waiting to die, tested her faith in a "God of love and mercy." Affectionately called "Miss Macy," she was described as emanating serene composure and innate goodness. Fern Britt wrote, "She was a central figure in the affairs of the whole town and exerted her influence for good in the most reprehensible people. Everyone trusted her implicitly."

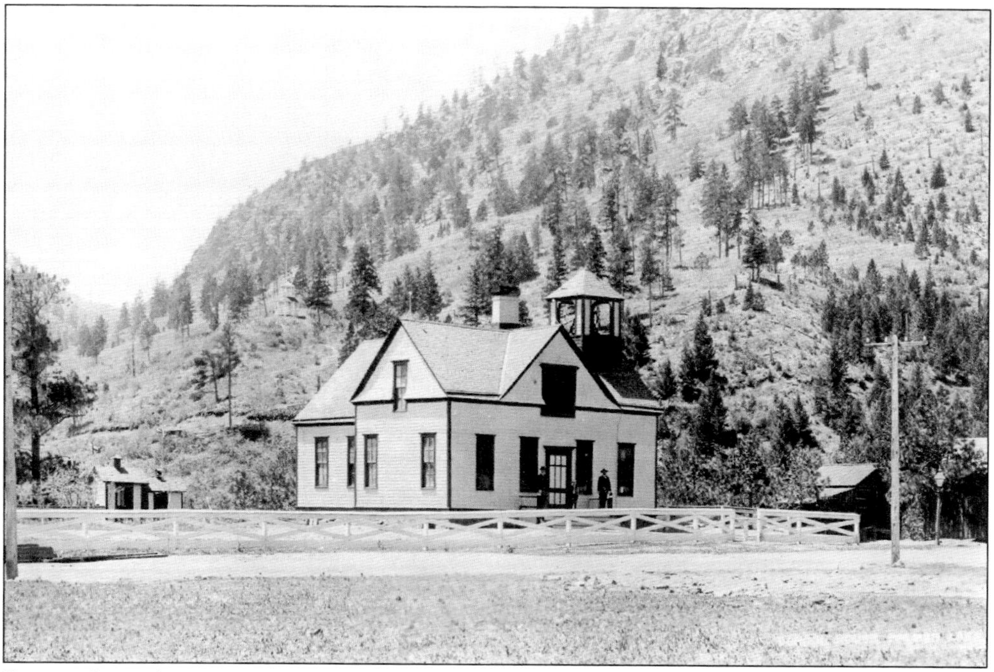

PALMER LAKE SCHOOLHOUSES. The schoolhouse above was donated to the town in 1888 by Dr. William F. Thompson. One teacher taught 20 to 30 pupils in grades one through eight. The bell in the belfry tolled at 8:30 a.m., 9:00 a.m., and again at 1:00 p.m. to alert students to arrive at school on time. Students played roll hoops, skip rope, dare base, blind man's bluff, baseball, hide and seek, run sheep run, and crack the whip in the school yard. The brick Palmer Lake Elementary School, built in 1934, is depicted below. This school also contained grades one through eight and replaced the old wooden school building, now a private residence, donated by Thompson.

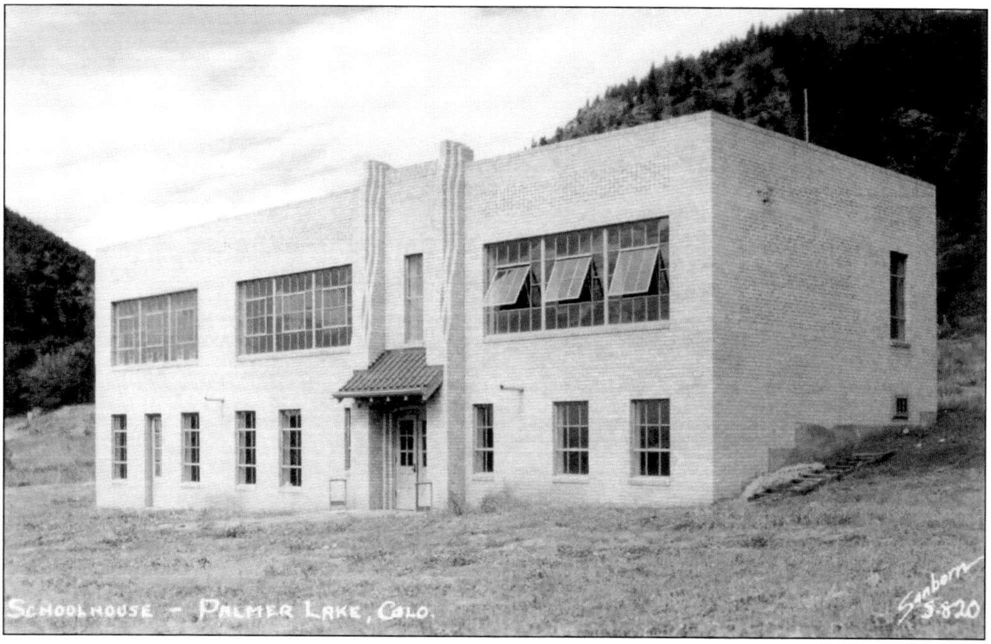

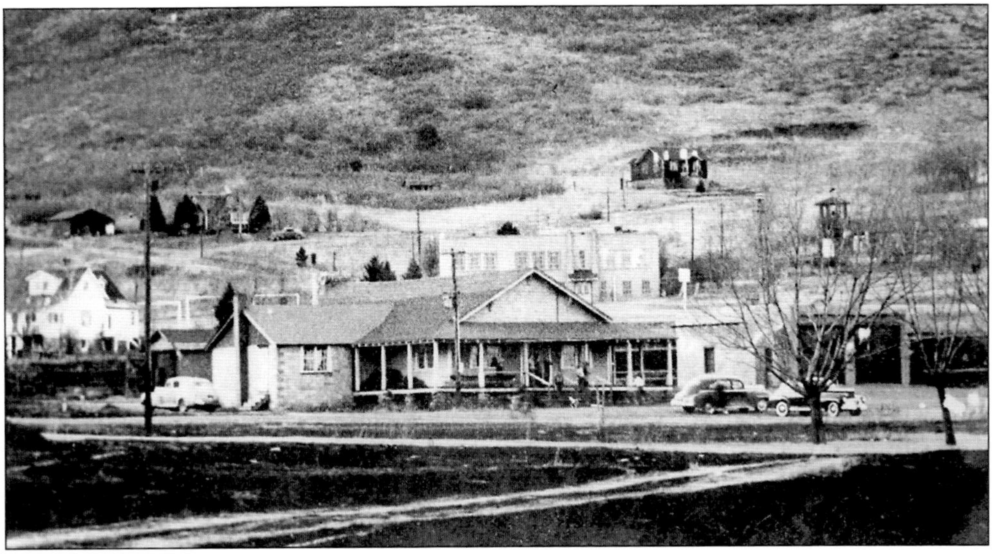

TOWN HALL. Construction of the Palmer Lake town hall building was financed in 1914 by warrants issued for the purchase of the land and building materials. Originally, to the right of the main room, there was a small library with shelves of books. This library was a gift from Dr. Francs Buchanan. A room to the left served as the town council chambers. Total cost of the building was about $1,600.

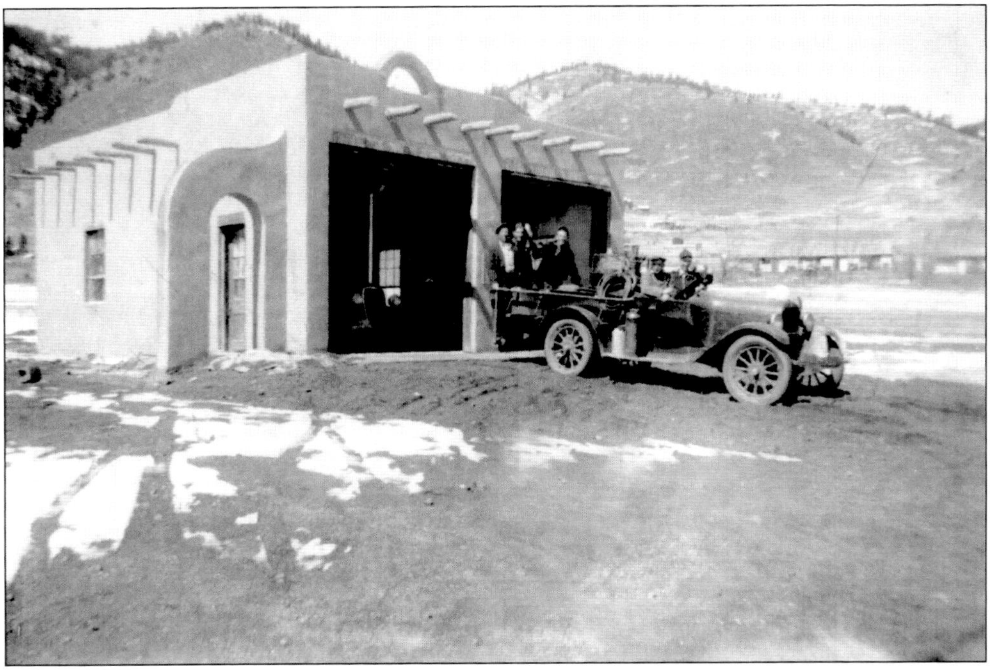

VOLUNTEER FIRE DEPARTMENT, C. 1938. The pueblo-style fire station was built through the Work Projects Administration in 1937. The Palmer Lake Volunteer Fire Department was organized by Byron Medlock, who purchased the first fire engine in 1927, the 1923 Dodge shown here. Charley Clark said, "Boys used to scramble all over it and, clinging like mad, ride to the fires." The fire department maintains the Palmer Lake Star on Sundance Mountain.

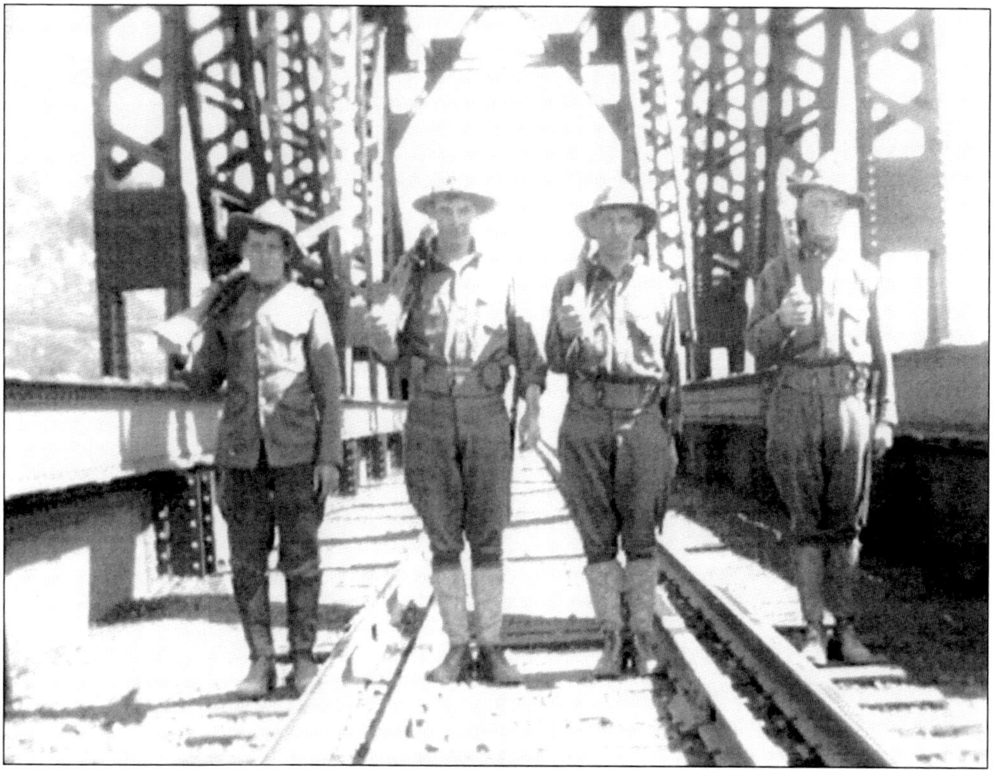

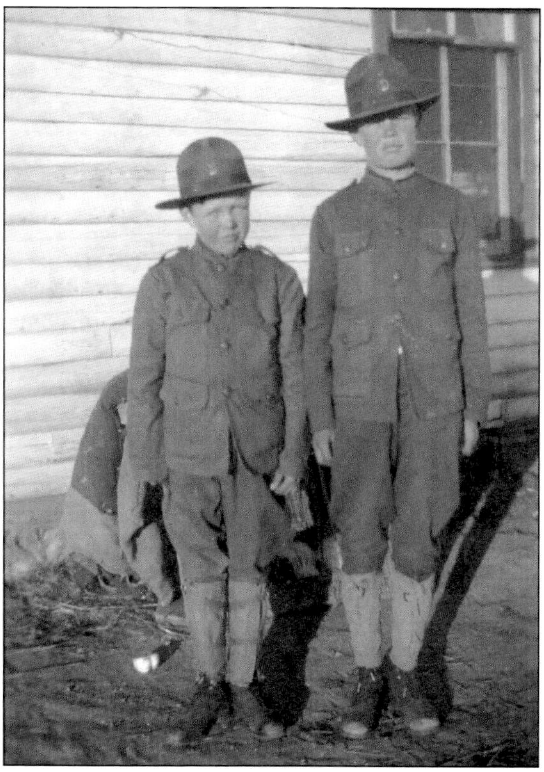

SOLDIERS PROTECTING COLORADO, C. 1917. When the United States entered into World War I with Germany, paranoia about German American loyalty to the United States swept the country. Many of Colorado's German Americans signed a pledge of loyalty to the country they chose to call home. Some changed their names and refused to speak the German language in their homes. Even though the testimonies of German American loyalty were numerous, they offered little comfort to many Coloradoans. Citizens were convinced that Colorado's power plants and water systems were prime targets of the German Kaiser. Armed guards were placed around Denver's water plants and reservoirs. Pictured above are unidentified soldiers guarding the bridge north of Palmer Lake. At left, from left to right, are Wilbur and Arthur Thompson, junior cadets in the Home Guard.

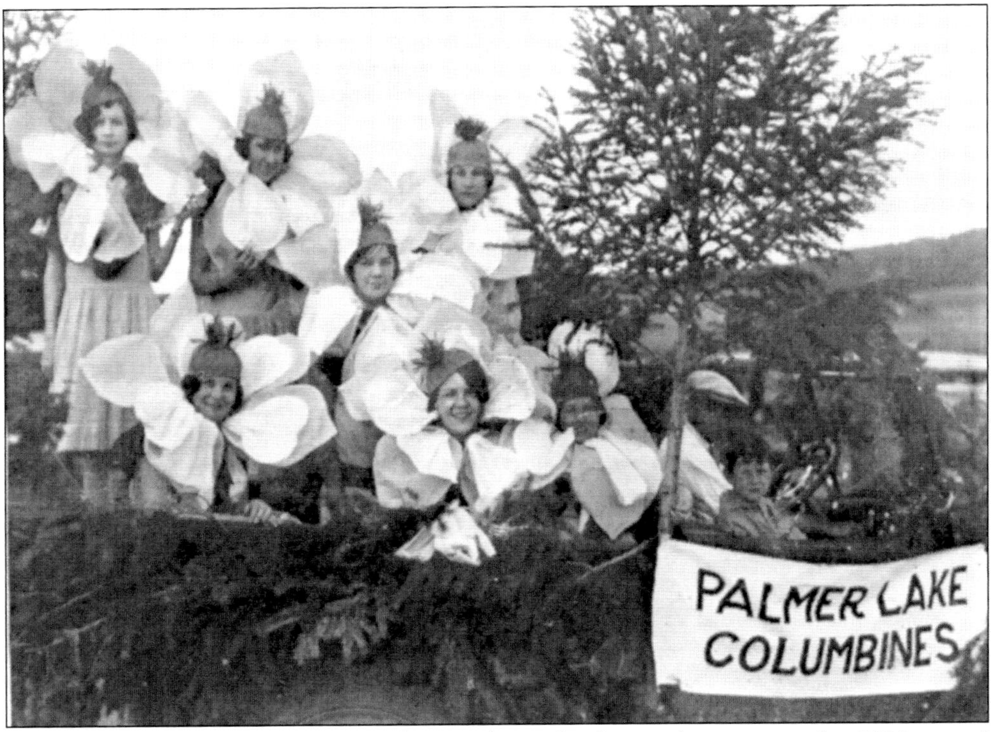

Ladies Having Fun. Lovely ladies decorated as columbines, above, enjoy the 1928 annual Palmer Lake Columbine Festival. The festival celebrated the Colorado Blue Columbine discovered by Dr. Edwin James during Maj. Stephen H. Long's expedition to the Palmer Divide in 1820. Pictured below are, from left to right, Agnes Shrull, Beatrice Niswanger, Evalena Macy, three unidentified, Freda Hubbard, Laura Stiffel, and an unidentified woman, kicking up their heels in glee. The ladies were members of a local homemakers club. This club, in existence from 1932 to 1996, was described as "a highly efficient group that was intent on learning anything and everything that pertained to the betterment of the home, family, community, and country."

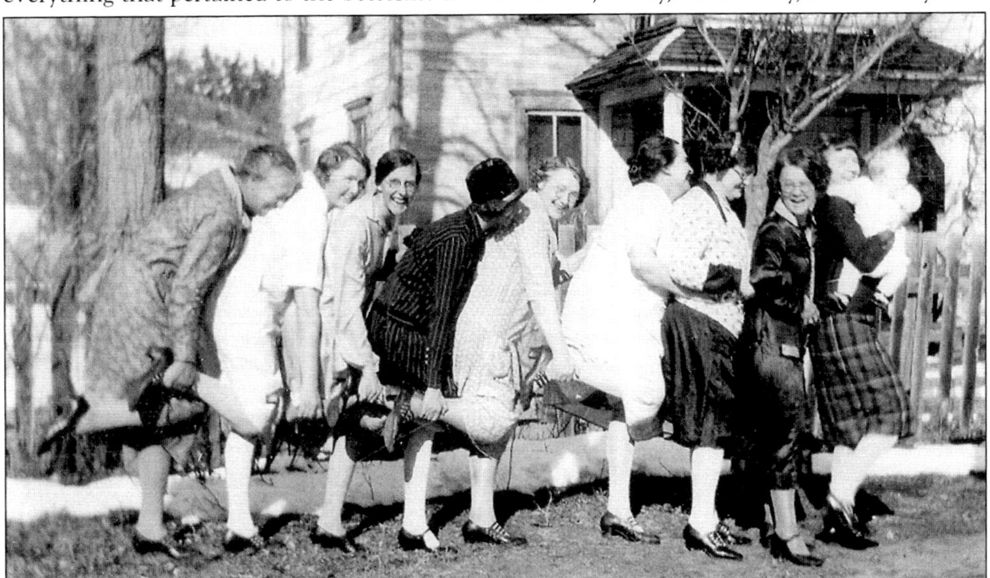

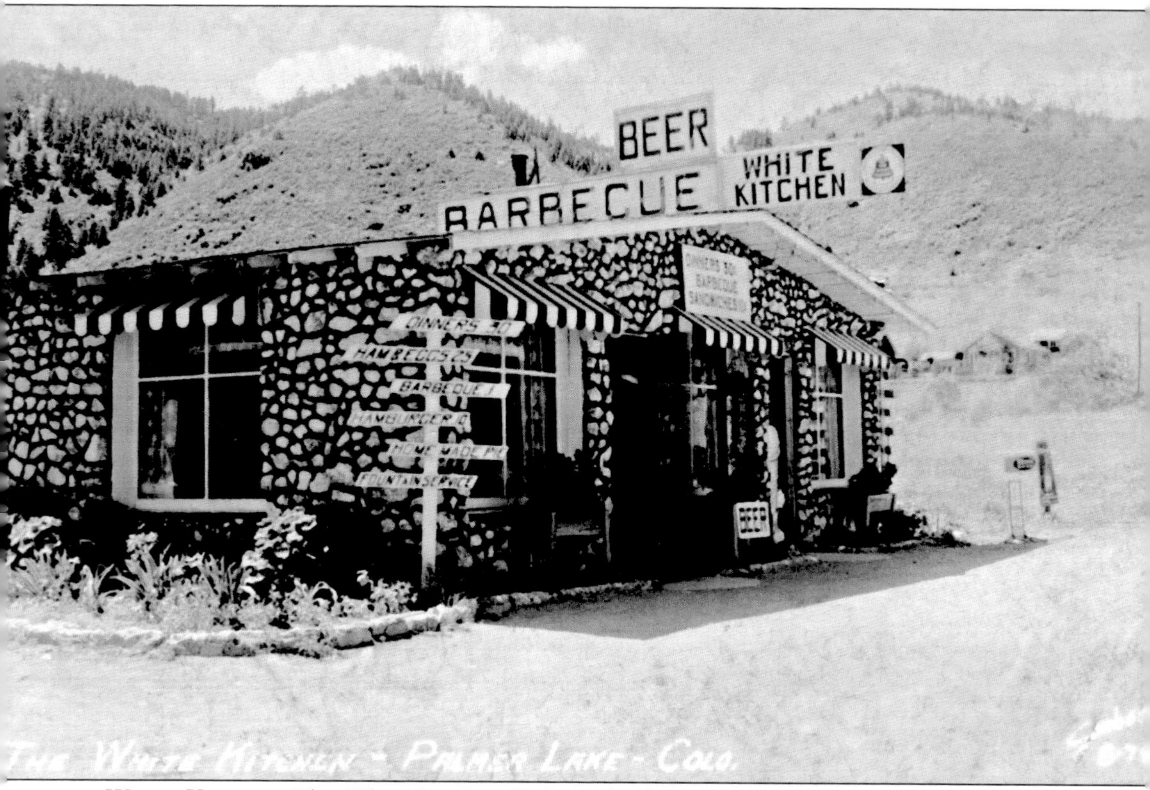

White Kitchen. The White Kitchen Café was built in 1927 by Freda Hubbard and her sister Faye Bellinger. Bellinger was a former postmaster of Palmer Lake. The white quartz rock was rolled down Sundance Mountain—seen here directly behind the building—by Hubbard, Bellinger, and their friend Jerry Kendrick. With the aid of a donkey cart, the rock was then hauled to the building site. The café operated as a 24-hour truck stop, servicing the heavy traffic that travelled State Highway 105 before the opening of Interstate 25 rerouted traffic away from Palmer Lake. For many years, the structure was the home of the Piper family. In 1998, Jeannine Engel purchased the structure and established the Rock House in 1999. It is famous for its ice cream and tasty lunch menu. (Courtesy of Victor Vaile.)

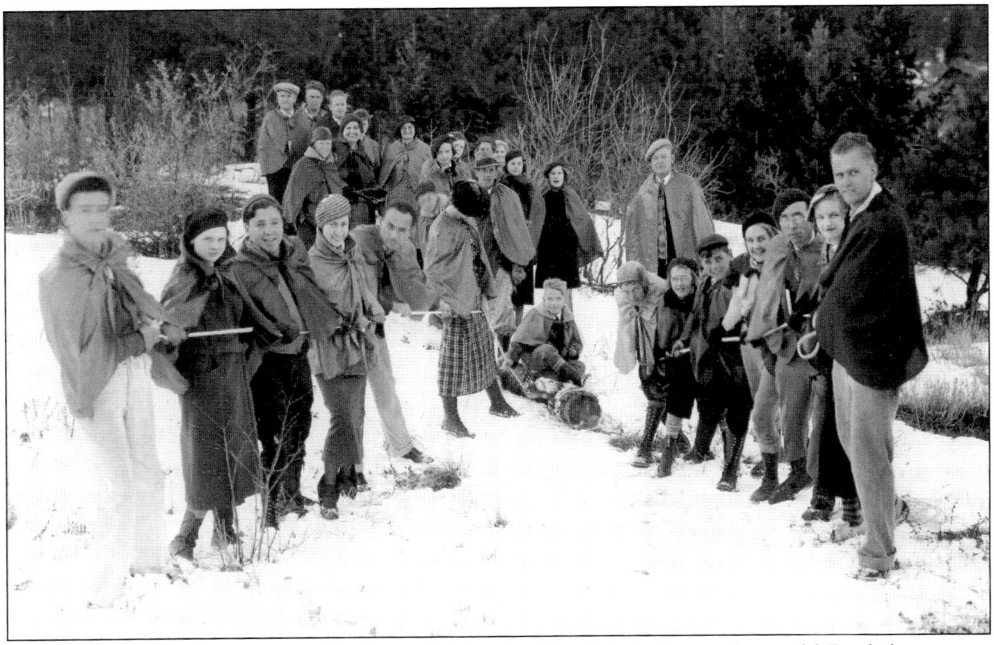

Yule Log Festivities. The American version of the Yule Log Festival, an old English custom, began in Lake Placid, New York. Palmer Lake's first festival was organized by Evalina Macy and Lucretia Vaile in 1933 and continues today. Pictured above are festival participants in about 1934. A log was marked with a red ribbon and hidden. A bugle would sound and the hunt would begin. Once found, the log was pulled back to the town hall with its finder and friends sitting astride. Attendees drank steaming bowls of wassail and toasted, "Be whole, good health to you." The log was burned in a fire started with a splinter from the previous years' log. The town's first log was ignited by splinters sent from the Lake Placid group. Pictured below is a group of attendees in the 1930s.

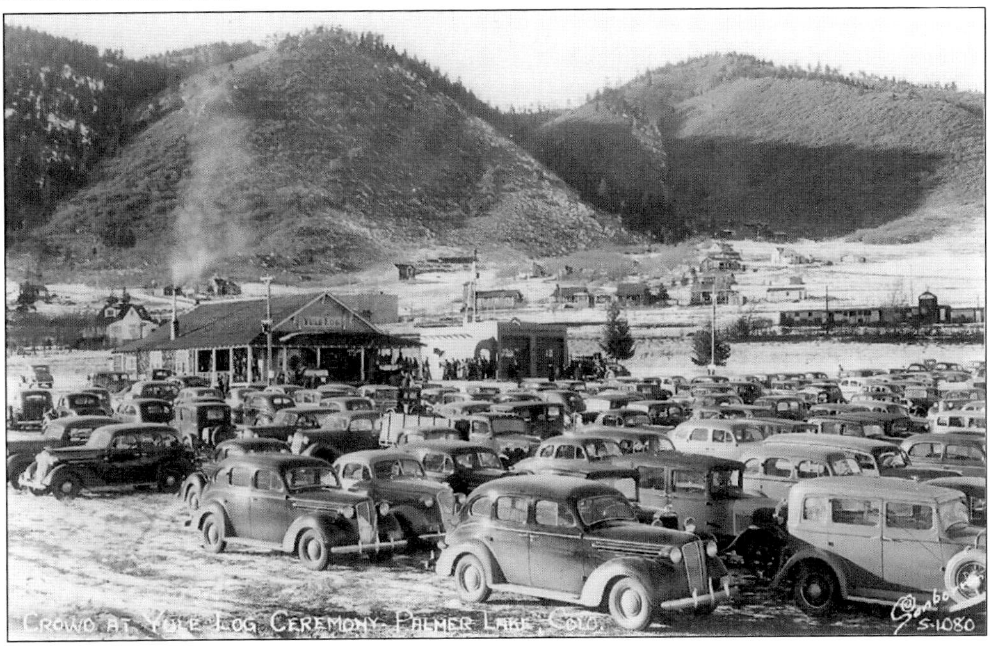

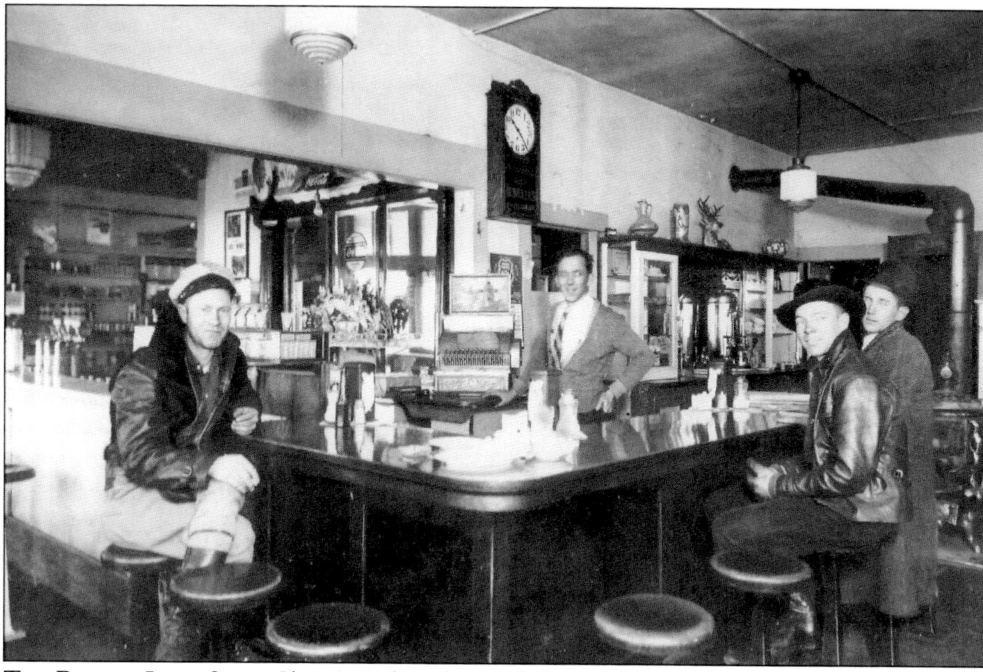

The Palmer Lake Star. Sloan's Cafe is depicted above in about 1935. In 1934, while at the cafe, Bert Sloan and B. E. Jack drew up plans for the Palmer Lake Star. The star was to be built on the side of Sundance Mountain above the town. A group of four men, including C. E. Rader, Byron Medlock, Richard Wolf, and Sloan began construction of the star. Dizzy, Sloan's German shepherd, carried a doggy pack stuffed with hammers, wires, and light bulbs across the rough mountainside, coming to whomever whistled or called his name. A bronze statue honoring Dizzy stands in the town commons. Pictured below is the Star in about 1936. Except during the blackouts of World War II, the Star, consisting of 91 lights, has shone brightly each December to proclaim the spirit of goodwill. (Above, courtesy of Sloan-Potts Collection.)

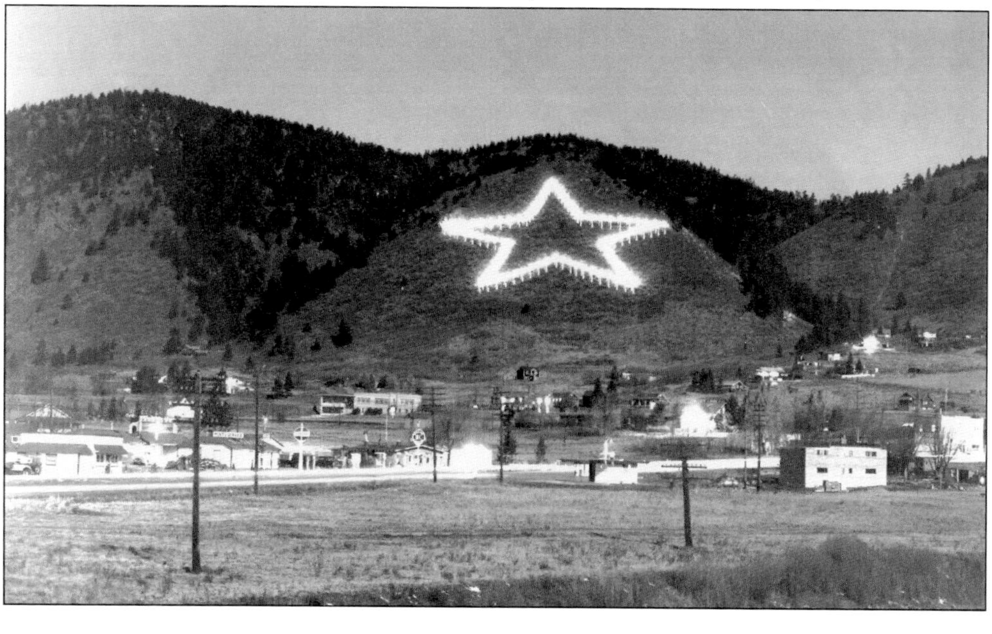

Four

Rocky Mountain Chautauqua and Glen Park

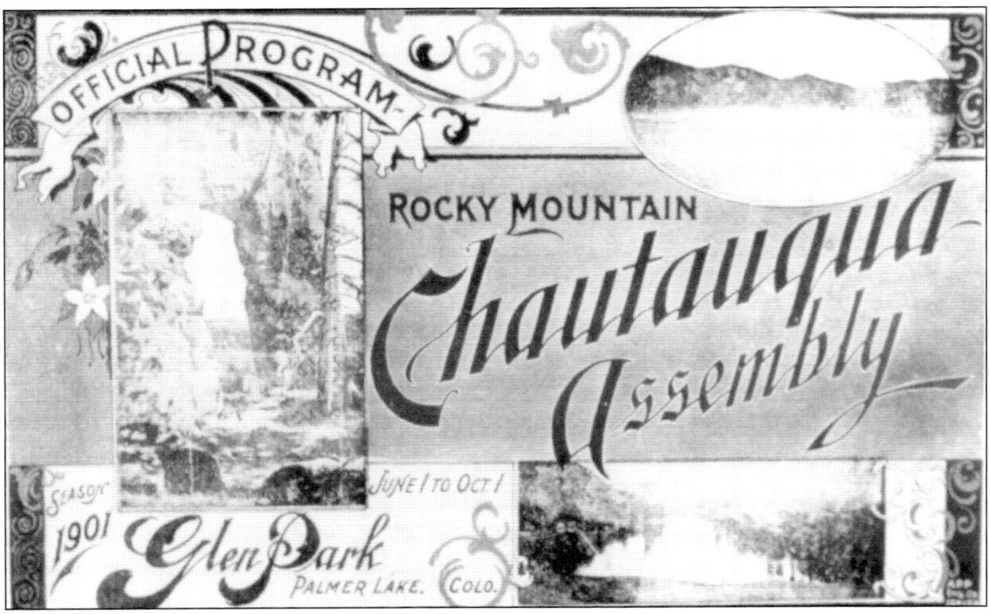

Rocky Mountain Chautauqua. The Chautauqua movement began in Lake Chautauqua, New York, in 1874 to provide educational lectures, cultural entertainment, spiritual enlightenment, and outdoor recreation to rural America. The First Rocky Mountain Chautauqua in Colorado was held at Glen Park in Palmer Lake in 1887. Its educational and cultural influence put Palmer Lake on the map, defining it as one of the most popular summer resorts on the Front Range.

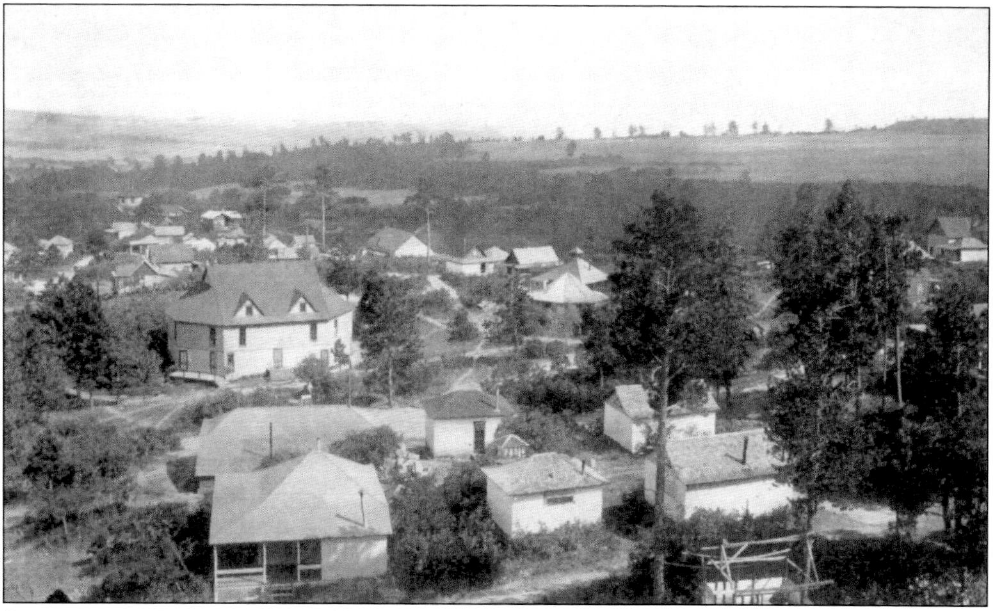

CHAUTAUQUA BEGINNINGS. Buildings from the early Chautauqua assemblies in Glen Park are depicted above. The Colorado Sunday School Association began plans to establish a Chautauqua in Colorado in the early 1880s. The intent was to create a resort equally as popular as New York's Chautauqua, which evolved into what was described as a university for the people. Palmer Lake was selected for its natural beauty and rail accessibility. The Glen Park Association was formed, and under the direction of R. H. Gilmore, construction began on roads, trails, rental cottages, and a large auditorium, shown center left, that seated 500 to 700 people. Pictured below is Glen Park's railroad station, which operated for more than 10 years. The Denver & Rio Grande Railroad agreed to charge $1 for a round trip from Denver to Glen Park. (Both courtesy of Herbert Edwards.)

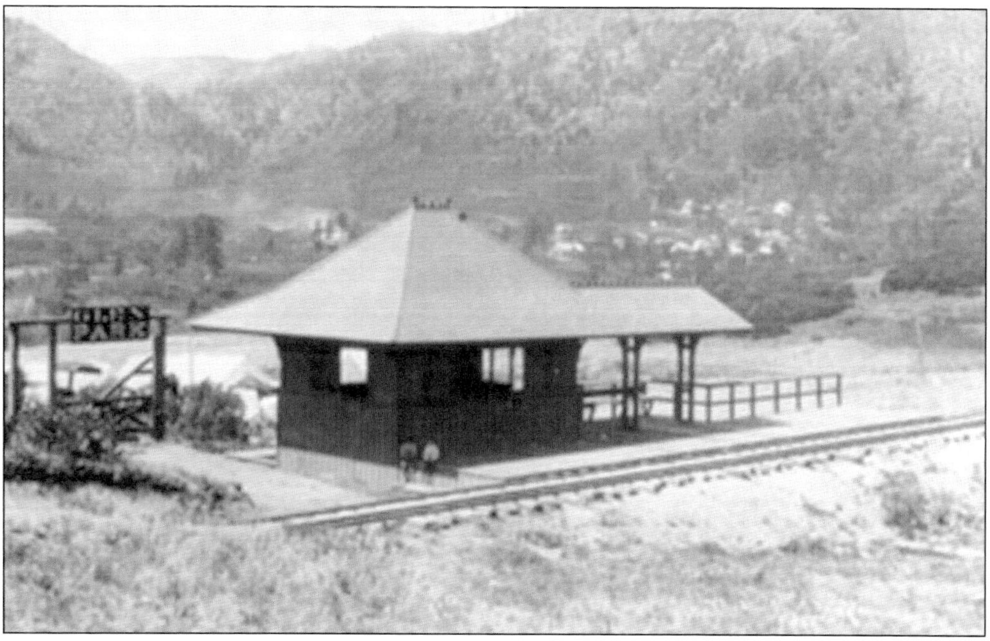

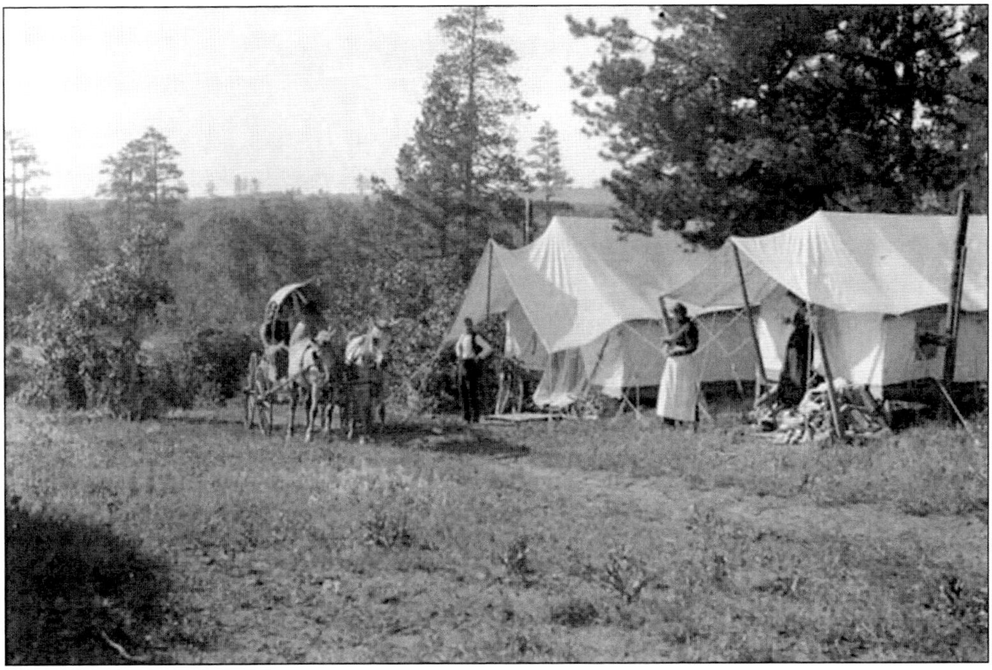

Early Glen Park Accommodations. Chautauqua attendees and summer residents could either bring tents or rent tents that ranged from the small "A" tents to big wall tents. Rents varied from $3.50 to $15 per month. In 1899, pitching your own tent required a $2.50 license fee, which increased to $5 by 1904. Many of the tent cottages had wooden floors, shingled roofs, and canvas sides. They were furnished with a spring bed, mattress, table, and chairs. An iron and cooking stove were available at an extra cost. Forrest Priestly, president of the Chautauqua Assembly and the Glen Park Improvement Company, is credited with introducing tent cottages as temporary housing for visitors to Glen Park.

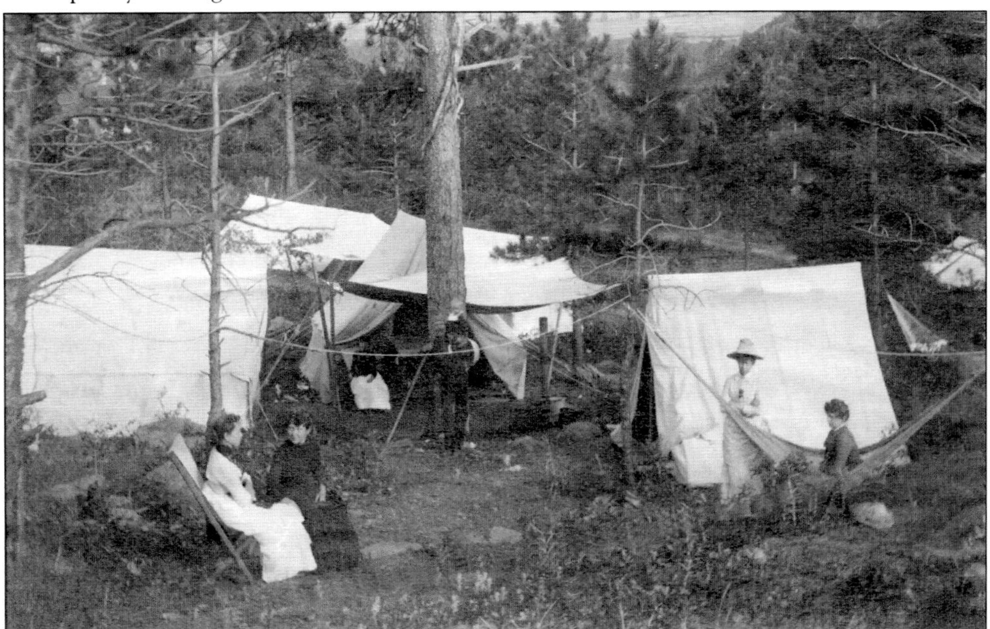

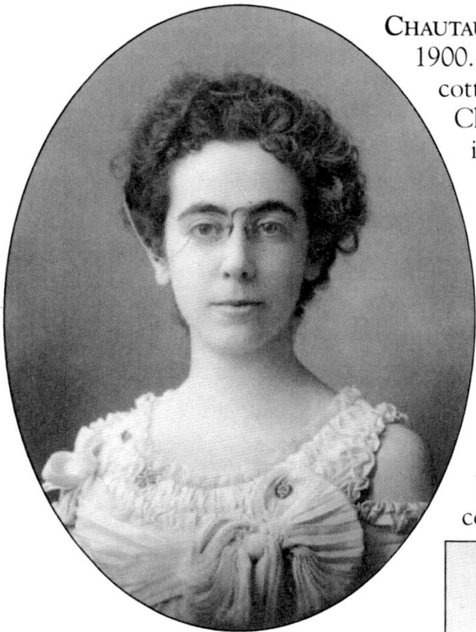

CHAUTAUQUA ACTIVITIES. At left is Mabel Edwards around 1900. She and her husband, Stanley, were among many cottage owners in Glen Park who supported the Chautauqua movement. Edwards was an instructor in oratory at Denver University and had studied elocution at Chautauqua, New York. She taught classes and gave performances at the 1901 Glen Park Chautauqua. Her lessons in vocal expression were concerned with interpretation of literature, while the Delsarte exercises she taught were to develop health, grace, and poise in women of all ages. This method was generally followed in Glen Park and was a must for every cultured young lady. Her husband served as secretary and treasurer of the Glen Park Improvement Company. Pictured below is a Chautauqua program from 1899. (Left, courtesy of Herbert Edwards.)

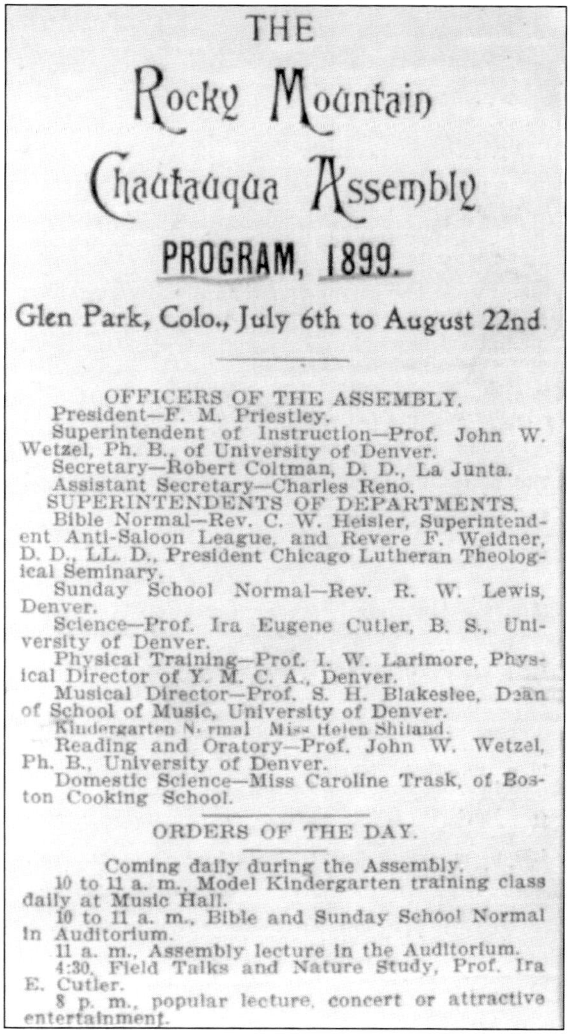

THE

Rocky Mountain

Chautauqua Assembly

PROGRAM, 1899.

Glen Park, Colo., July 6th to August 22nd.

OFFICERS OF THE ASSEMBLY.

President—F. M. Priestley.

Superintendent of Instruction—Prof. John W. Wetzel, Ph. B., of University of Denver.

Secretary—Robert Coltman, D. D., La Junta.

Assistant Secretary—Charles Reno.

SUPERINTENDENTS OF DEPARTMENTS.

Bible Normal—Rev. C. W. Heisler, Superintendent Anti-Saloon League, and Revere F. Weidner, D. D., LL. D., President Chicago Lutheran Theological Seminary.

Sunday School Normal—Rev. R. W. Lewis, Denver.

Science—Prof. Ira Eugene Cutler, B. S., University of Denver.

Physical Training—Prof. I. W. Larimore, Physical Director of Y. M. C. A., Denver.

Musical Director—Prof. S. H. Blakeslee, Dean of School of Music, University of Denver.

Kindergarten Normal—Miss Helen Shiland.

Reading and Oratory—Prof. John W. Wetzel, Ph. B., University of Denver.

Domestic Science—Miss Caroline Trask, of Boston Cooking School.

ORDERS OF THE DAY.

Coming daily during the Assembly.

10 to 11 a. m., Model Kindergarten training class daily at Music Hall.

10 to 11 a. m., Bible and Sunday School Normal in Auditorium.

11 a. m., Assembly lecture in the Auditorium.

4:30, Field Talks and Nature Study, Prof. Ira E. Cutler.

8 p. m., popular lecture, concert or attractive entertainment.

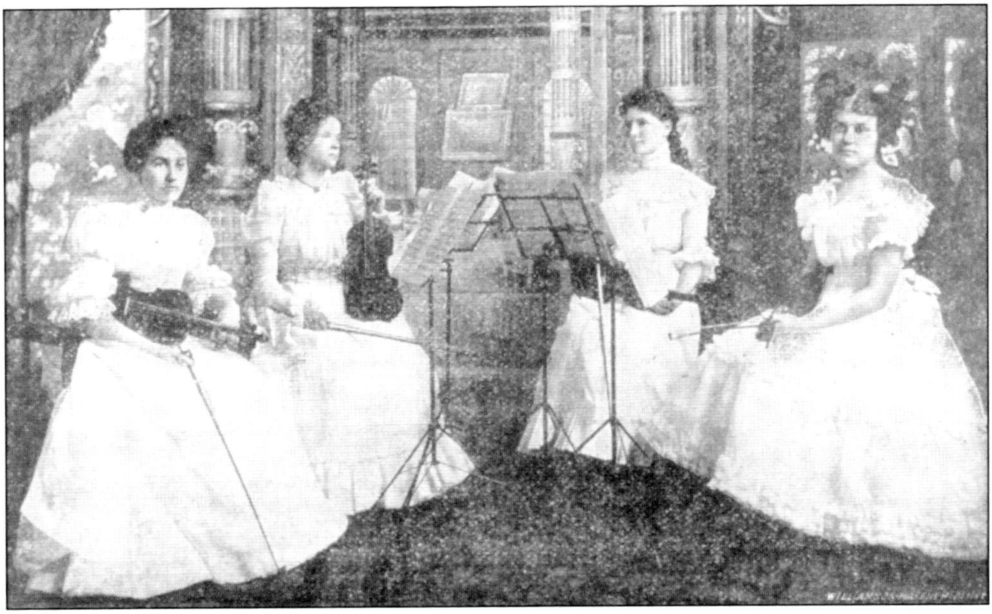

Ladies' Social Activities. The Chautauqua at Glen Park provided the atmosphere of a quiet retreat, but offered programs in music, art, drama, current events, religious study groups, secular lecture courses, and nature study. Social events included picnics, receptions, and moonlight rides. Participants held songfests and recitals, and gave dramatic presentations. Pictured above is the Dawkins violin quartet, which was comprised of these unidentified young ladies from Denver. This group became one of the main musical features of the Chautauqua. Accommodations were austere and sparse and people took pride in roughing it in the rustic cabins. Nonetheless, the women maintained Victorian grace, elegance, and genteel manners in the campground atmosphere. Pictured below are several unidentified ladies who gathered between sessions for social interaction while they did piecework on a quilt. (Above, courtesy of Herbert Edwards; below, courtesy of Lori Suddeth.)

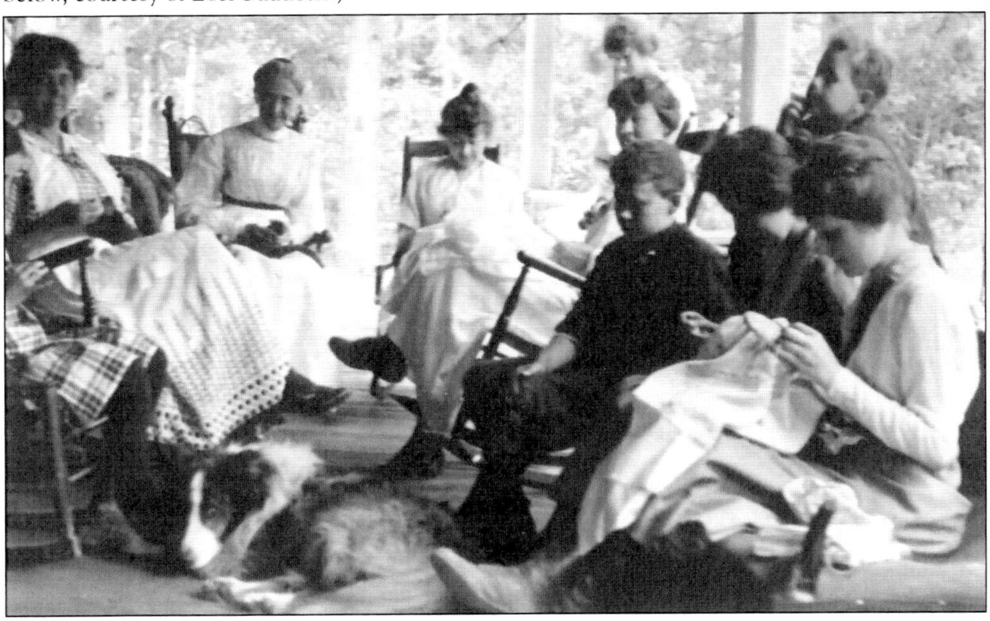

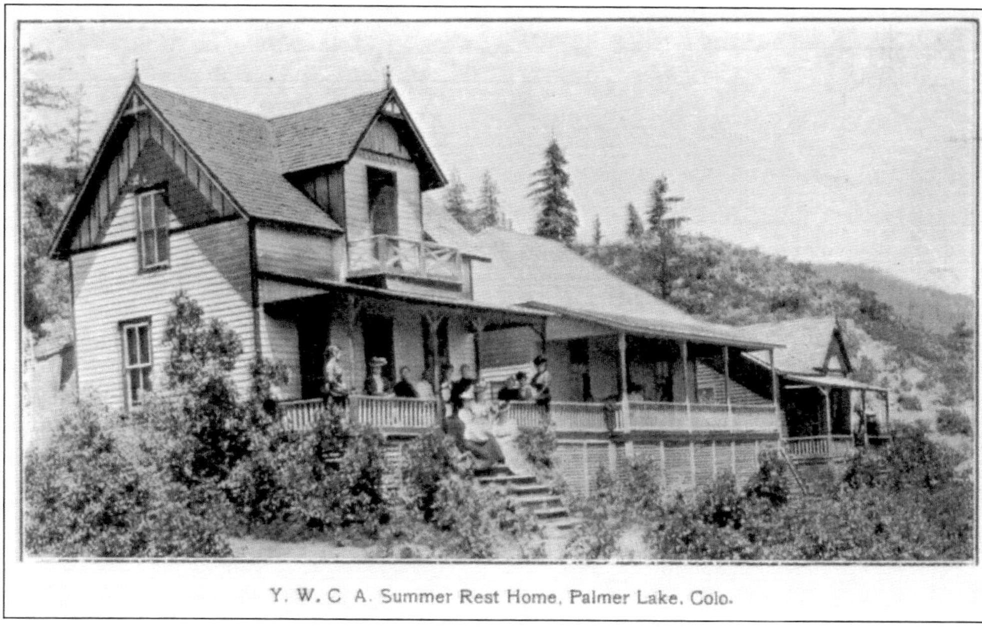

Youth Accommodations and Activities. The Young Women's Christian Association home in Glen Park, depicted above, opened in 1893. The price for room and board was $3.50 a week. Their slogan was "to furnish an outing and rest in the mountains for self-supporting women at a price within their reach." A dining hall and tent annex were added that could accommodate 50 guests. The association operated this home until the late 1920s. This building still stands on Largo Avenue. Glen Park also boasted a vacation hostel for boys founded by Fanny Manly in 1898. The hostel was known as the Home for Manly Boys. Outdoor activity was encouraged and was deemed a healthful and useful way to use one's leisure time. Pictured below is a group at a campsite near the reservoir. (Both courtesy of Victor Vaile.)

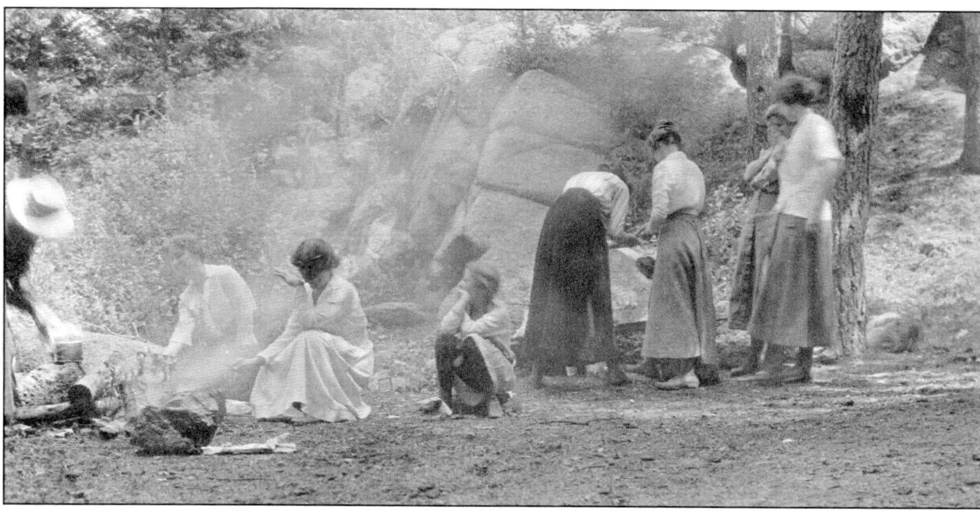

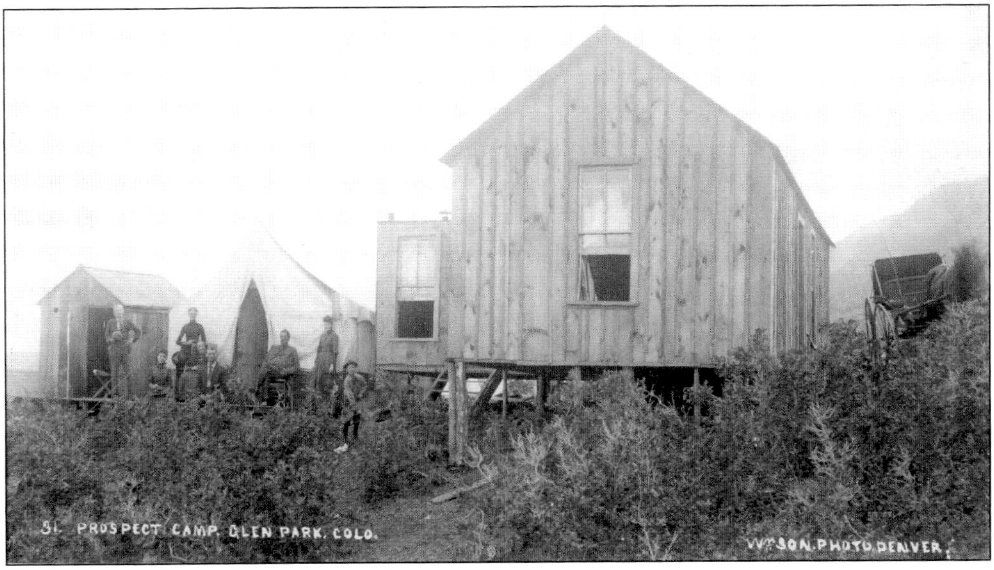

LIFE IN GLEN PARK. The Cory family came to Glen Park in 1886. Pictured above is the family's cabin. In 1898, a dispute erupted between the town's people, and the Chautauqua and the Glen Park Association after the town council allowed a temporary fence to be built across the roads leading into the property. This allowed the Chautauqua to collect entrance fees to their grounds. The tollgate war ensued for several years, and led one individual to chop down the gate during the night! The Bread Store, where fresh bread was available daily, is seen below. This was one of the small stores that sprang up to support the many guests in Glen Park.

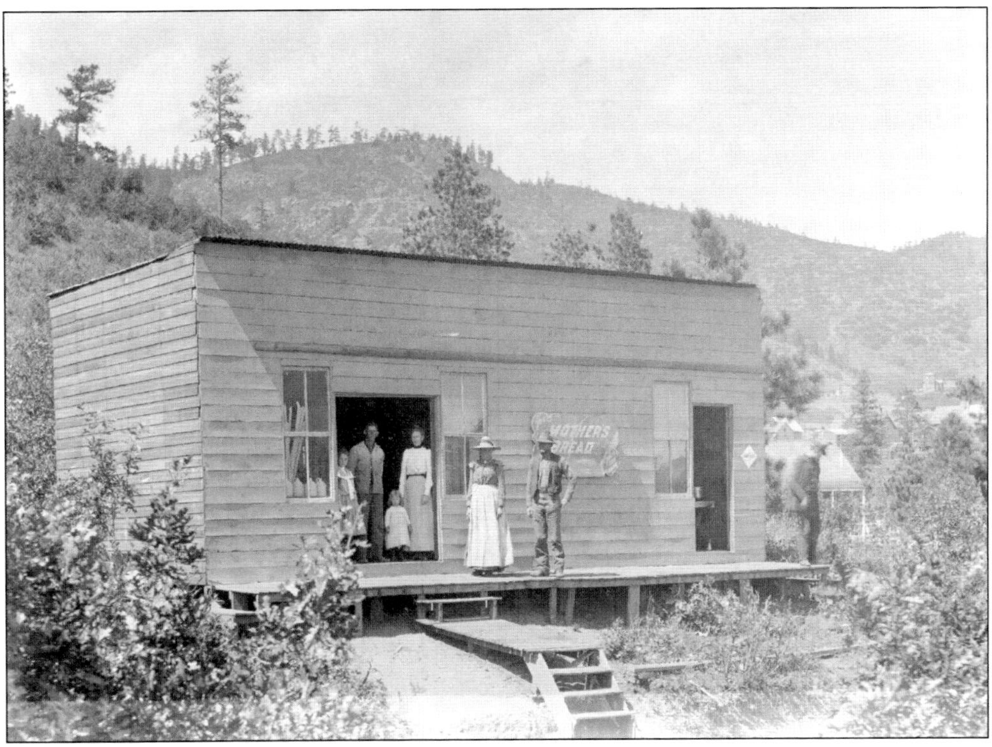

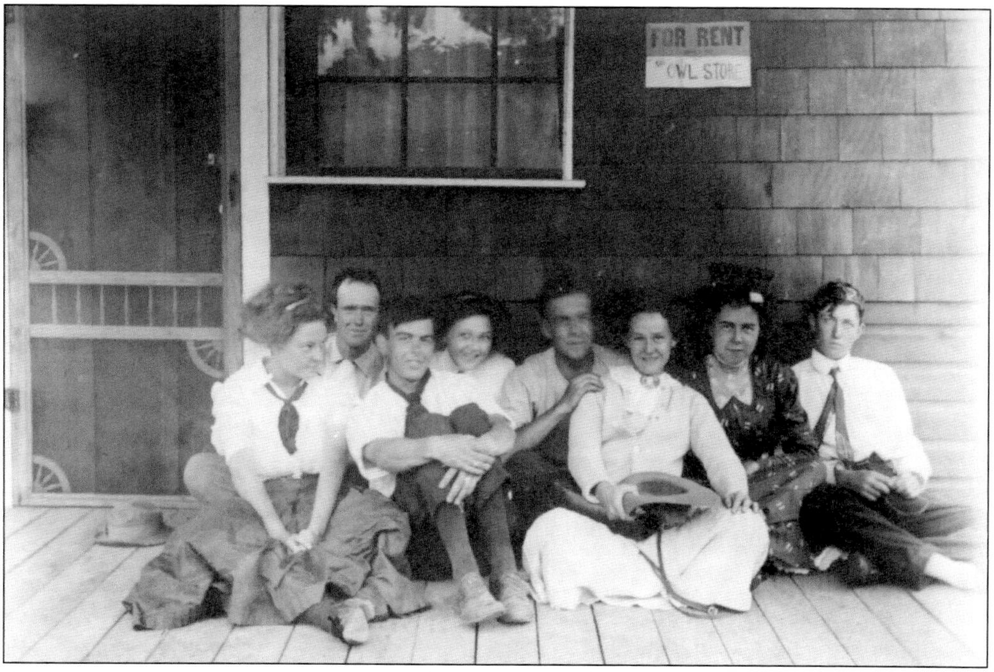

ENJOYING NATURE. A group of unidentified young people, above, pose outside the Owl Store, west of the auditorium. Tramping, hiking, burro riding, and horseback riding were some of the activities the young people enjoyed. Lucretia Vaile recalled, "We liked to explore where we believed no one else had ever been." Favorite haunts were the ice caves, the Indian caves, the beaver dam, the red rocks behind the golf course, and a place locally known as the bottomless pit on Mount Herman. There, the young people constructed a cabin of crisscrossed logs over the deep crevice. Vaile recalled, "Inside the cabin were ladders for descending into this awesome chasm." The pit was a gathering place for boys and girls. Pictured below are unidentified young people from about 1894, possibly returning from one of their nature adventures.

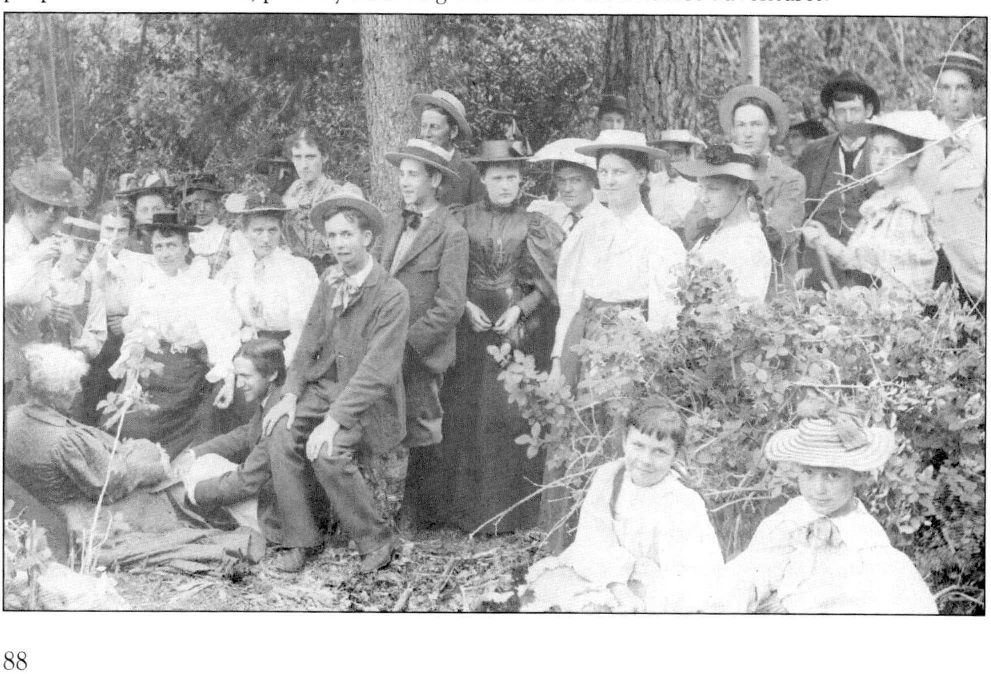

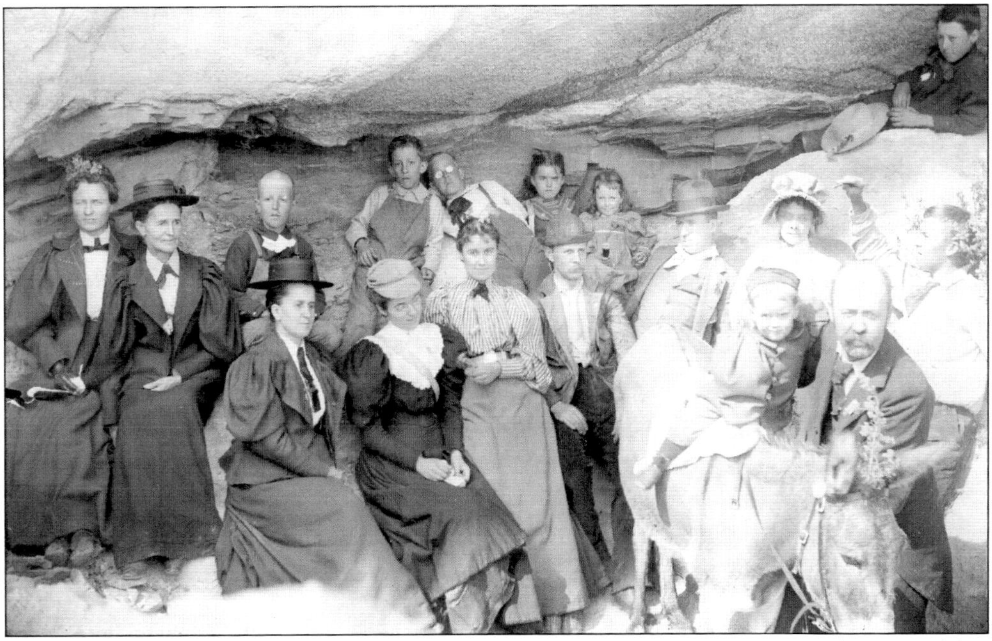

ICE CAVES EXCURSION. A group of unidentified visitors to the ice caves are seen above. Boulders tumbled together to form the caves, a popular hiking destination for the town's people and Chautauqua visitors residing in Glen Park. The caves are located west of the first reservoir in Palmer Lake, and to reach them, even today, requires a hike up steep terrain and over rocky outcroppings. Since many of these local hikes were arduous, burros were well suited for such trips in the mountains. During the heat of the day, ladies hiked in long sleeved blouses and long skirts with layers of petticoats, while the men wore suits and ties. Pictured below are unidentified travelers entering the area of the caves.

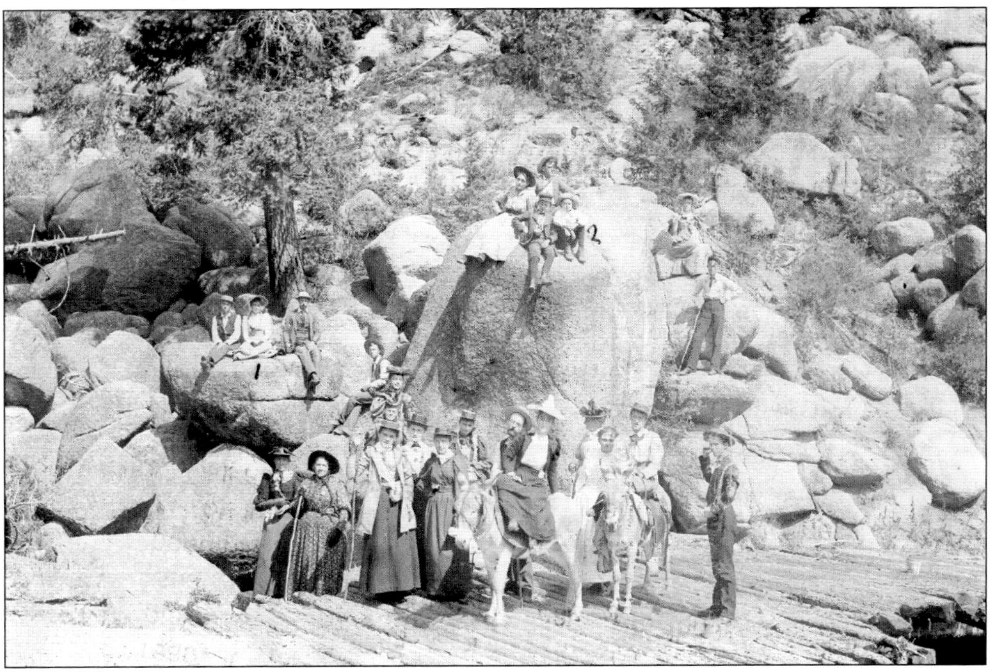

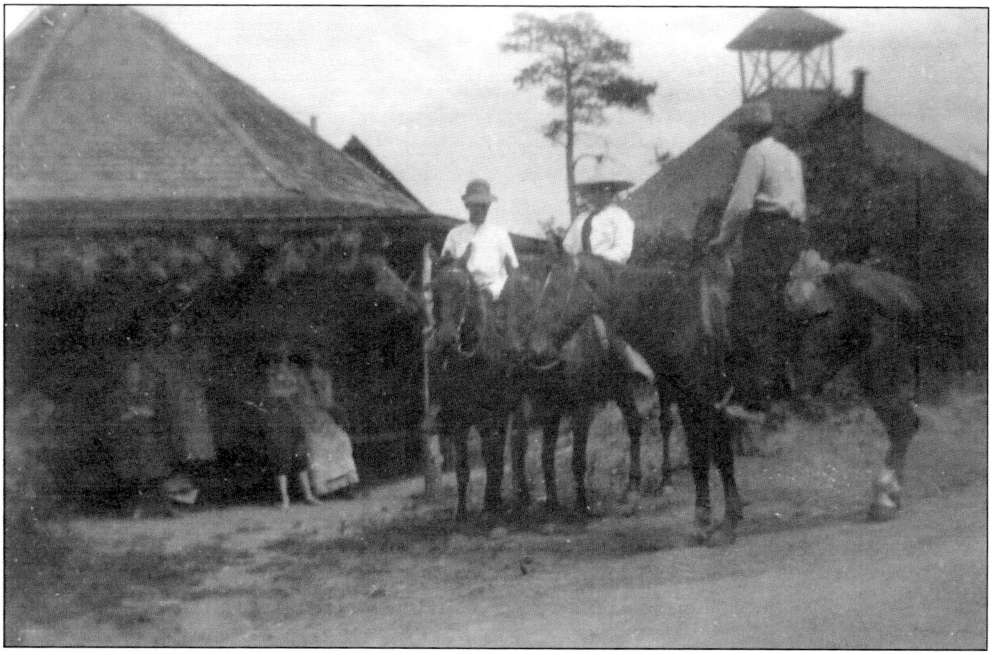

Octavia, c. 1900. The Octavia Cottage, an eight-sided slab wood structure, was believed to have been built by the Glen Park Association as a rental for the Rocky Mountain Chautauqua. Reportedly, it was once a drugstore and later a meat market. It was also believed to have been a refreshment stand for the Pine Crest Methodist Youth Camp. The structure still stands today.

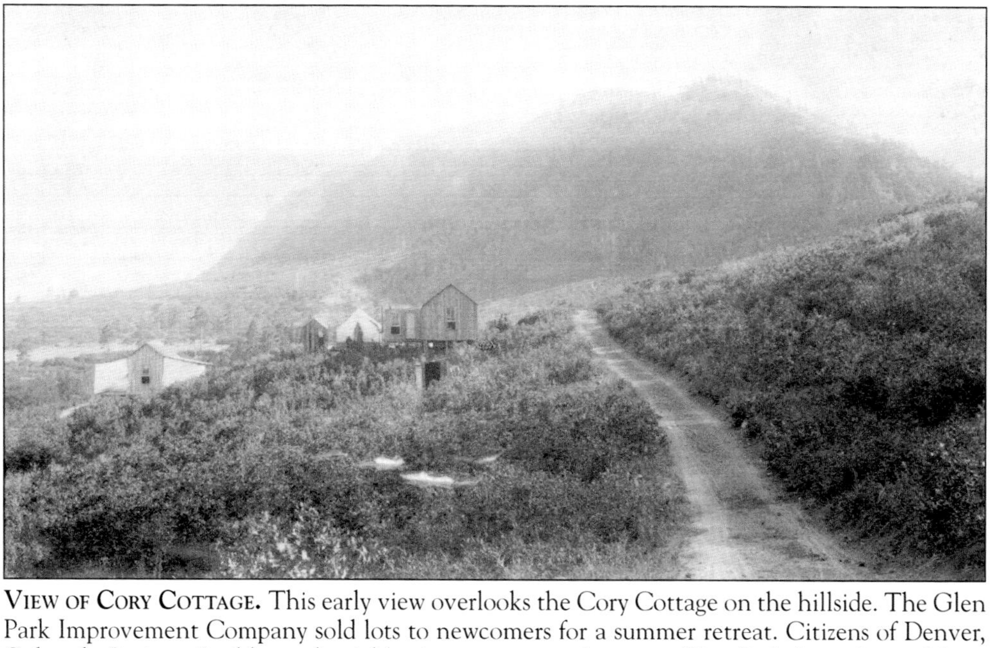

View of Cory Cottage. This early view overlooks the Cory Cottage on the hillside. The Glen Park Improvement Company sold lots to newcomers for a summer retreat. Citizens of Denver, Colorado Springs, Pueblo, and neighboring states were drawn to Glen Park for its beautiful yet rustic surroundings, the serenity of its location, and the cultural events offered by the Rocky Mountain Chautauqua.

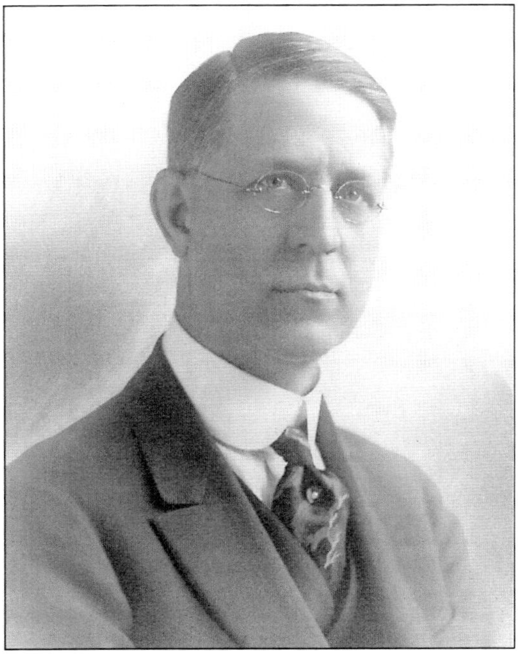

JUDGE FRANK McDONOUGH SR., c. 1930. Forrest Priestley was the leading figure in the Chautauqua in Glen Park and later the Glen Park Improvement Company from 1891 until his death in 1903, when Frank McDonough Sr. assumed both positions. The declining popularity of the Chautauqua movement, coupled with changing vacation habits resulting from the introduction of the automobile, brought about the decline of the Chautauqua in Glen Park. (Courtesy of Rogers Davis.)

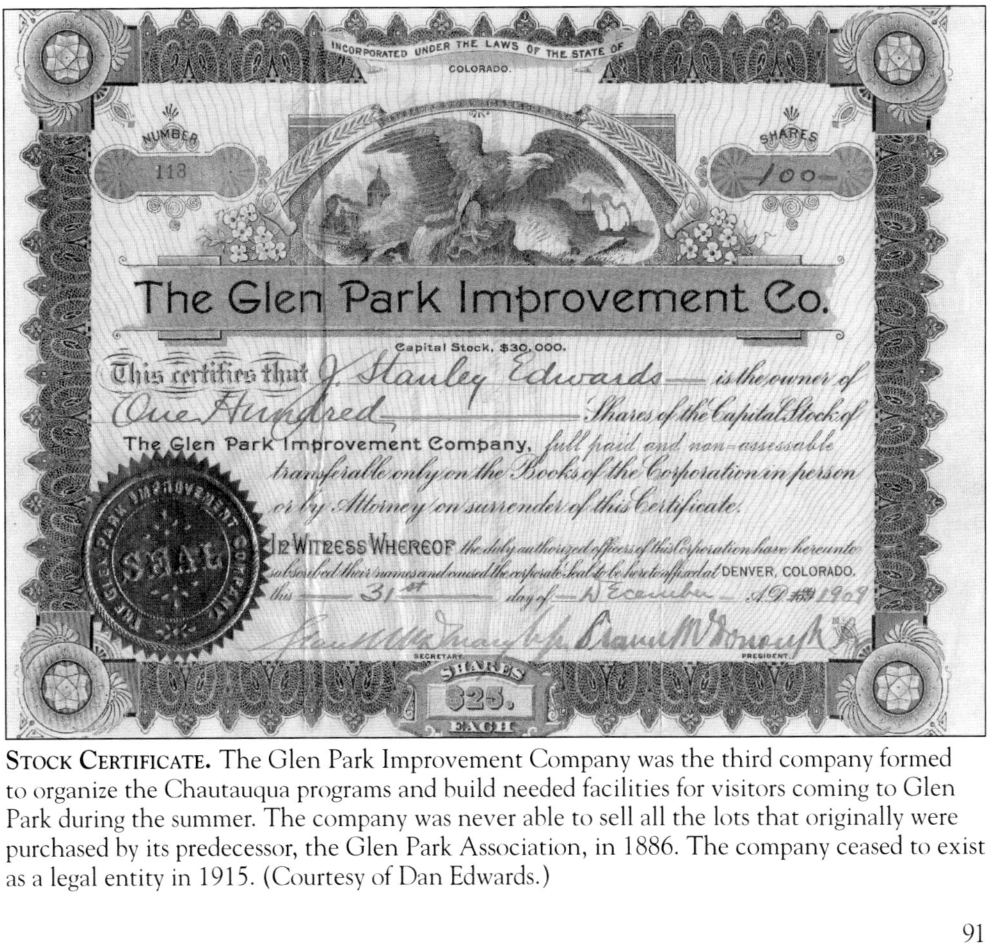

INCORPORATED UNDER THE LAWS OF THE STATE OF COLORADO.

NUMBER 113

SHARES 100

The Glen Park Improvement Co.

Capital Stock, $30,000.

This certifies that J. Stanley Edwards is the owner of One Hundred Shares of the Capital Stock of The Glen Park Improvement Company, full paid and non-assessable transferable only on the Books of the Corporation in person or by Attorney on surrender of this Certificate.

In Witness Whereof the duly authorized officers of this Corporation have hereunto subscribed their names and caused the corporate Seal to be hereto affixed at DENVER, COLORADO. this 31st day of December A.D. 1909

THE GLEN PARK IMPROVEMENT COMPANY SEAL

SECRETARY PRESIDENT

SHARES $25. EACH

STOCK CERTIFICATE. The Glen Park Improvement Company was the third company formed to organize the Chautauqua programs and build needed facilities for visitors coming to Glen Park during the summer. The company was never able to sell all the lots that originally were purchased by its predecessor, the Glen Park Association, in 1886. The company ceased to exist as a legal entity in 1915. (Courtesy of Dan Edwards.)

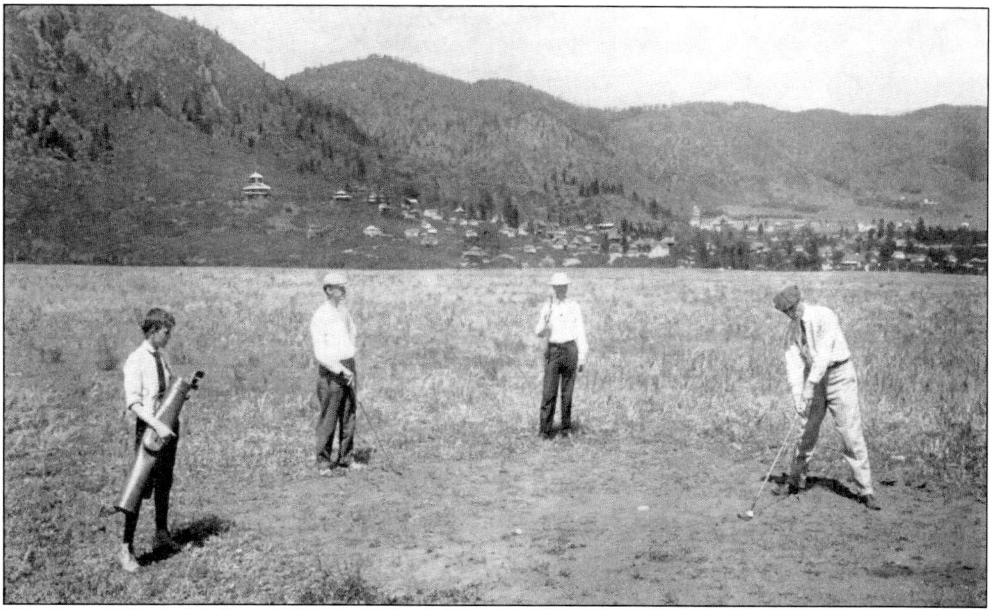

Recreational Activities. Around 1898, Frank McDonough Sr. and Prof. Walter Arundel, a fine tennis player and golfer, developed the nine-hole golf course and a tennis court on the mountainside. Pictured above is the golf course, which was on the plateau above where the Romoca Lodge once stood. Both men and ladies enjoyed golf and tennis. Pictured below is the tennis court. If these unidentified tennis players were to suffer strained muscles, they could seek the advice of Emil Tiffero, who practiced the philosophy of osteopathy, a therapy based on manipulation of bones and muscles. In the 1901 Chautauqua program, Tiffero advertised that he would cordially receive inquirers who may like to know more of the new philosophy.

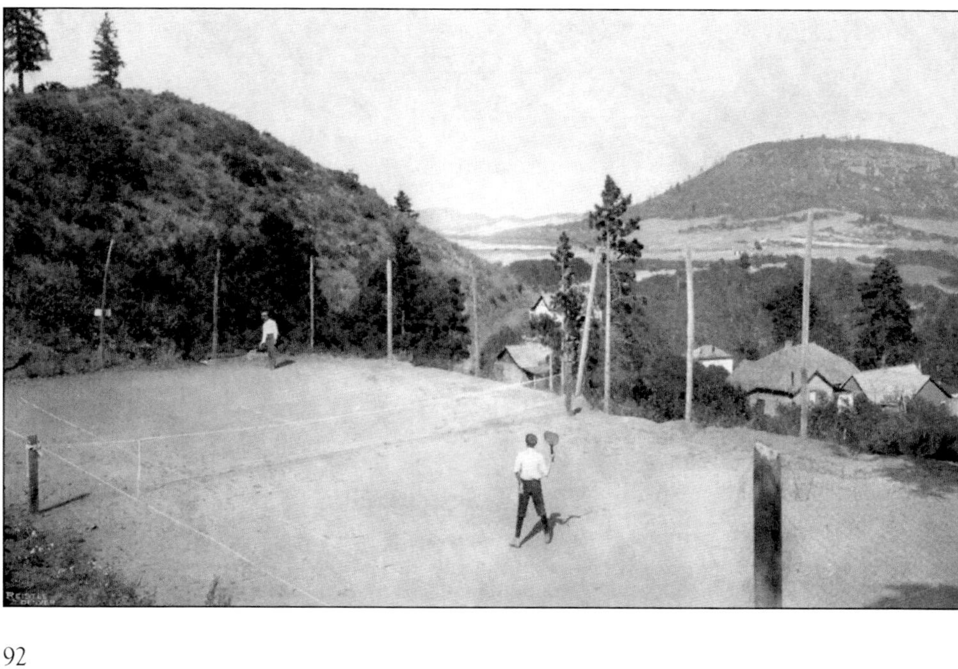

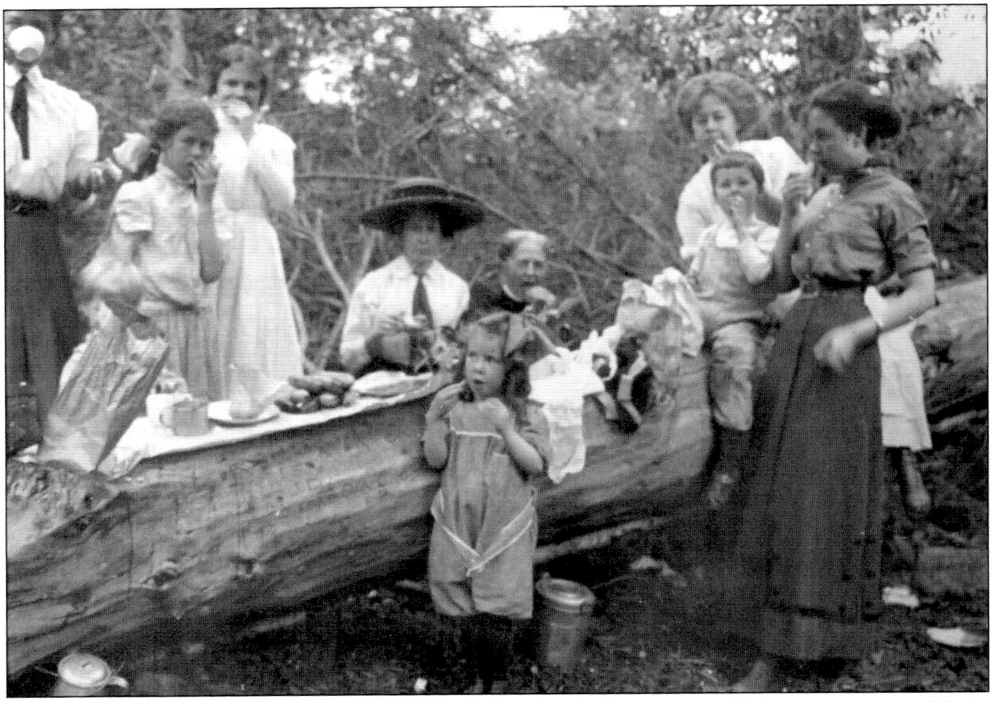

PICNICS AND HAYRIDES. A group of unidentified individuals using an old log as a picnic table in Glen Park is seen above. During the Chautauqua season, Wednesday afternoons and Saturdays were given up to picnics, hikes, boating, horseback riding, fishing, sports, mountain climbing, and hayrides. On most days, excursions departed for scenic attractions such as Elephant Rock, Fern Glen, the courts, and the loop trail up Monument Canyon. Longer trips went north to Perry Park, south to the stone formations in Monument Park and Garden of the Gods, and to Woodland Park and Cripple Creek, via the reservoir canyon. Pictured below about 1913 are unidentified excursionists traveling in one of Thomas Hanks's touring wagons, which seated 12 people. (Above, courtesy of Lori Suddeth; below, courtesy of Victor Vaile.)

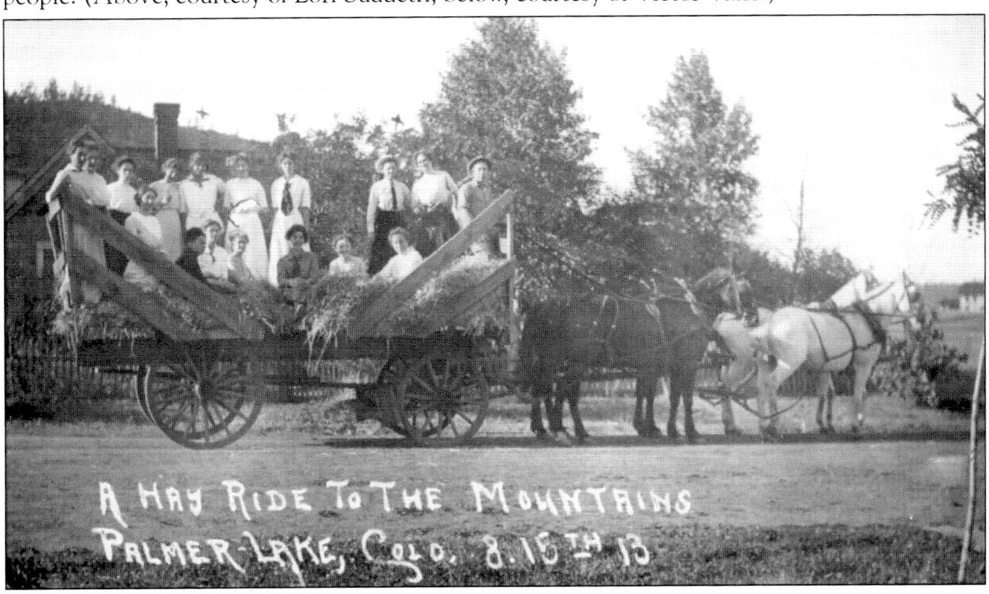

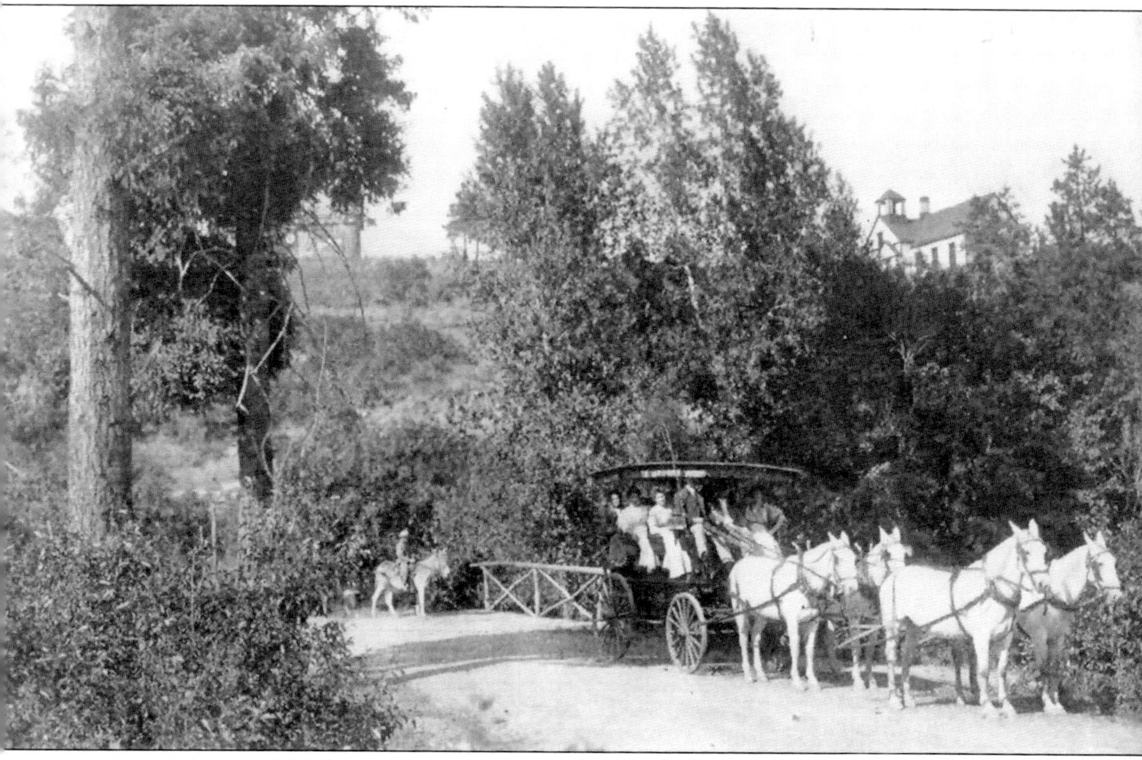

Tally-Ho, c. 1906. In the background is the Palmer Lake one-room schoolhouse while in the foreground is Thomas Hanks's handsome tally-ho wagon and beautiful team of white horses, in which he took great pride. One summer day in 1905, Hanks reluctantly rented his team and carriage to an arrogant show-off. Frank McDonough Jr. reported that the man drove the horses so hard, they swerved on a curve, tipping the tally-ho over the edge of the road and dumping its cargo of screaming girls and McDonough's brother, Rogers, into the flooded waters of the creek. Two horses drowned, but the heroic efforts of the girls and Rogers, who ran 2 miles with a broken arm for help, saved the man's life.

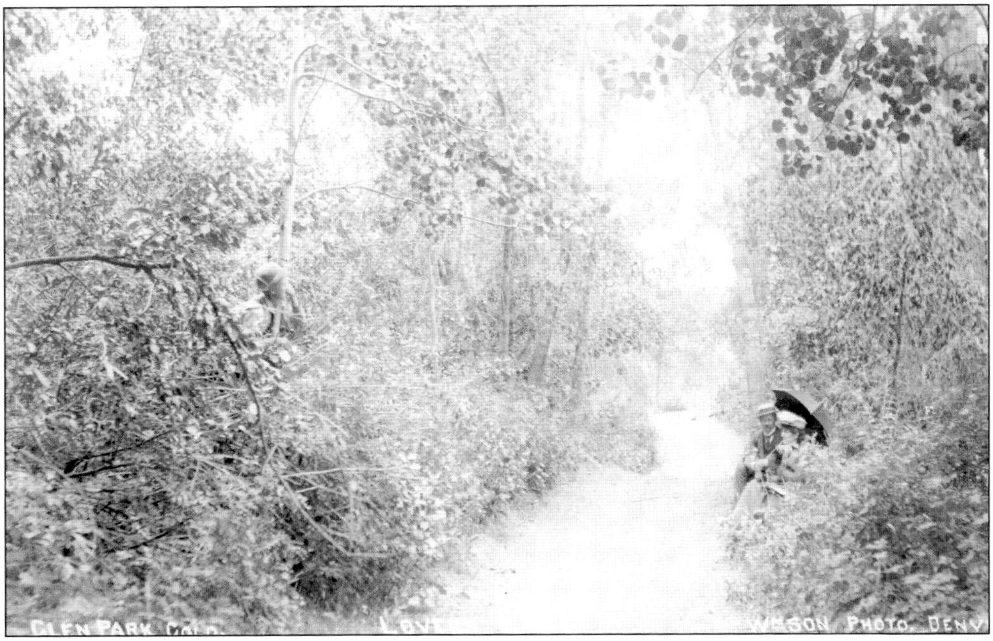

Romantic Escapes. Lovers' Lane, pictured above, began at the mouth of reservoir canyon and followed the creek through Glen Park. Across from the unidentified couple on the bench is a peeping tom, hidden in the bushes. Below is an unidentified man at a footbridge that crossed Limbach Creek where it joined Monument Creek. Eleanor Romack recalled a time when she felt troubled, so she and her husband took a walk one evening across the footbridge and to the end of Lovers' Lane. They sat on a rock under a soft mist that had begun to fall, holding hands while they listened to the strains of music from the Salvation Army band playing at the old inn. Romack said that she left most of her troubles and grief by the creek.

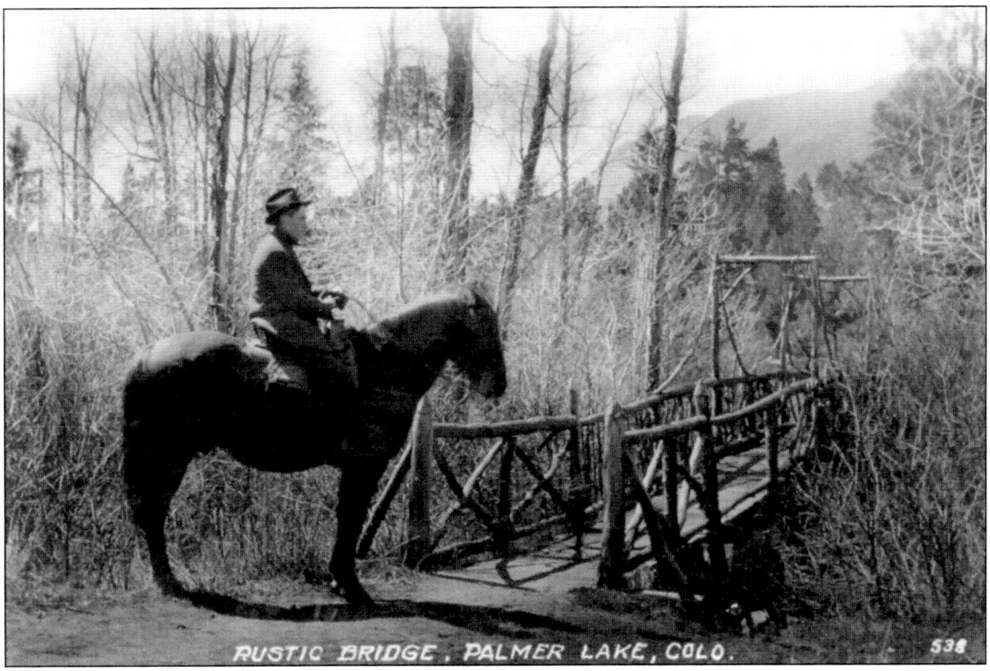

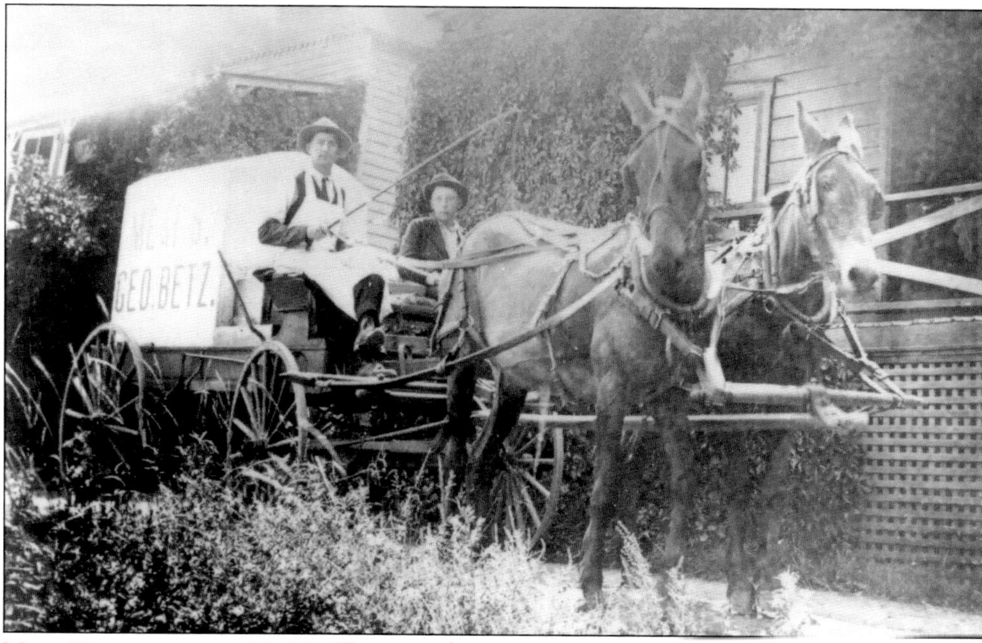

Meat Delivery, c. 1913. Mr. Turner and Mark Schubarth deliver meat from George Betz's market in Monument to the "Pines" cabin in Glen Park. The enclosed wagon was equipped with hooks to hang the meat, a meat block, and scales. During summer, large tubs of ice kept the meat cold. Twice a week deliveries were made to Palmer Lake and small communities as far east as Table Rock.

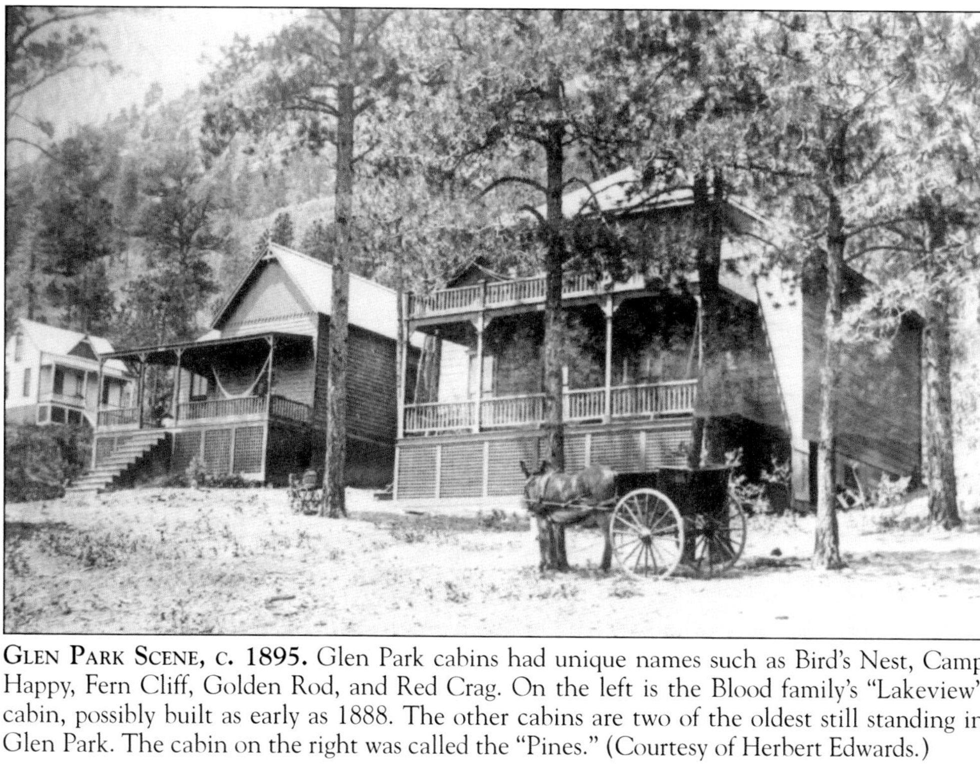

Glen Park Scene, c. 1895. Glen Park cabins had unique names such as Bird's Nest, Camp Happy, Fern Cliff, Golden Rod, and Red Crag. On the left is the Blood family's "Lakeview" cabin, possibly built as early as 1888. The other cabins are two of the oldest still standing in Glen Park. The cabin on the right was called the "Pines." (Courtesy of Herbert Edwards.)

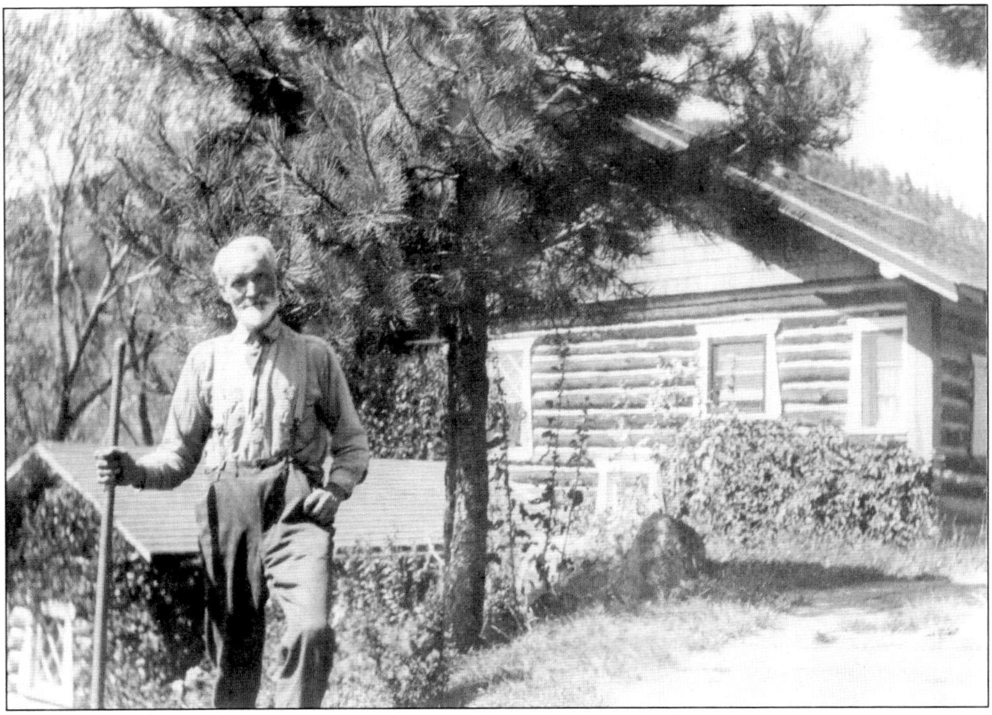

Peter Paul Blass. Peter Paul Blass, above, was an Austrian who came to America to avoid compulsory military service. He found his way to Palmer Lake by way of the Cripple Creek gold rush and acquired a 40-acre tract of land. Pictured below is the house he built. Although a newcomer to the town, Blass was elected mayor in 1901. Around his home, he developed Columbine Park, perhaps on the very spot where the Colorado Blue Columbine was discovered in 1820. In 1901, Columbine Park was described as "one of the most beautiful sights in Colorado." Although the area was fenced in, Blass could not prevent excursionists from invading the park and carrying the flowers away in baskets. The fiery newspaperwoman Kate Sherwin blasted the behavior of the weekend visitors as barbaric. (Both courtesy of the Blass Family.)

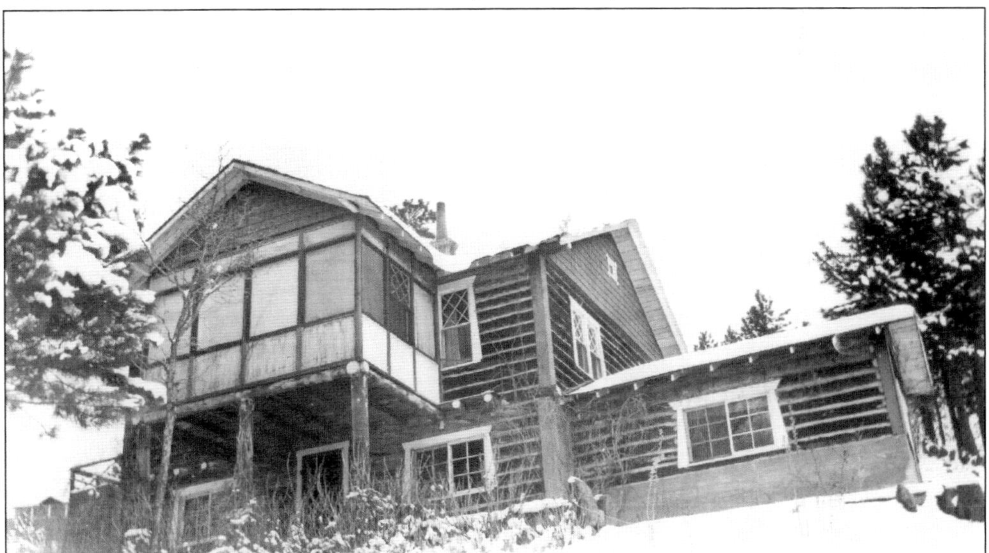

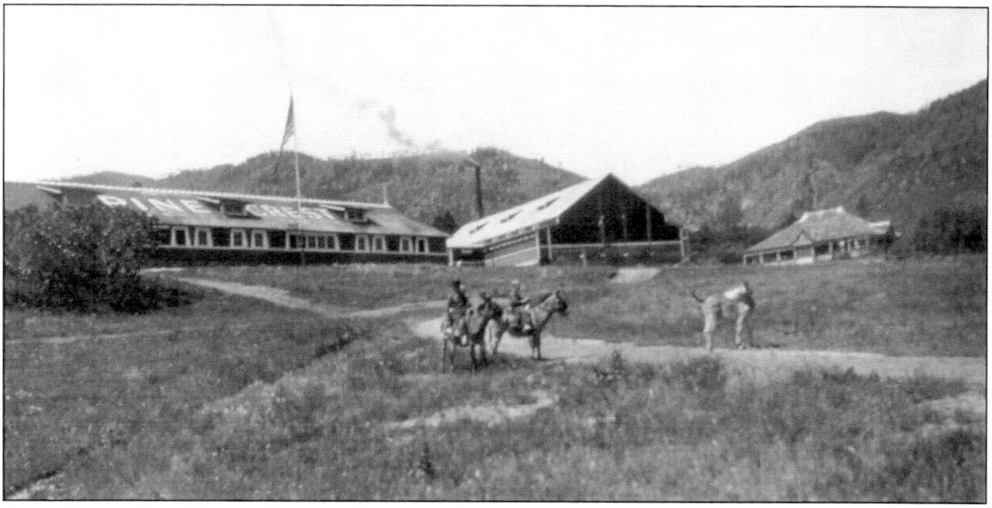

PINE CREST. In 1908, William Pickens purchased 20 acres from the Peter Blass family. Pickens was eager to build and promote a recreational facility to be called Pine Crest. Although he had limited capital, he built a bowling alley, a billiard hall, a tennis court, and a large swimming pool. Pictured above, to the right, is the Denver & Rio Grande Railroad pavilion that was moved to the site. Pictured below is the professional baseball team that Pickens assembled by hiring players from Florida, Mississippi, and Louisiana and paying high salaries. His promotional slogan "Pickens of Pine Crest" failed to catch on and his business reverted to his business partner, Fred Baker. Baker managed Pine Crest until 1920. Pine Crest was then sold to Newton E. Medlock, who served several terms as Palmer Lake's mayor.

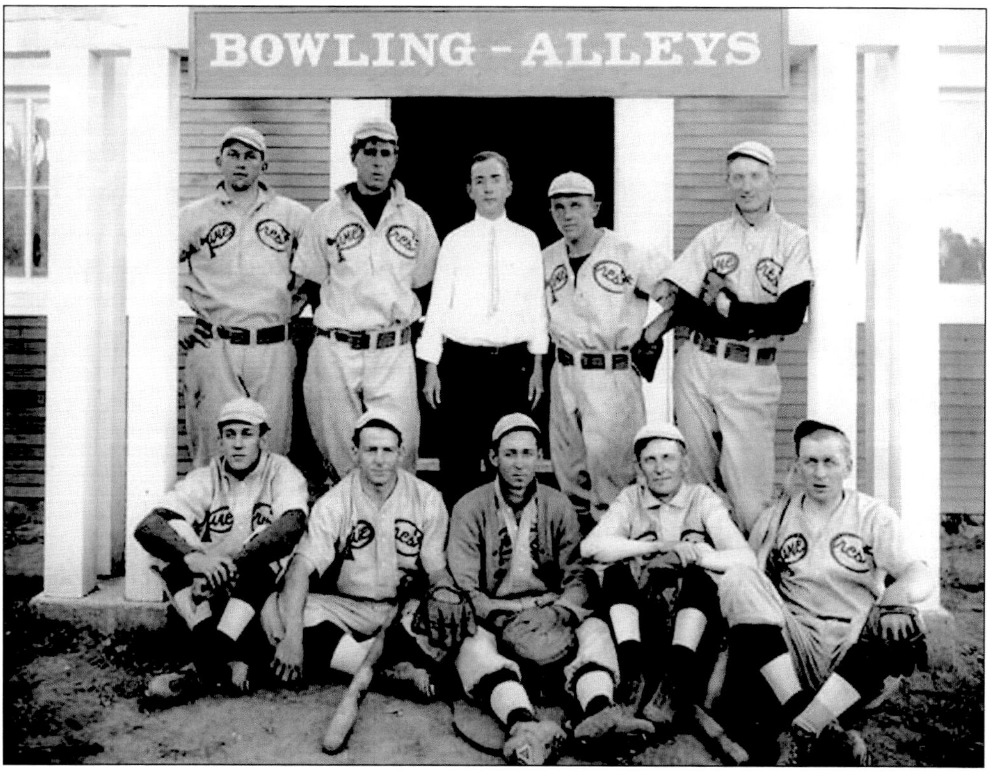

Five

Life in the Outlying Areas

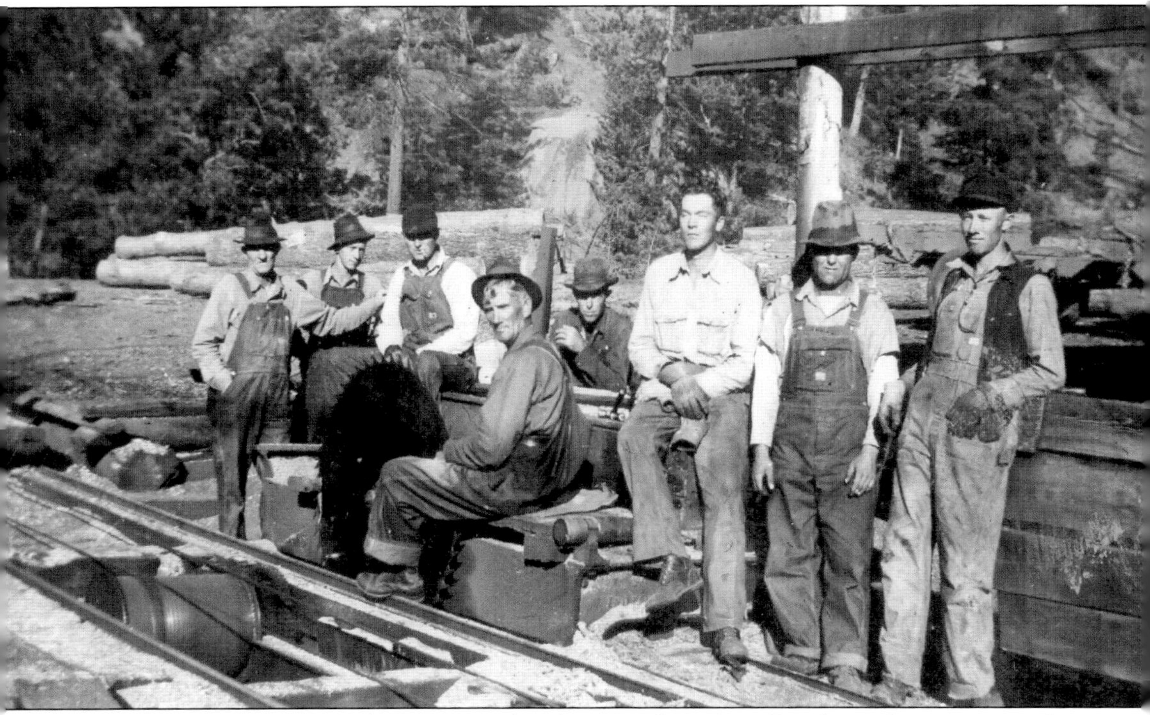

Early Lumber Mill. In the late 1800s and early1900s, the Palmer Divide was home to several small communities and towns, most of which have faded away. Settlers in these communities farmed, raised cattle, and harvested the forests. Lumber mills dotted the area. Neighbors lived far apart, yet were a close-knit group and willing to help each other. Charles Schubarth is shown seated with his crew. (Courtesy of Jean Rathburn.)

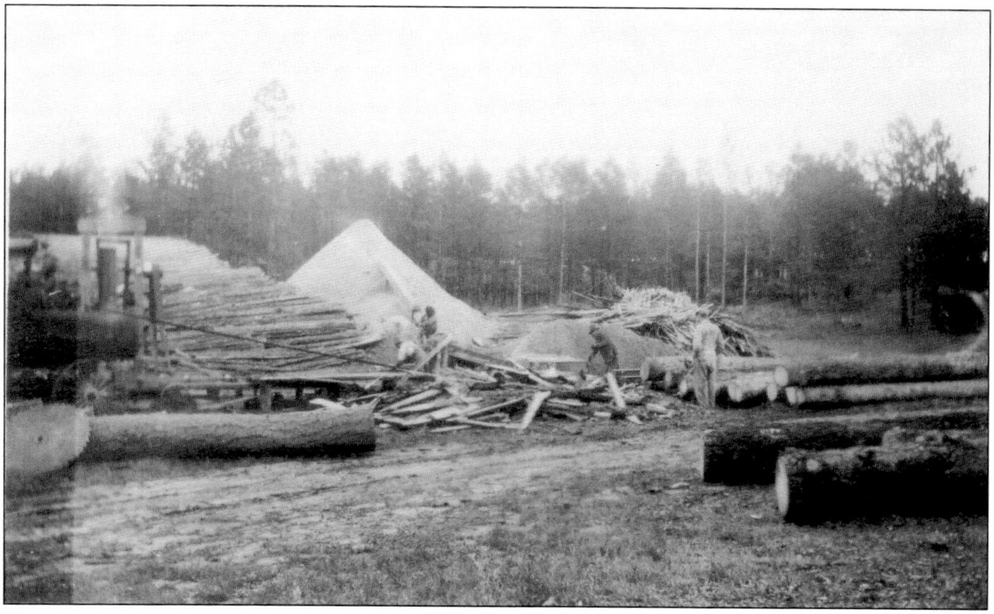

Timber Industry. Early settlers on the Palmer Divide found extensive forests of cottonwood, pine, and scrub oak. The arrival of the railroads created an enormous demand for wood to use as railroad ties and to fuel the locomotives, leading to the harvesting of large swaths of virgin forests. Today the remaining forests on the Palmer Divide consist primarily of second growth trees. (Courtesy of Jean Rathburn.)

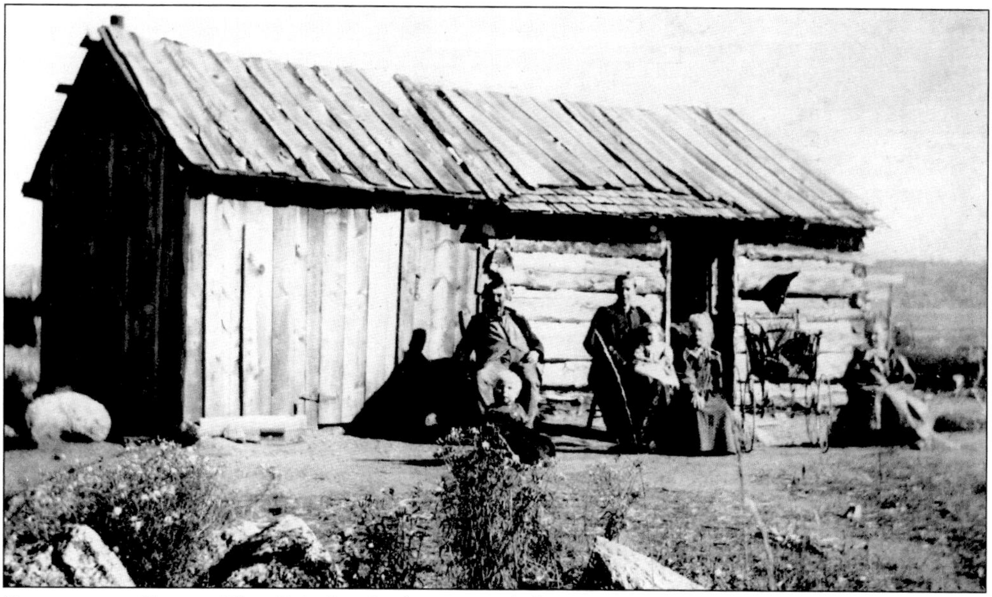

Schubarth Cabin. The Schubarths homesteaded near Cathedral Rock below Dead Man's Canyon, where settlers hanged cattle rustlers and horse thieves. Pictured here are Charles Schubarth and his family. Charles and his brothers, Hugo and Herman, operated a sawmill on Mount Herman. Charles's nephew, a Monument lawman, brought home prisoners to eat and sleep because there was no jail. Other Schubarths became farmers and merchants in Spring Valley. (Courtesy of Jean Rathburn.)

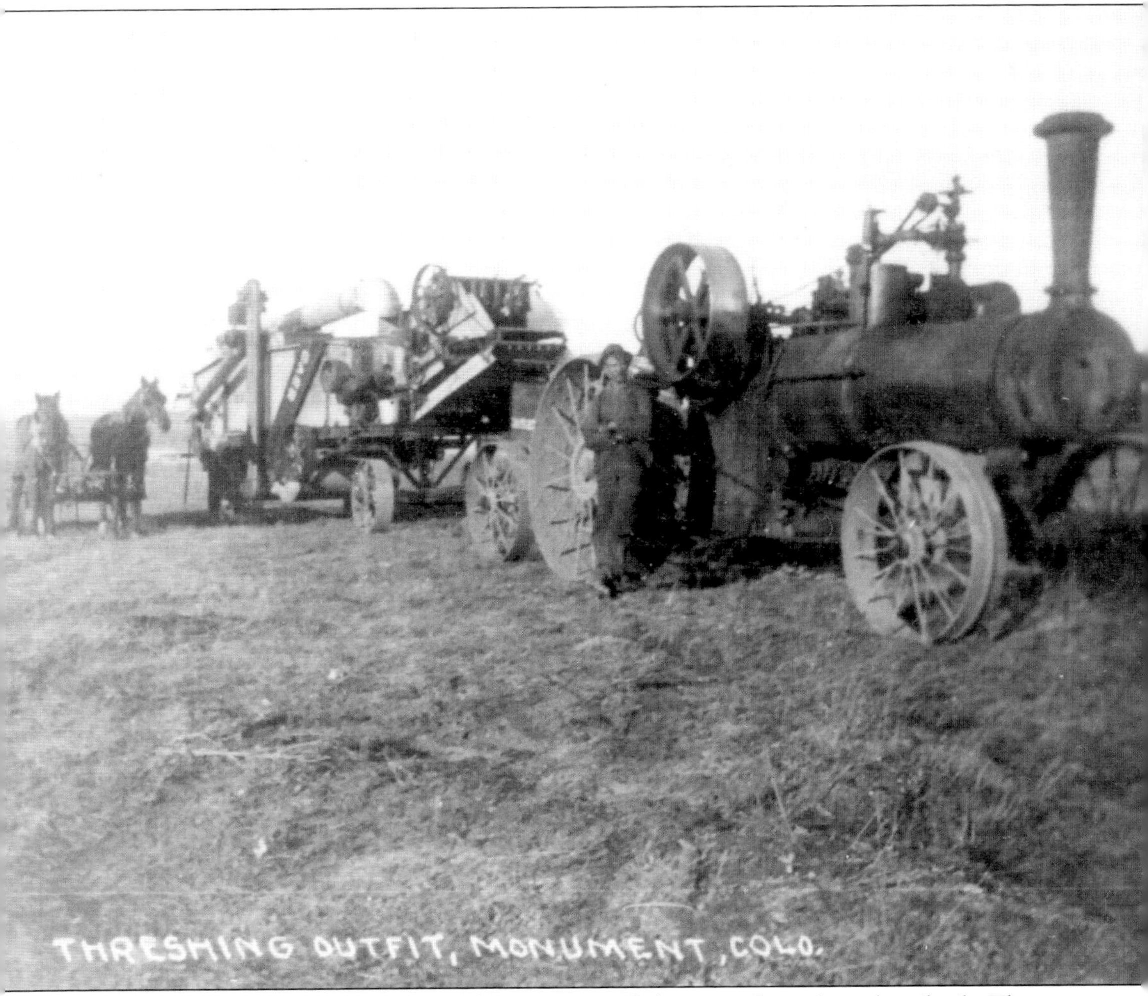

THRESHING MACHINES. Threshing machines separated the grain from the cob or husk. These machines were initially powered by horses and later by steam engines or steam tractors. Small farmers could not afford to buy a threshing machine, so the owner or operator of a threshing machine or threshing rig and his crew would hire themselves out, traveling from farm to farm to thresh grain during the harvest season. On threshing day, everyone would gather at the farm to complete the massive job. The engineer would back the grain separator between the large stacks of grain, and the men would climb up on top of the thresher to pitch grain bundles into the threshing machine. As the grain came out a spout, a gauge told how many bushels the grain crop was yielding. The cob or husk was saved for animal bedding. This photograph shows the Hugo Schubarth and Sons steam engine threshing machine. The Schubarths' steam engine also powered the conveyor chains in Doyle's Ice House. (Courtesy of Jean Rathburn.)

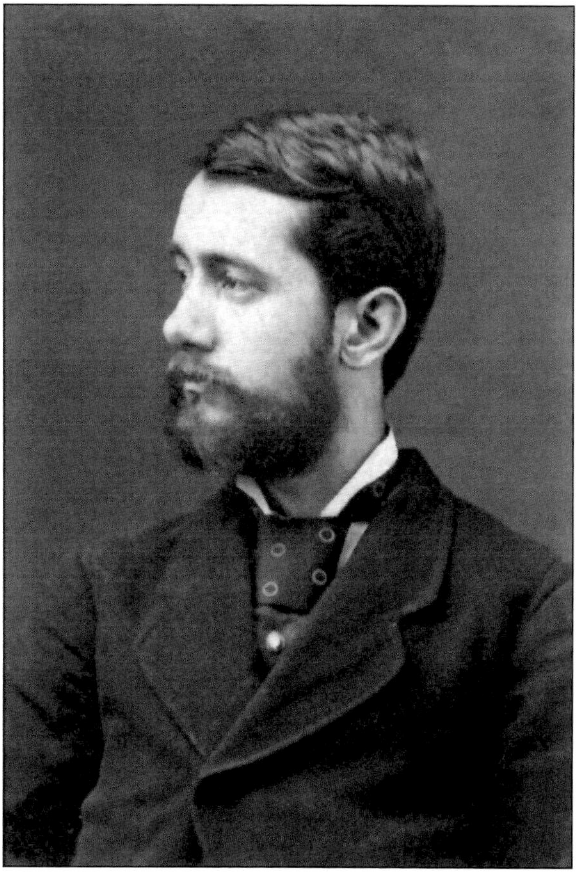

William Bangs Young, c. 1871. William Bangs Young, at left, and his wife Mary Eliza, along with their children Marian and Russell, left their comfortable life in Chicago to head to Colorado via wagon because of Mary's health. The family came by wagon because Mary's doctor thought the train, at a speed of 20 to 30 miles per hour, would be too fast for Mary's fragile heart, as she would gain altitude too quickly. They traveled with a doctor and the Tomlinsons, another family traveling west. Pictured below is Young's sketch of an encampment during their journey. This shows what might be his daughter, Marian, giving flowers to another child, a woman washing clothes, a man tending a campfire, and their Newfoundland dog, Chase. Among his accomplishments, Young started the First National Bank in Colorado Springs. (Both courtesy of Rogers Davis.)

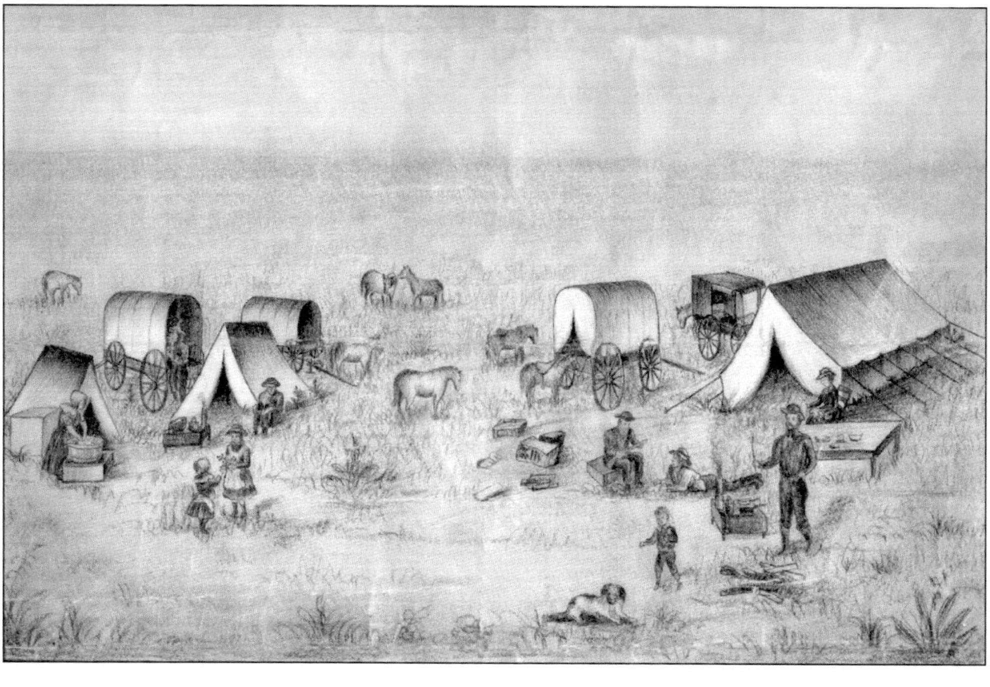

First Impressions. Mary Young and her daughter, Marian, are photographed at right before their trip to Colorado. As they crossed the Kansas-Colorado border, Young was unimpressed with her new surroundings and wrote in her diary, "this country ought to have the redeeming feature, healthfulness, for never was I in so Godforsaken a country, the sun pours down and bakes the ground till it cracks open. There is not a spear of anything green, nothing but grass and dirt." Arriving in Colorado Springs, she soon changed her opinion and loved the area. Pictured below is the cabin the Youngs built, on what is now the U.S. Air Force Academy. It had 3-inch gaps to let in healthy Colorado air. The dry medicinal air did seem to help, as Mary was able to fully engage in ranch life. (Both courtesy of Rogers Davis.)

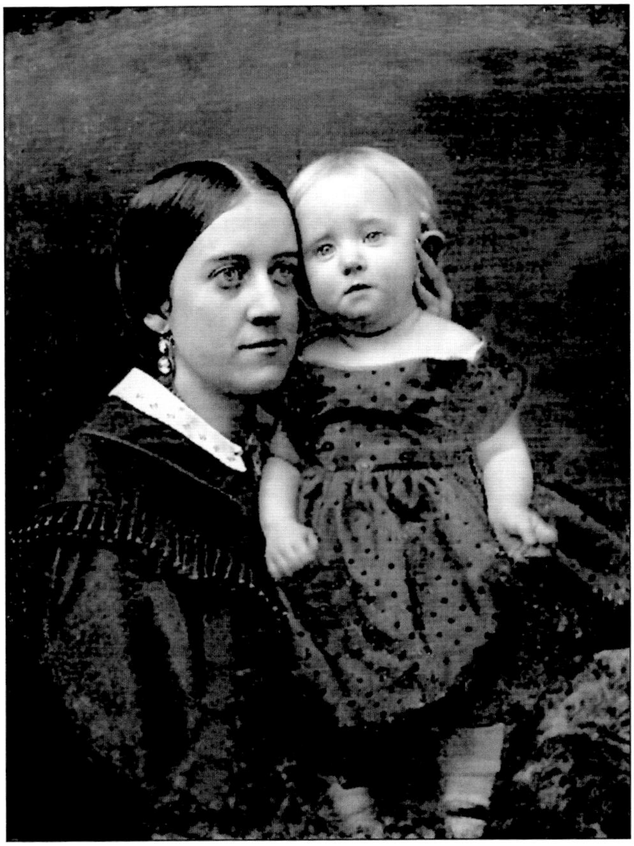

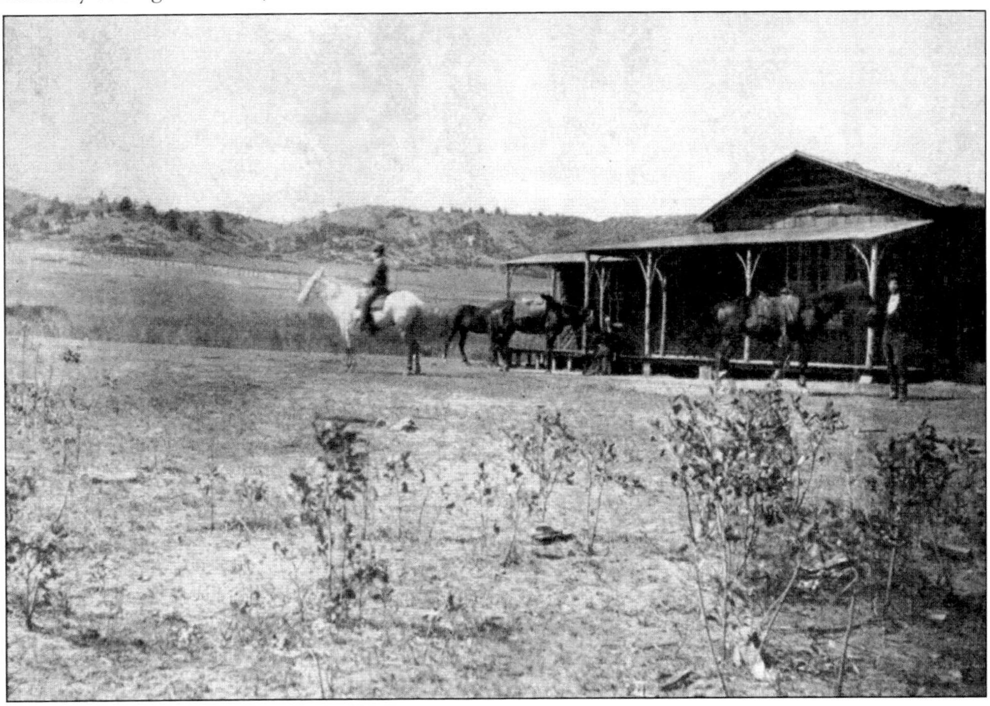

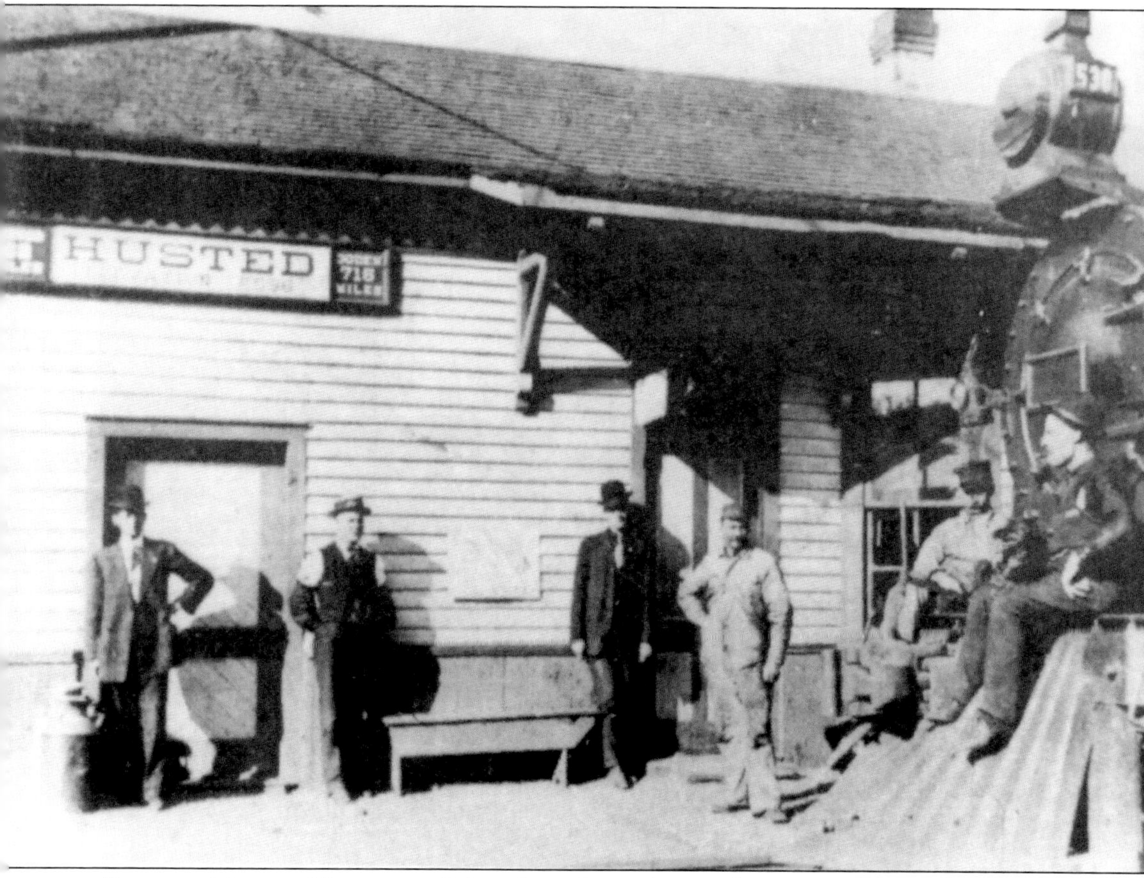

Town of Husted. The town of Husted was located near what is now the north entrance to the U.S. Air Force Academy. It was named after Calvin Husted, who established a lumber mill around 1878. Husted's lumber mill used timber from the pineries to build the railroad and homes in growing Colorado Springs. The town of Husted was actually comprised of East Husted and West Husted. Pictured is the Denver & Rio Grande Railroad Depot of West Husted. At one time, the depot was a converted boxcar housing a post office. There was a station for the Santa Fe Railroad at East Husted. Husted had two hotels, a general store, a saloon, a clay pit, and a church. In addition, there was a restaurant called the Branding Iron, where one could get a ham sandwich for 48¢ or, on cold Palmer Divide days, a pint or quart of hot, homemade soup.

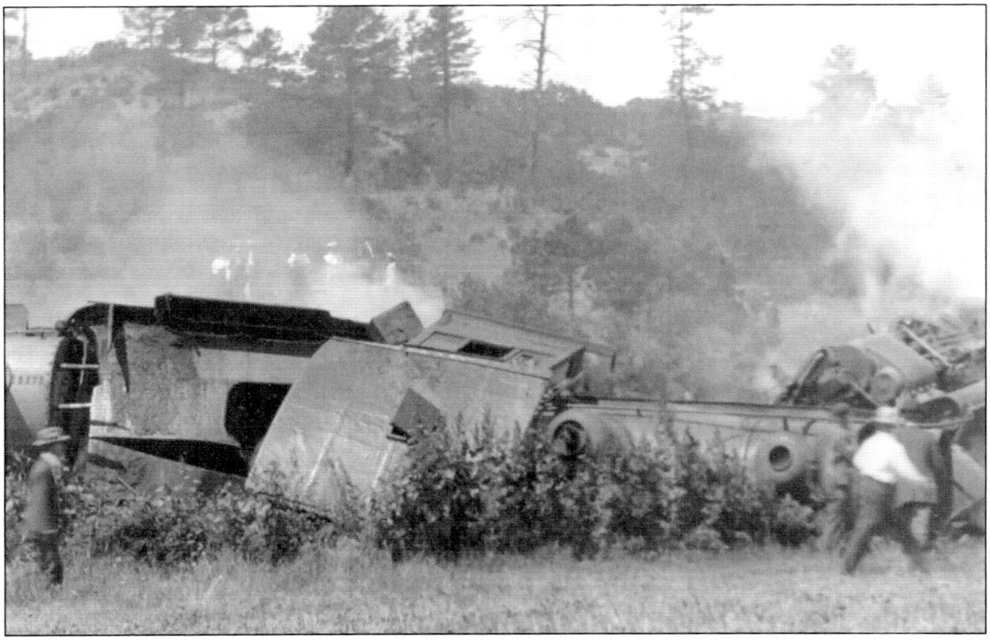

Husted Train Wreck, c. 1909. These are photographs of the aftermath of a local train wreck. Because of the high elevation, trains would need helper engines to pull them over the Palmer Divide. After the helper engine did its job, it would use a roundabout to get into position for the next train. On August 14, 1909, Jack Gossage, a fireman on a helper engine, waved to his wife as the engine passed his home. He was never to see her again. That day, northbound and southbound trains accidently shared the same track and, traveling at full speed, collided just north of Husted. Gossage was trapped in the horrific collision and died. Seven others perished in the wreck that injured 50 people. Gossage's grandson, Rick "Goose" Gossage, would later become a Hall of Fame baseball pitcher. (Both courtesy of Norma Lavelett.)

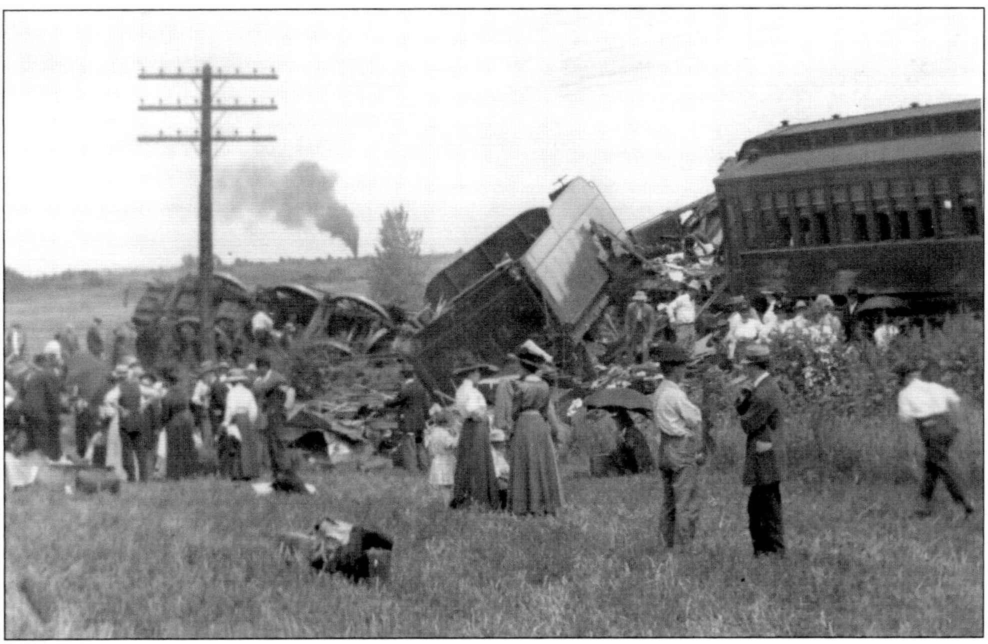

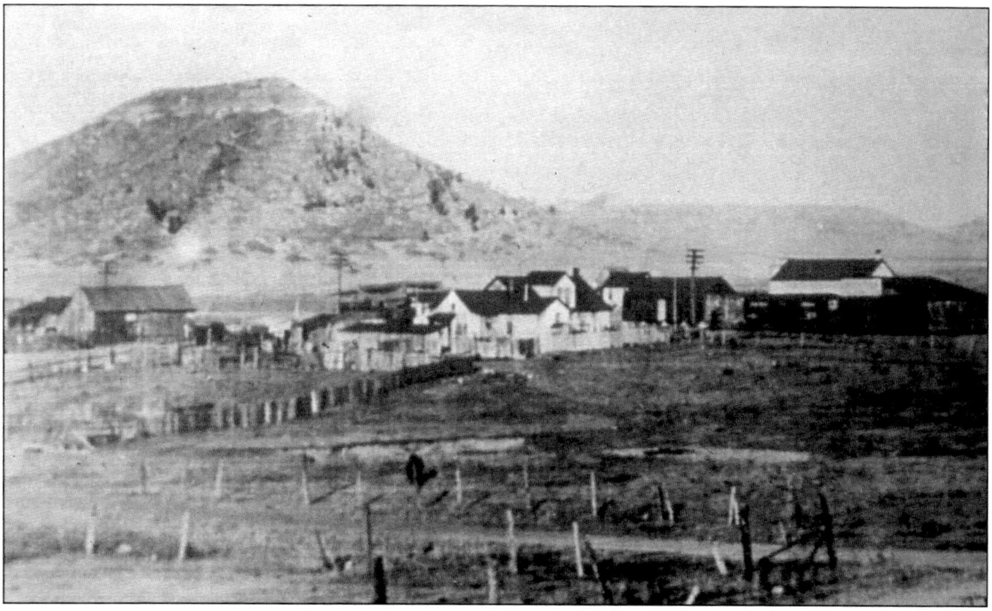

Greenland Ranch. When the famous author Helen Hunt Jackson traveled through this area and saw how green the flats and foothills looked, she said, "This town site should be called Greenland." The Greenland Breeding Farm, also known as the Greenland Stock Farm, was one of the largest ranches in Douglas County in the 1880s. There were several buildings on the property, including a horse barn, a blacksmith shop, and residences for ranch overseers. In 1906, John William Higby purchased the land after operating a store in Monument. Pictured above is Higby's Greenland Ranch in 1915. Below are the Higbys at the ranch house. They owned this property until the 1980s. The help of many organizations and individuals allowed the Greenland Ranch to later be set aside as a reserve between Colorado Springs and Denver. (Both courtesy of Jim Sawatzki.)

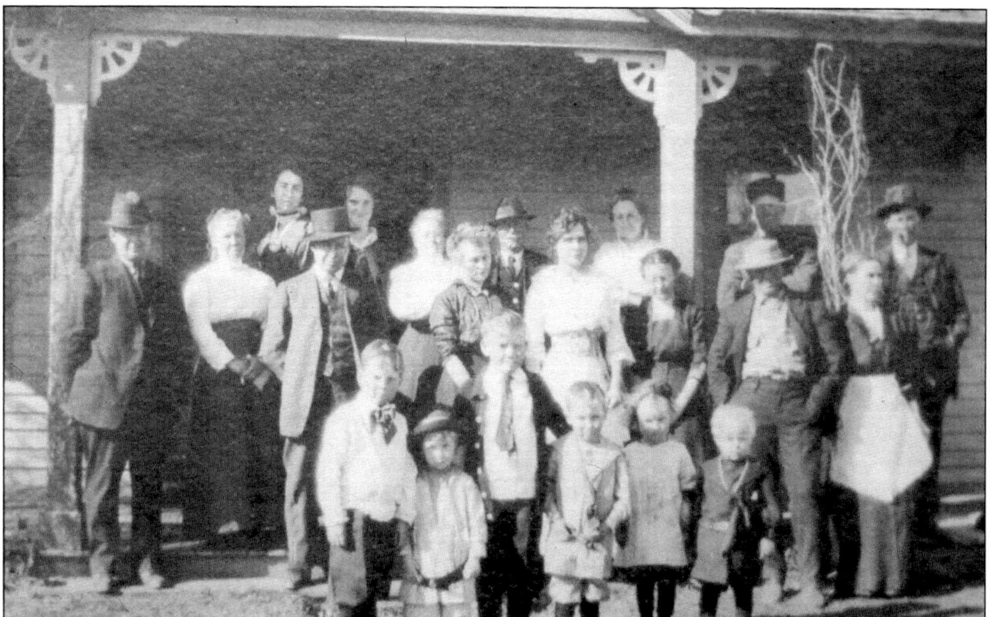

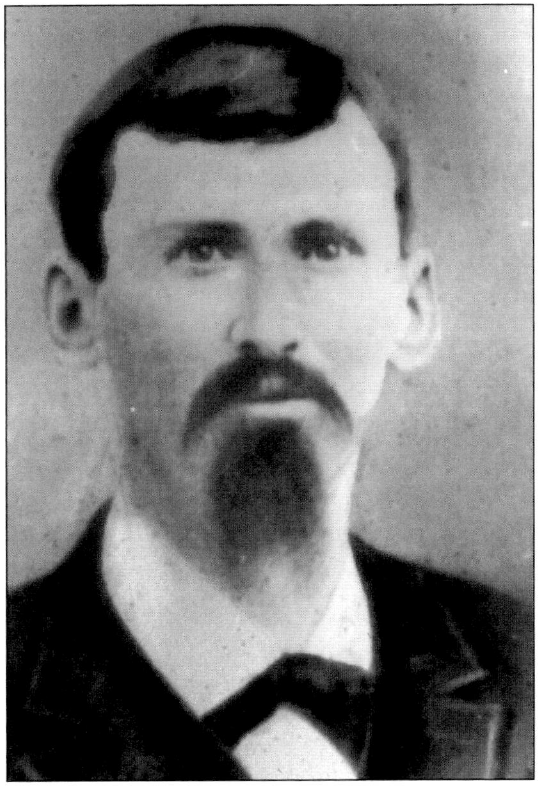

Noe Family and the Eagle Mountain Ranch. Issac Jegirtha Noe, right, also known as I. J., came west in 1878 with his wife, Jennie, to his brother's ranch in Greenland. I. J. quickly secured employment at the Greenland Breeding Farm. He became the manager in 1881, and later a partner with C. B. Kountz, who purchased the ranch. Kountz was not happy when I. J. purchased 160 acres owned by a Mr. Moorhead to add to the ranch. In 1890, I. J. and his son, Fred, decided to keep that property for themselves, naming it the Eagle Mountain Ranch. The ranch grew to 1,400 acres. They raised shorthorn cattle, prize-winning bulls, trotting horses, and Berkshire hogs. Fred Noe later took over the ranch, married Jennie Katherine Higby, and raised 10 children. Pictured below is the ranch house I. J. built in 1890. The ranch is recognized as a Centennial Farm by the State of Colorado for being in use by the Noe family for over 100 years. (Both courtesy of Bill Noe.)

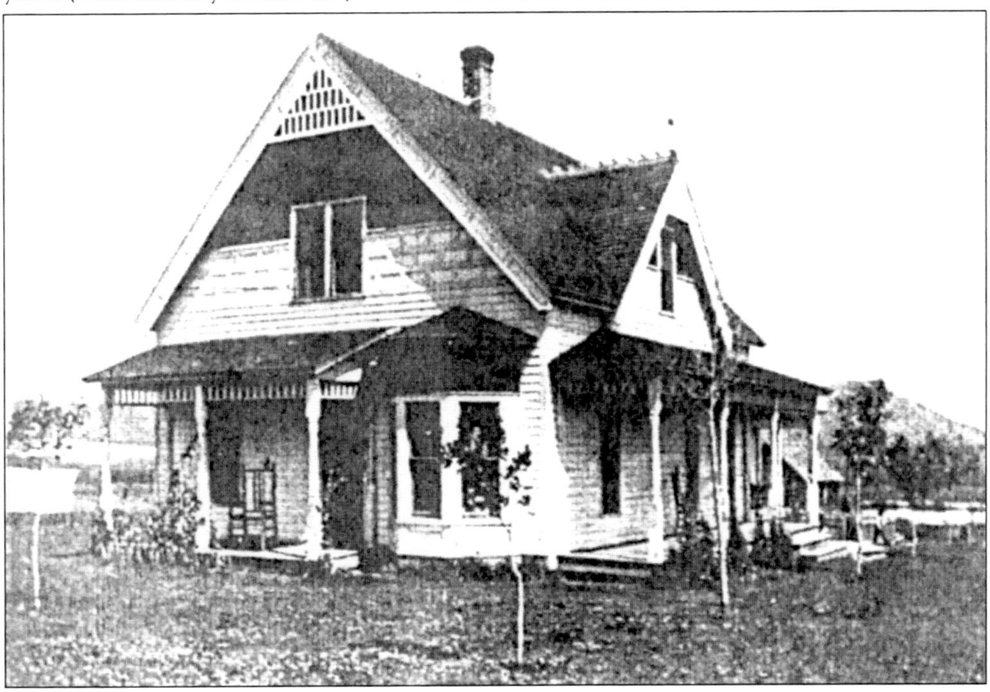

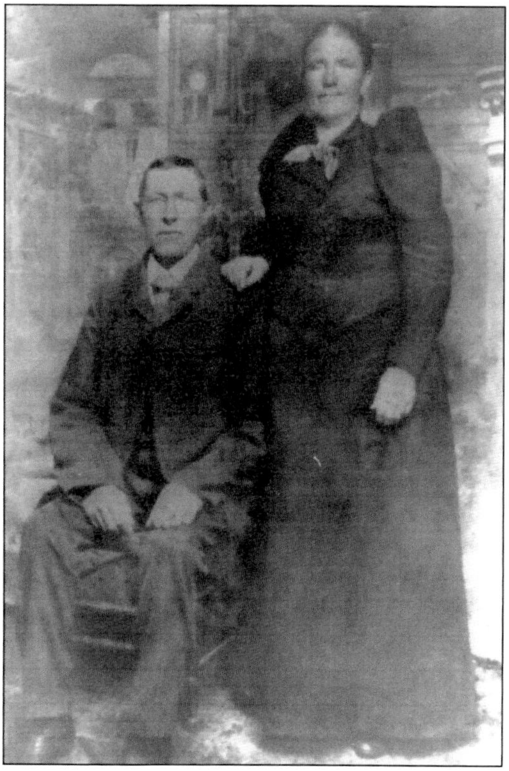

John and Christina Olfs. John Olfs and his wife, Christina, are shown at left. Olfs was born about 1840 in Germany and immigrated to America in 1860 to avoid serving in the German military. Interestingly, Olfs later fought in the Union army during the Civil War. In 1870, he left the army, and by 1871, he had homesteaded 160 acres east of Monument. Pictured below is the house he built. It had 12-foot-high ceilings, a large parlor, and a staircase leading to bedrooms on the second floor. Olfs's neighbors, the Swanbecks, told him about Christina Schacht, who lived in Germany with her daughter, Dora. Olfs sent for them in 1872, and married Christina in Denver. Monument's Presbyterian Church bell rang out one last time for Christina upon her death. (Both courtesy of Evelyn McCune.)

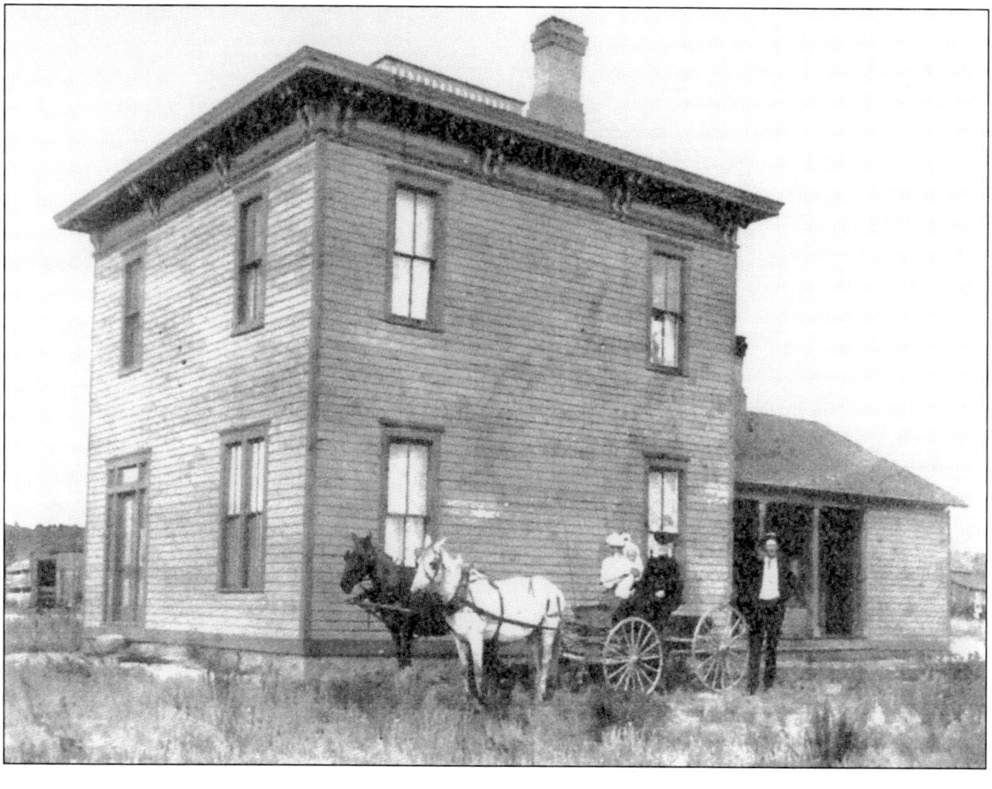

DEATH OF MRS. HAGEDORN.

Mary Catharine Olfs first saw the light of day at the Olfs ranch one mile northeast of Monument April 27, 1874, where all her life, until her marrige, was passed. She was educated in the Monument school.

December 31, 1891, she was united in marriage to Philip Hagedorn of Colorado Springs, where they resided for 15 years, he being an employe of the Tramway company. Later they removed to the Divide, again living part of the time on the old home place. Six children were born to this union, four boys and two girls, two of whom preceded her to "The Great Beyond." Harry, the eldest, who died at the age of 2 and one-half years and George, next eldest, who died July 17, 1918, in the service, and which came as such a shock to this devoted mother, that she was nearly prostrated. Another son, Marion, is in the navy at San Pedro, and was unable to come to his mother's bedside on account of quarantine.

Friday, October 18, she was stricken with the fatal influenza and only lived six days, leaving a heartbroken husband, one son, Bryan, and two little daughters, Lucille and Mildred, in the home. Bryan and Lucile are both ill of the same disease. Besides the above mentioned, three brothers and three sisters survive.

On account of the malignant form of the disease, the funeral was private, interment being at the Monument cemetery, with short services at the grave. The floral offerings were mute tributes of the esteem in which this woman was held. What more can be said than "to know her was to love her."

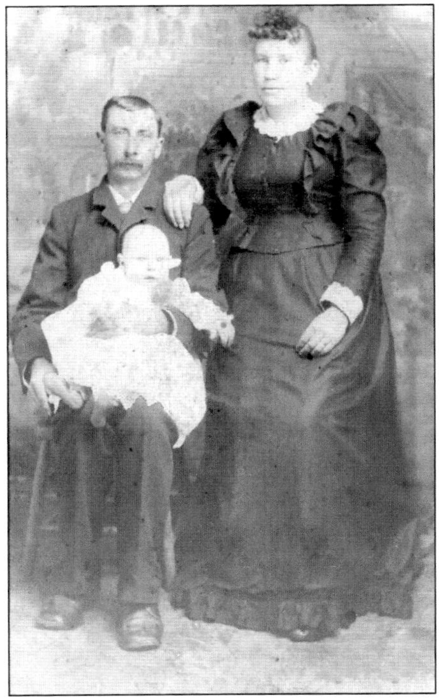

The Hagedorns and the 1918 Flu Pandemic. Phillip and Mary Hagedorn, the daughter of John and Christina Olfs, married in 1891. They had six children. Pictured above are the Hagedorns with their eldest child, Harry, in about 1892. He died at the young age of two. Two other children were Mildred and Lucille. Hagedorn's wife had the unfortunate fate of catching the notoriously lethal 1918 influenza, which led to her demise in just six days. Pictured at left is her obituary. The flu was so virulent and feared that funeral services were held to a minimum. It is estimated that 40 million people died from this flu worldwide. Although Lucille and another brother, Bryan, caught the flu, they survived. (Both courtesy of Evelyn McCune.)

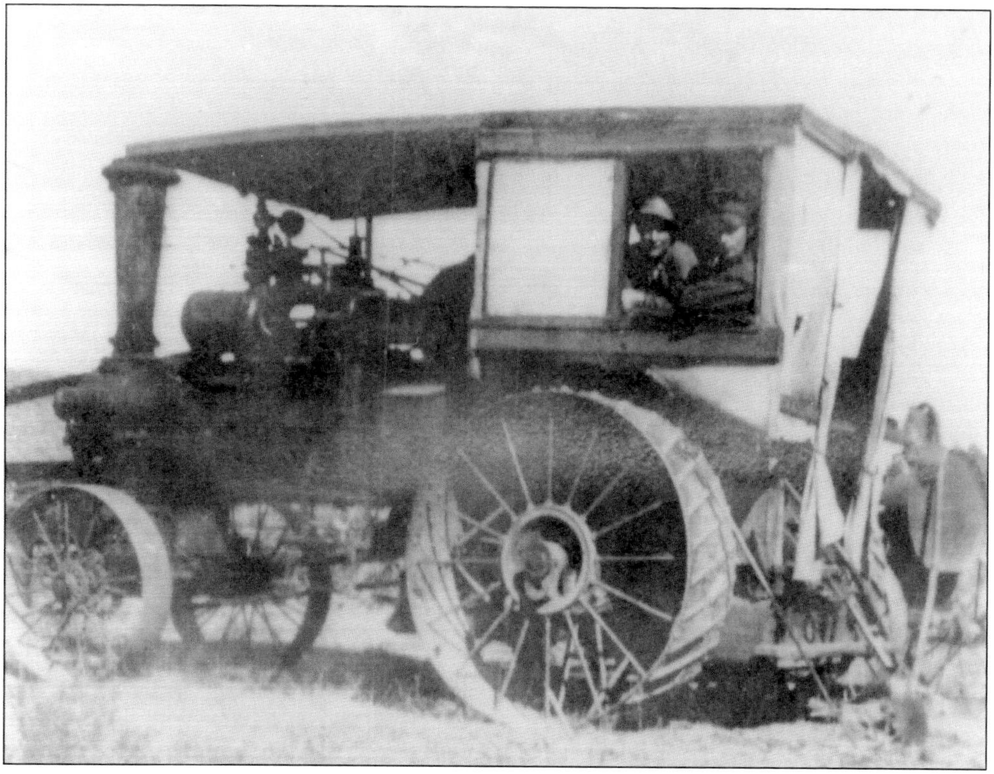

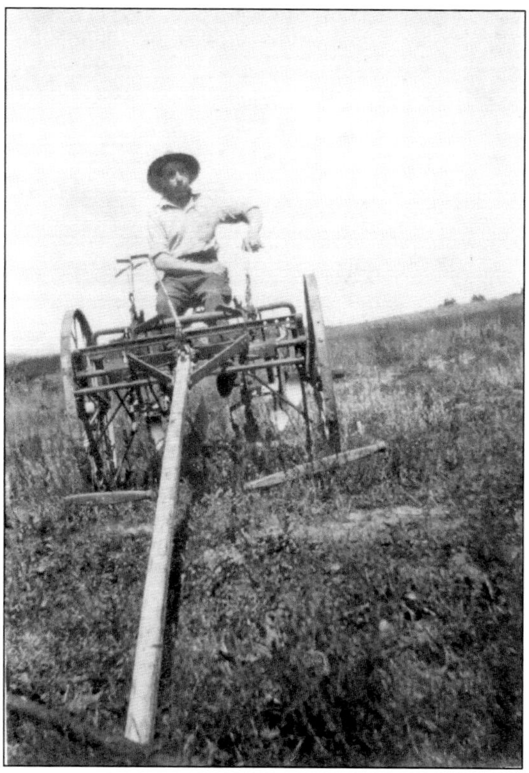

HAGEDORN THRESHING. Steam engines, such as the one above, ran the threshing machines at harvest time. On threshing day, everyone would gather to help with the massive job of harvesting the crops in one day. Women and older girls were in charge of cooking the noon meal. Children, depending on their age, would supply water for the men and the steam engine, haul away the freshly threshed grain, or scoop the grain into the granary. At the end of the day, everyone would go to bed early, so they would be ready to do it all over again the next day at the neighbor's farm. Pictured at left is Bryan Hagedorn, who survived the 1918 flu that claimed the life of his mother. (Left, courtesy of Evelyn McCune.)

LUCILLE AND MILDRED HAGEDORN (LAVELETT), C. 1910. Pictured at right is five-year-old Lucille Hagedorn with her six-month-old sister, Mildred. Both sisters married Lavelett brothers. In her high school yearbook, Lucille, who was already married, said her ambition was to "be the perfect housewife." She became a lover of local history and went on to write several pivotal books about the Palmer Divide. (Courtesy of Evelyn McCune.)

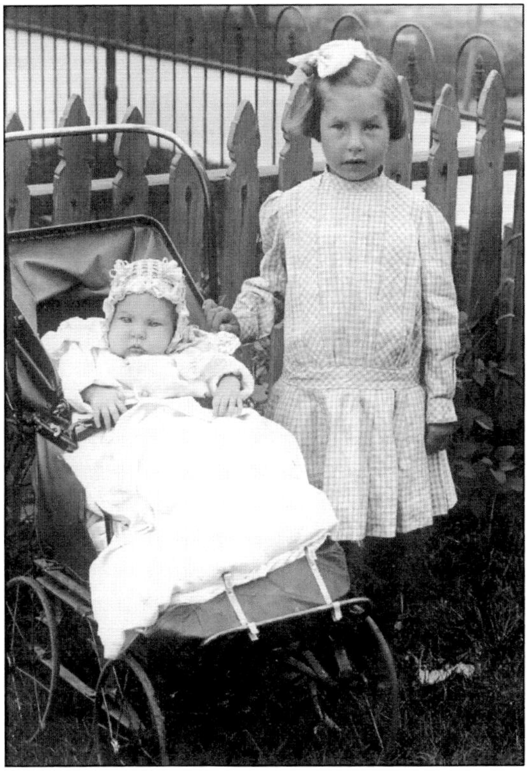

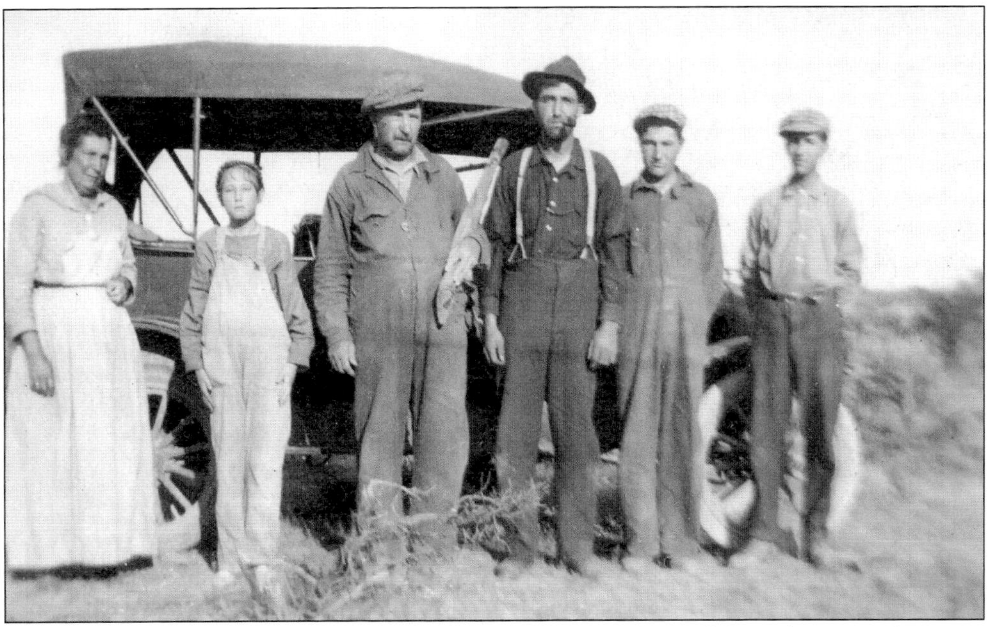

NEIGHBORS COMING TOGETHER, C. 1920. Living on the outskirts of the Palmer Divide, it was common for members of local families to marry into each other's families. This photograph shows members of two pioneering families. They include, from left to right, Priscilla Lavelett, her granddaughter Leona Aubuchon, two Aubuchon brothers, and Steve and Clarence Lavelett. Steve and Clarence married Mildred and Lucille Hagedorn, respectively. (Courtesy of Evelyn McCune.)

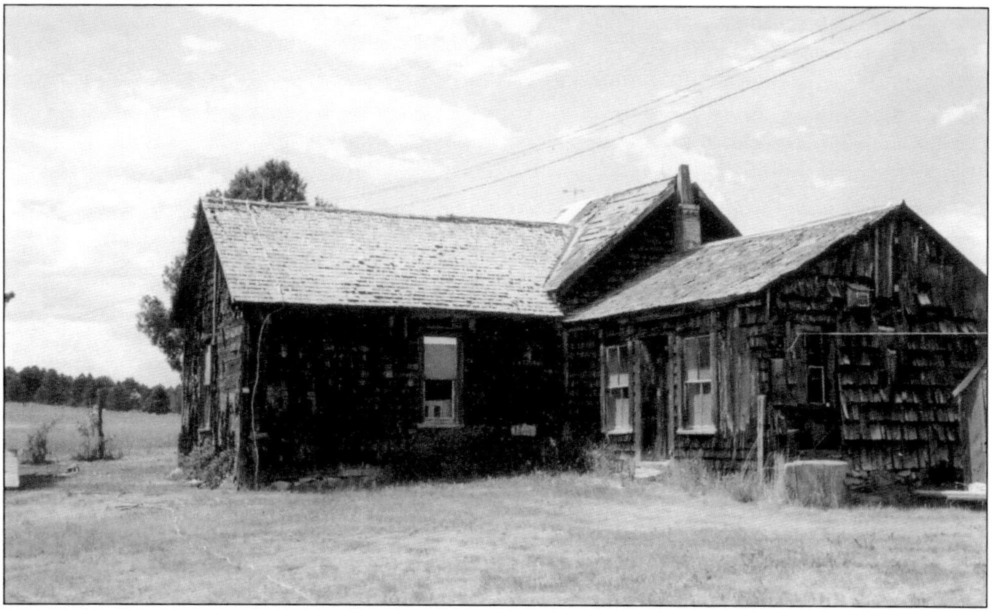

The Wissler Ranch. In 1910, Charles Wissler and his wife Selma moved to the Palmer Divide from Minnesota with their 10-year-old son Walter and Selma's father, Red Nadelhofer. The Wisslers originally purchased land at Furrow and County Line Roads for their farm. Pictured above is the Wissler ranch house. There were many trees on their land, which were cut for bridges and railroad ties. They later bought more acreage east of State Highway 83 for summer pastures. The ranch is still occupied by the family. Pictured below around 1920, from left to right, are Selma Wissler and her daughter, Lucy, posing on a spring wagon in front of a new barn on their property. (Both courtesy of Fern Britt.)

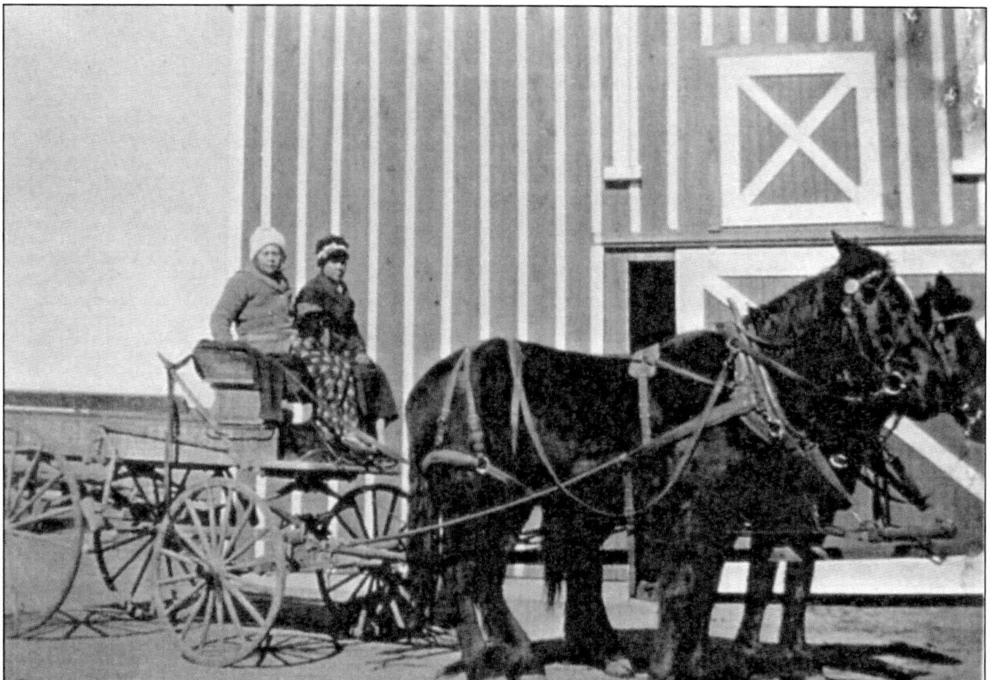

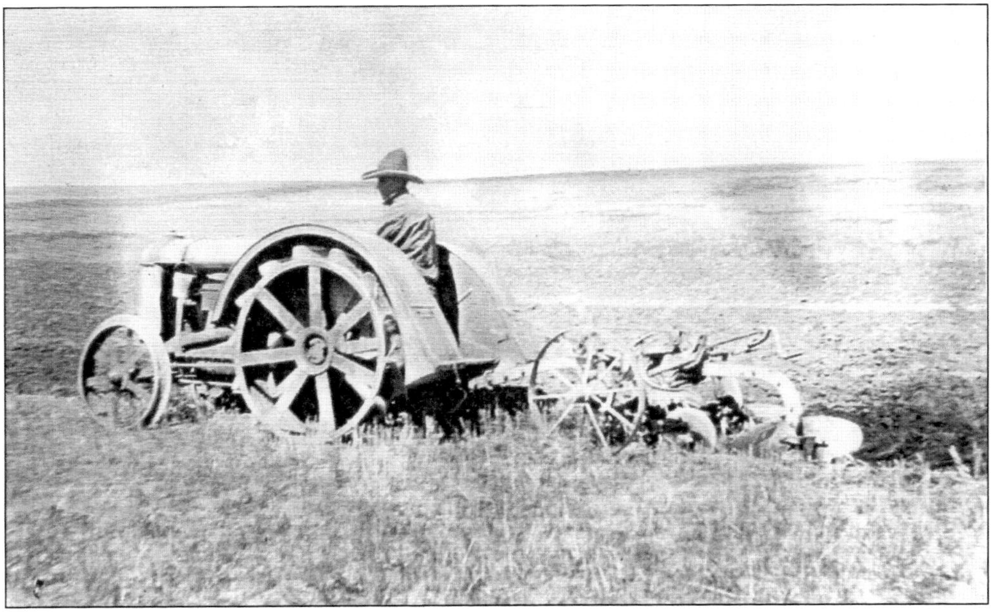

Wissler's Fordson Tractor, c. 1928. Walter William Wissler and his brother, Charles Jr., farmed the family land together and built a duplex where their families lived, one on each side. Walter once ran this tractor into a hornet's nest and was stung so many times that he could not get out of bed for quite some time. (Courtesy of Fern Britt.)

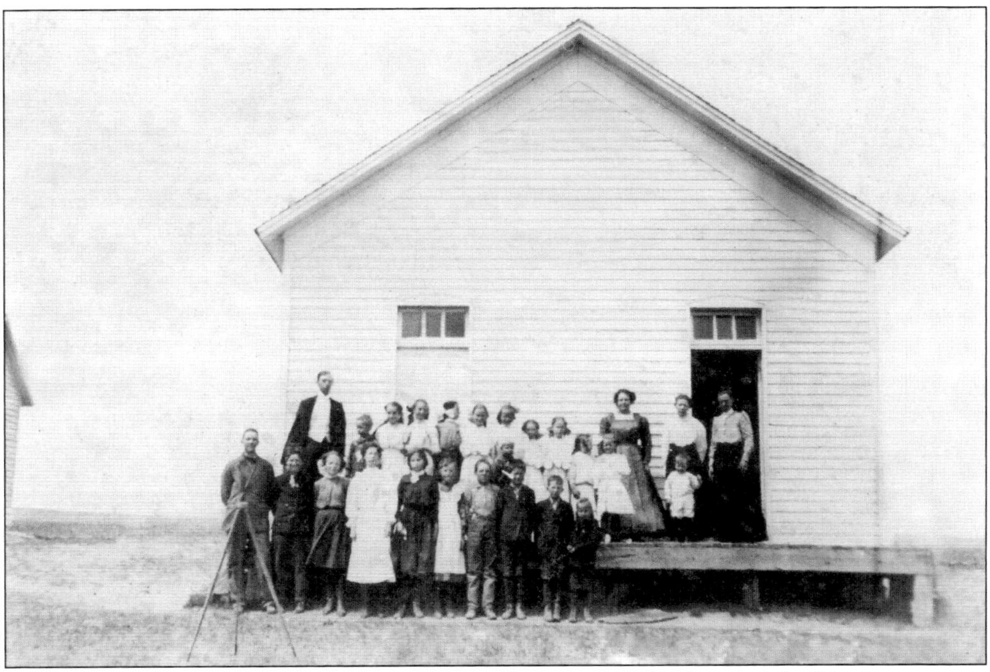

Columbine School. Located at County Line and Furrow Roads adjoining the Wissler property, Columbine school opened in the 1870s as a joint El Paso County and Douglas County school. Unfortunately the school burned to the ground in 1940 due to a stove fire. The Wissler family boarded the teacher, Elizabeth Harrington, in their home, and the "teacherage," her former residence, became the school building. (Courtesy of Fern Britt.)

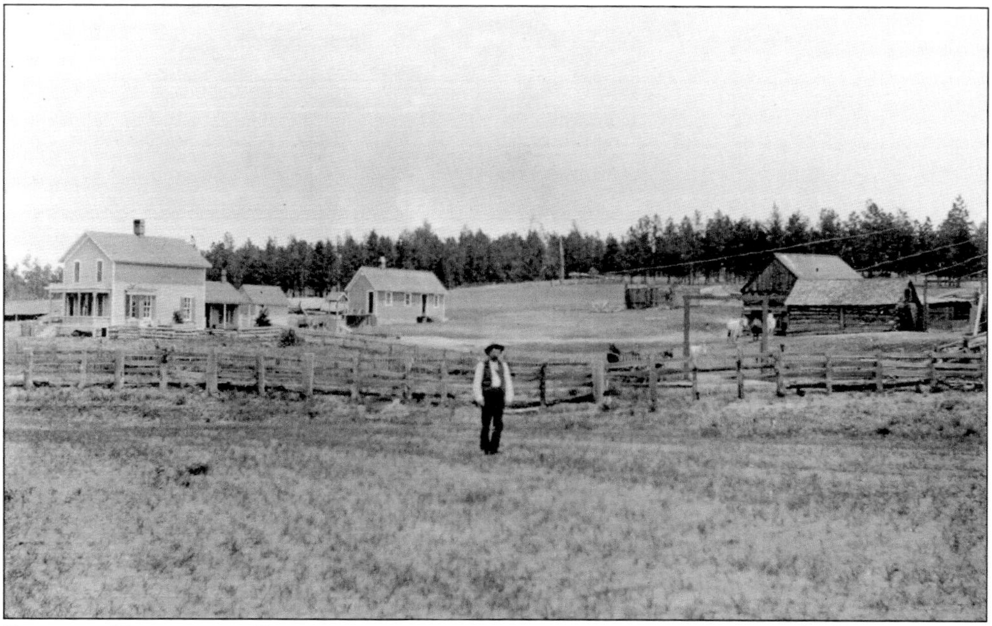

RANCHES, PEOPLE, AND FORTS, C. 1900. Joe Pettigrew was discharged from the Union army at Fort Bent after the Civil War. He met Patrick Murphy when Murphy was a cook at Fort Bent and they became best friends. Murphy convinced Pettigrew to homestead in the Palmer Divide area. Pettigrew's homestead, adjoining Murphy's, was along what is now State Highway 83. Rube Pribble is shown above enjoying happier times on the Pettigrew Ranch. Pribble would later kill his best friend, William Neff, at Limbach's Saloon in Monument. Fear of Indian attacks prompted many pioneers to seek protection in forts built as safe havens. Pictured below are the remains of John Iron's Indian fort in Spring Valley, not too far from Pettigrew's ranch. (Both courtesy of Jim Sawatzki.)

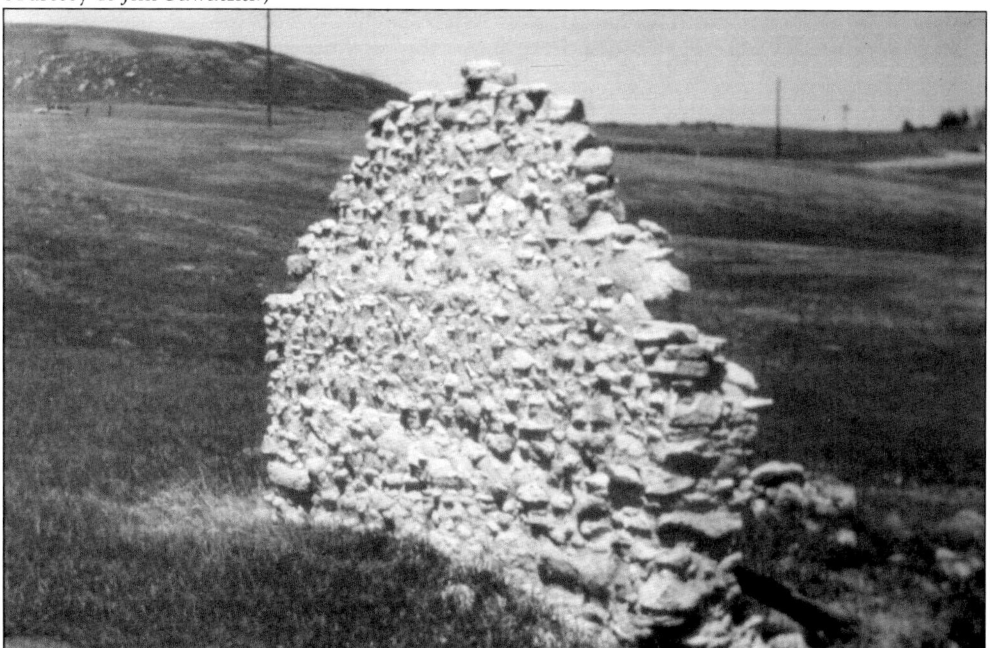

PATRICK MURPHY AND HIS CABIN. Patrick Murphy, right, was born in Ireland and came to America in 1864. He walked everywhere, from the Palmer Divide to places in Colorado like Denver, Colorado Springs, and Fort Bent. He made his last trip up Pikes Peak at age 101. It is rumored that he once turned down a ride to Colorado Springs because he said he could get there quicker by walking. Although he could neither read nor write, he had a sharp mind and quick wit. Pictured below is his two-room log cabin located in Spring Valley. From left to right are his two good friends, Joe Pettigrew and George Stamm. When he died in 1926, Murphy was 105. He was the oldest member of the Knights of Columbus and the oldest rancher in Colorado.

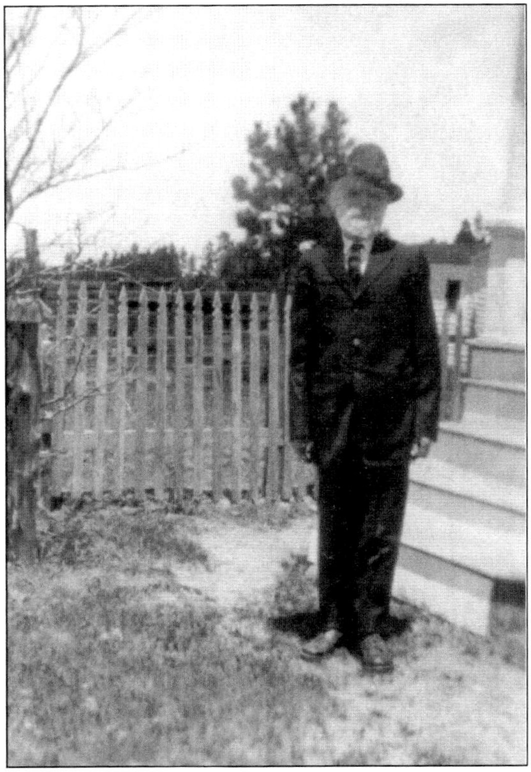

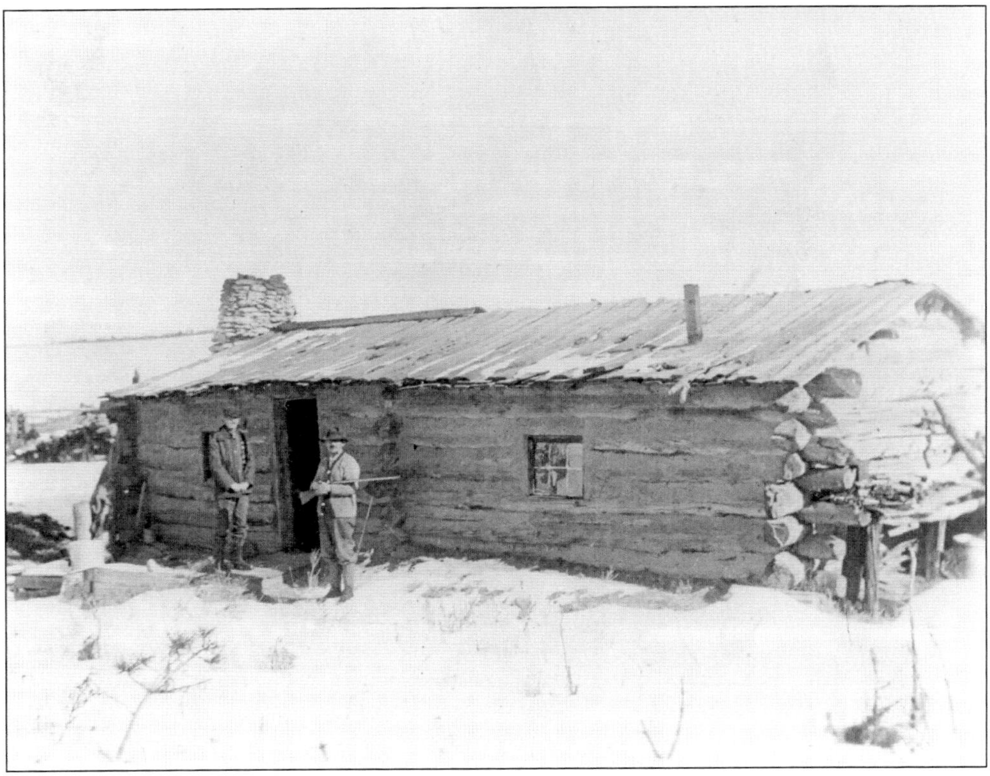

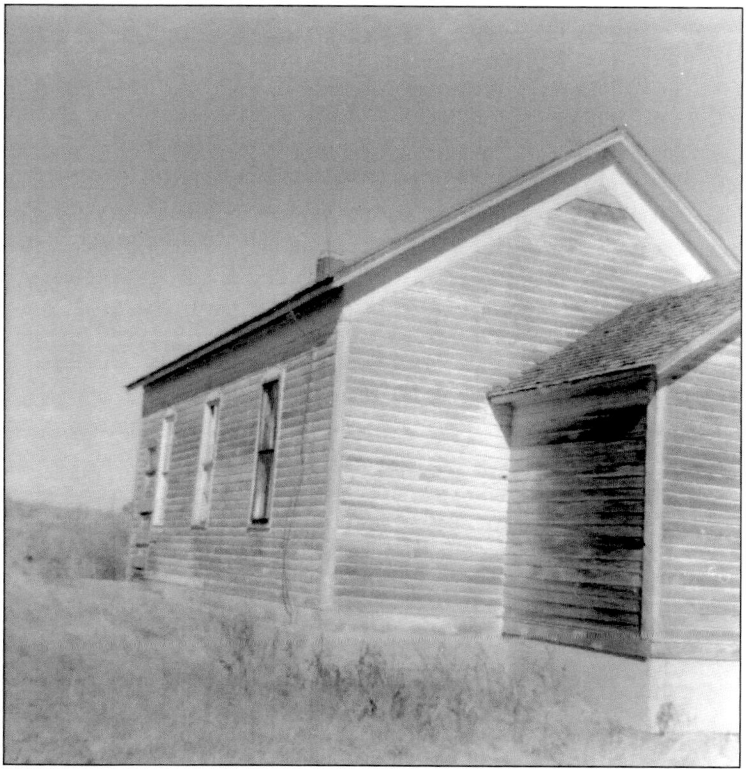

Spring Valley School. This single-story white schoolhouse was built prior to 1875 by Harrison Bucks and John Geiger. The building served as the hub of the community where weddings, funerals, religious services, parties, and court trials were held. Community dances were held with tunes belted out on the piano by Ramona Wissler, Charles Wissler's wife. She was accompanied by their son, Roy, on the fiddle.

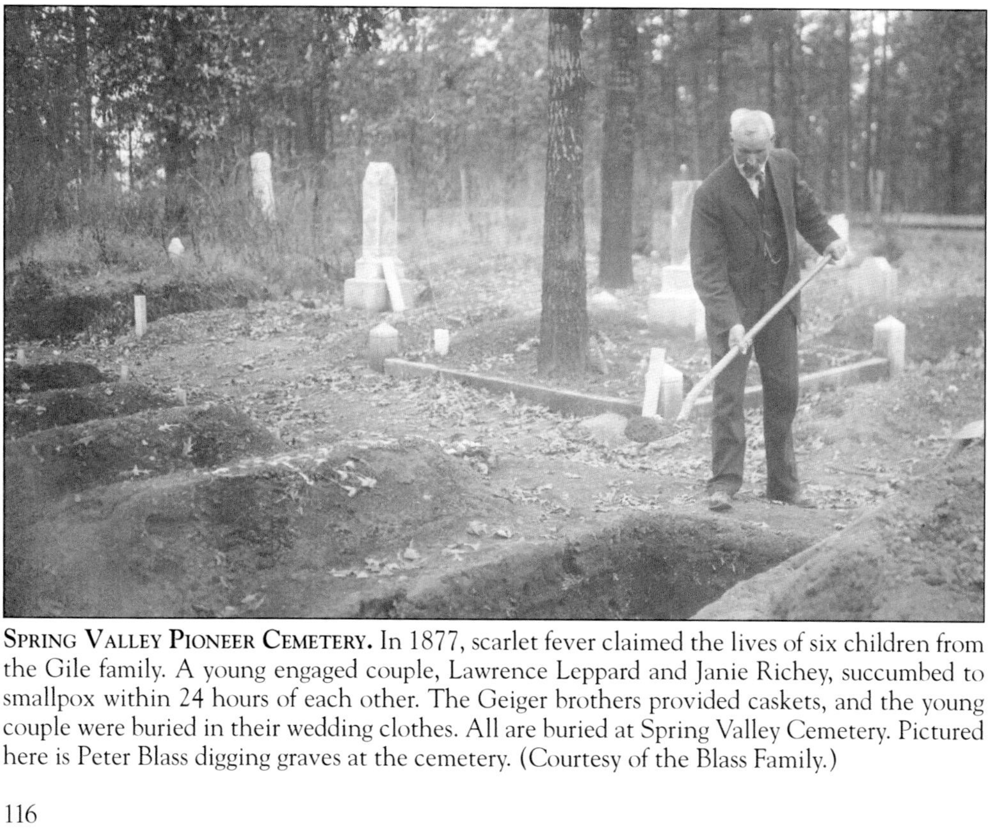

Spring Valley Pioneer Cemetery. In 1877, scarlet fever claimed the lives of six children from the Gile family. A young engaged couple, Lawrence Leppard and Janie Richey, succumbed to smallpox within 24 hours of each other. The Geiger brothers provided caskets, and the young couple were buried in their wedding clothes. All are buried at Spring Valley Cemetery. Pictured here is Peter Blass digging graves at the cemetery. (Courtesy of the Blass Family.)

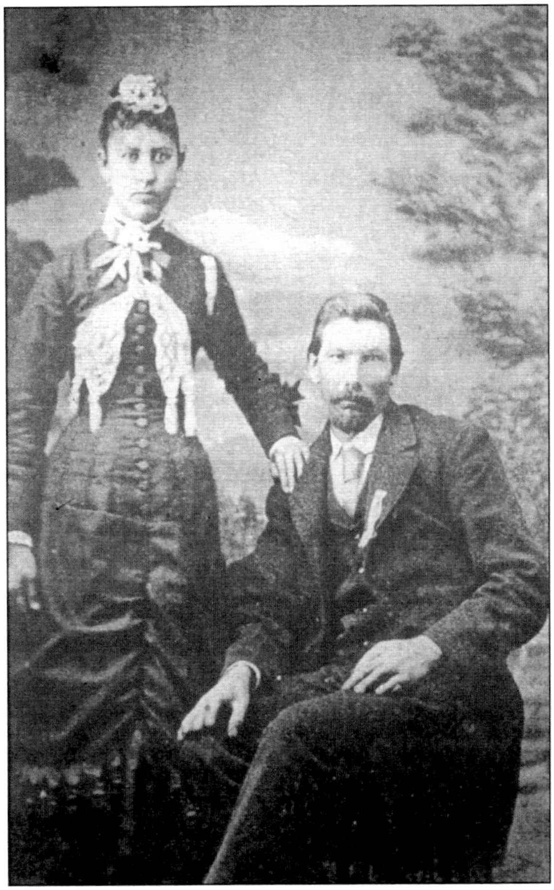

John and Anna Geiger, Spring Valley. John Geiger and his wife, Anna, are in the photograph at right. Geiger first saw this area in 1864 when escorting Confederate prisoners to Fort Bent with his brother, Jacob. He returned and filed a homestead claim in 1879. Geiger, a talented carpenter, built many wooden bridges and the courthouse in Castle Rock. He became a Douglas County commissioner and lived to see his grandchildren attend the Spring Valley School, which he also built. Ranching was a major way of life in Spring Valley and all around the Palmer Divide. Hay was a staple crop of the area. Standing on the wagon below are Francis and Richard Geiger. Their father Fred and little sister Dorothy stand below. The Geiger Ranch was one of the earliest homesteads in the area and remains in the family today.

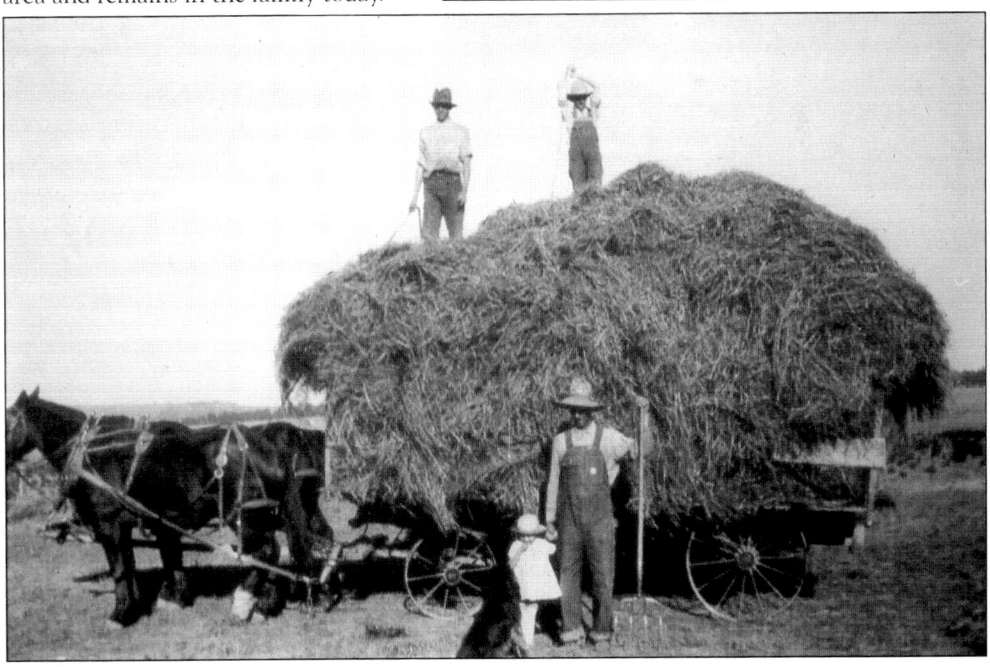

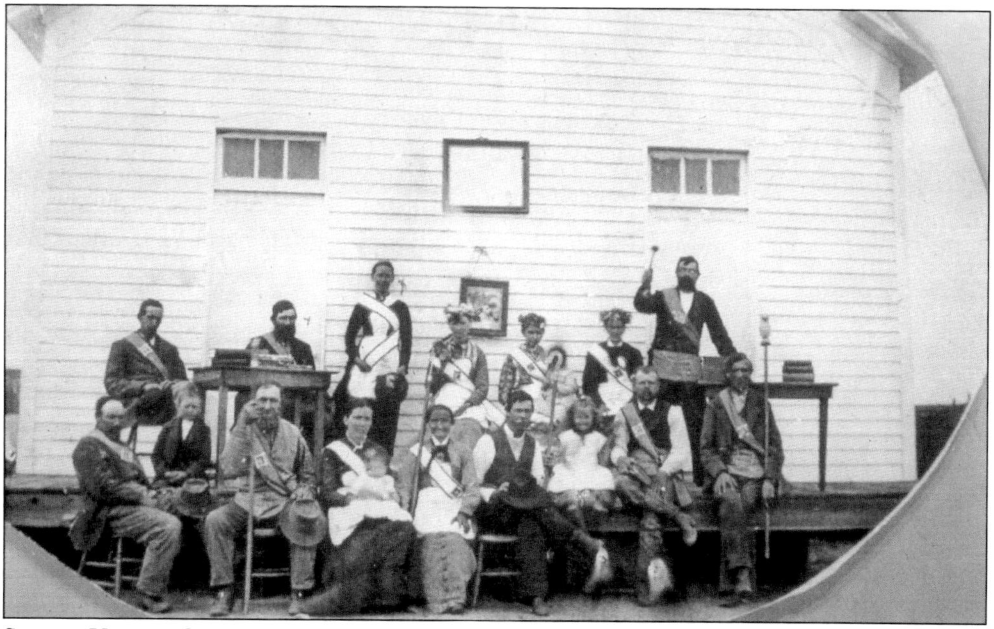

Spring Valley Grange. c. 1870. This building in Spring Valley, once managed by Jacob Geiger, contained an active Grange (farmers' association) and store. Secretary John Geiger is seated top row, second from left. Jacob is holding a gavel with his arm up. Lawrence Leppard lived in the back of the building. Leppard was the first person to contract smallpox. Fear of the disease and its spread led to the store being set ablaze around 1886.

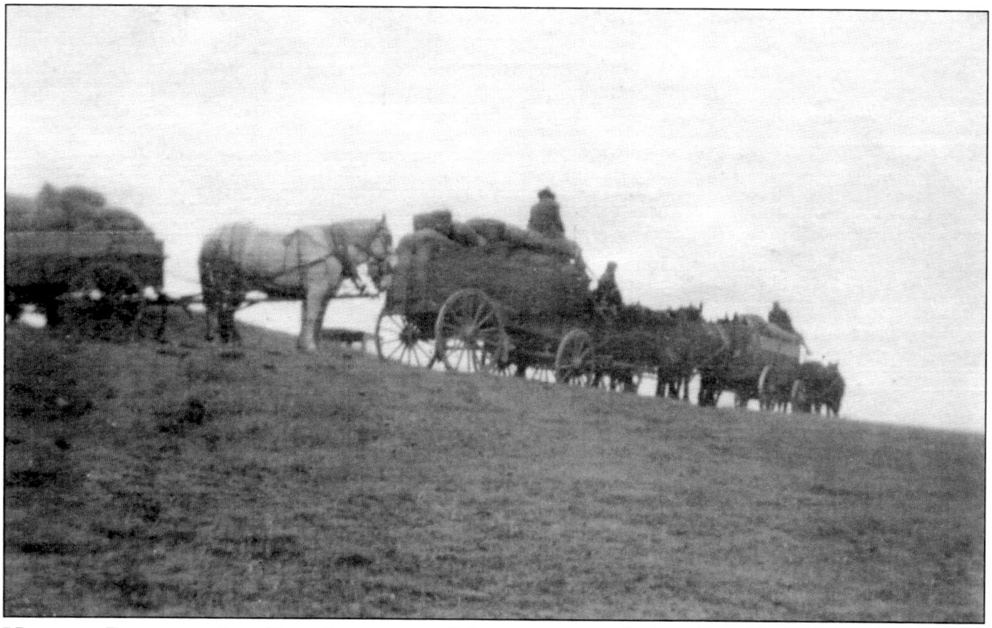

Hauling Potatoes. Lou Steppler was a well-known potato farmer from the area of Table Rock. He was often referred to as the "Potato King." During harvest time it was not uncommon to see 60 wagon loads of potatoes being hauled from Table Rock to Gwillimville to be stored in W. B. "Rod" Walker's potato cellar until they were distributed. In 1875, potatoes sold for 75¢ per hundred.

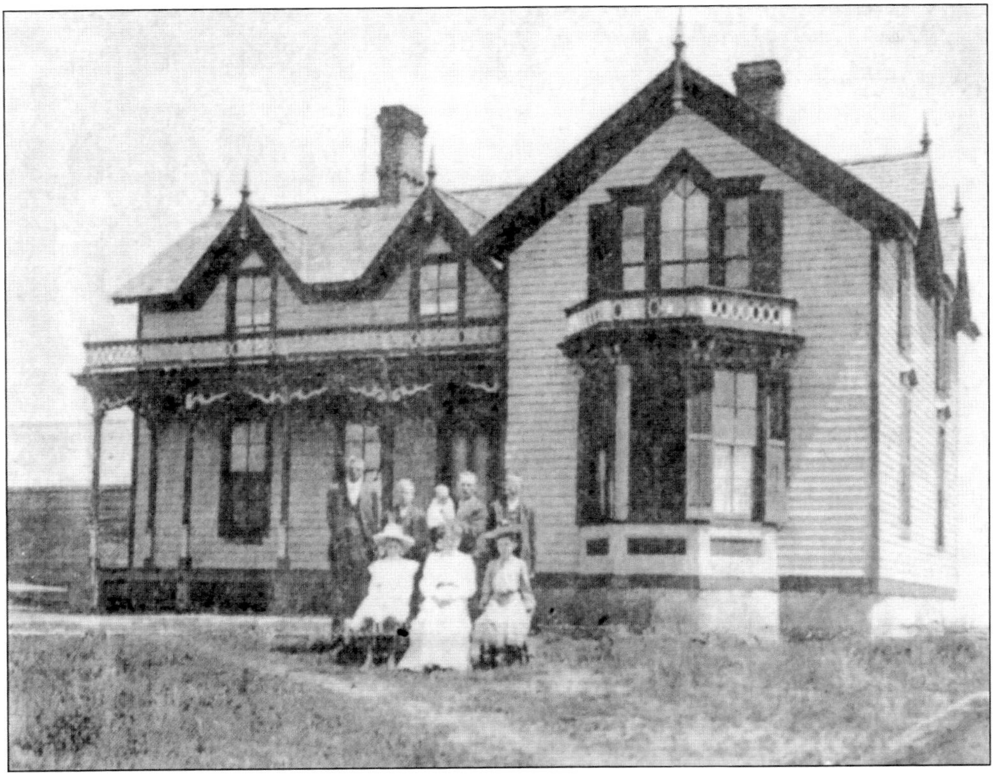

GWILLIMVILLE. The Gwillim brothers, Gwillim R. and Richard J., left South Wales between 1869 and 1870 and established the community of Gwillimville. Pictured above is the Gwillim family home. The Gwillims had several thousand acres of land adjacent to each other. The community included several families from Wales and England, a church, the first school in the area, a post office, creamery, store, blacksmith shop, saloons, and a cheese factory that was established in 1878. The Gwillims sold 25 pounds of butter a week in Colorado Springs. Mrs. Gwillim's butter was so good it took first place at the state fair. Her prize was a brass lamp. Pictured at right is Richard Gwillim, who was justice of the peace in Colorado Springs and El Paso County assessor from 1913 to 1915.

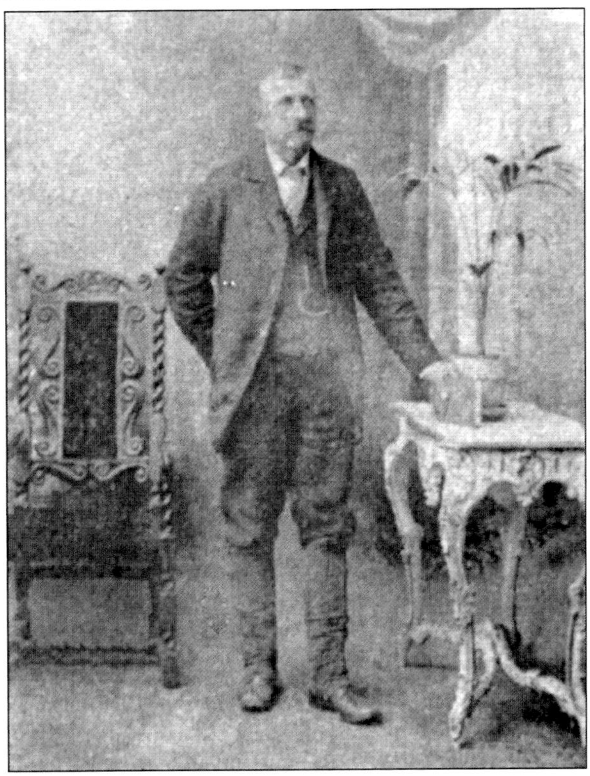

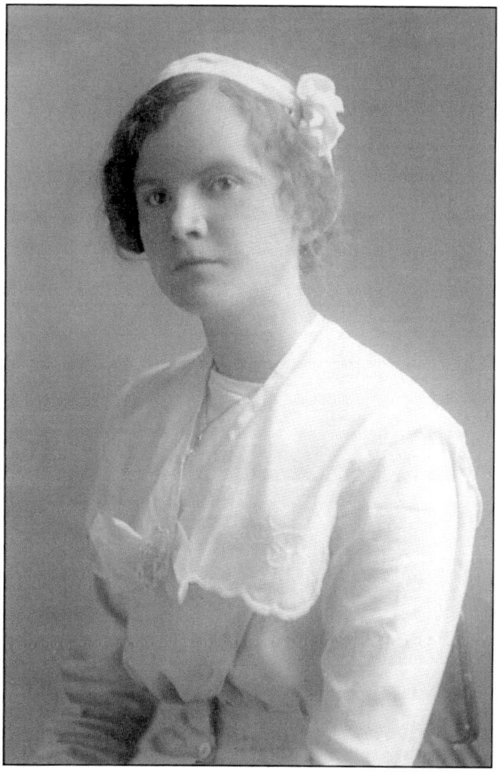

EDNA BENNETT, C. 1915. Edna Bennett, at left, was a local Douglas County girl who became the first teacher of the Pine Grove School in 1913. The school was located along the border of El Paso and Douglas County. She made $50 a month teaching every grade during the six-month school year. One of her students, Pearl Dutton, wrote that Bennett was "a wonderful teacher." The school calendar adjusted to the growing season and, because children had chores on the farm, school hours had to adapt to the farm schedule. Pictured below is a souvenir of the 1915 school year. A list of pupils was on the back. Pine Grove School was restored and relocated to Kilmer Elementary School to be used as a history classroom. (Both courtesy of Evelyn McCune.)

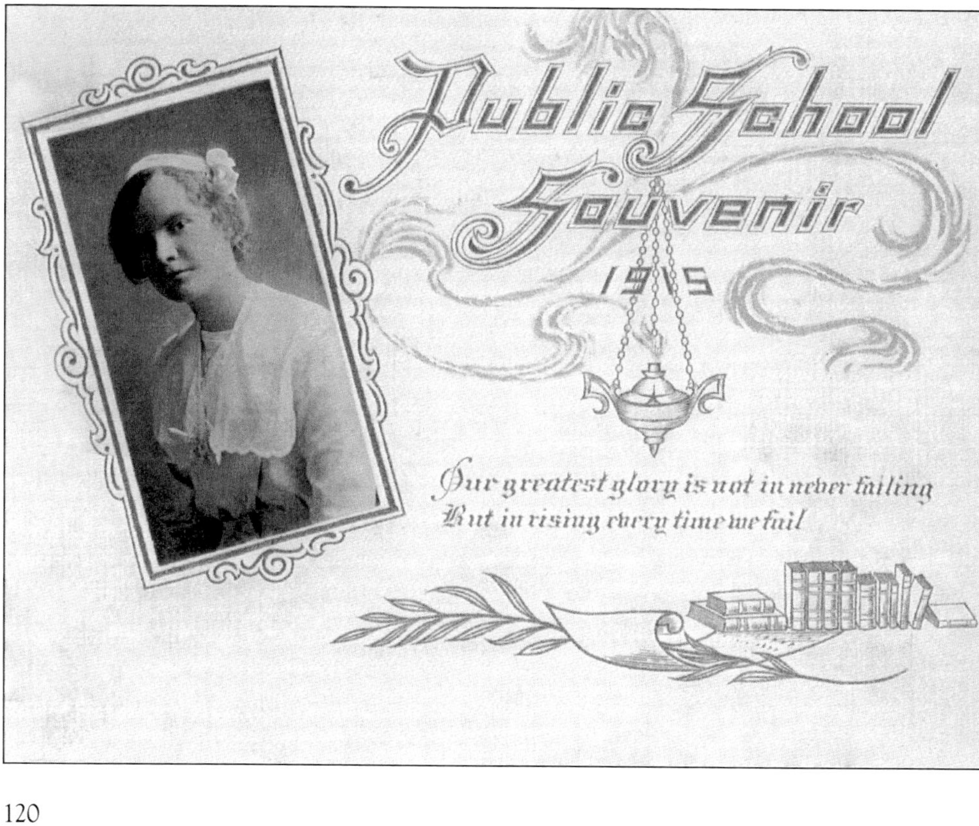

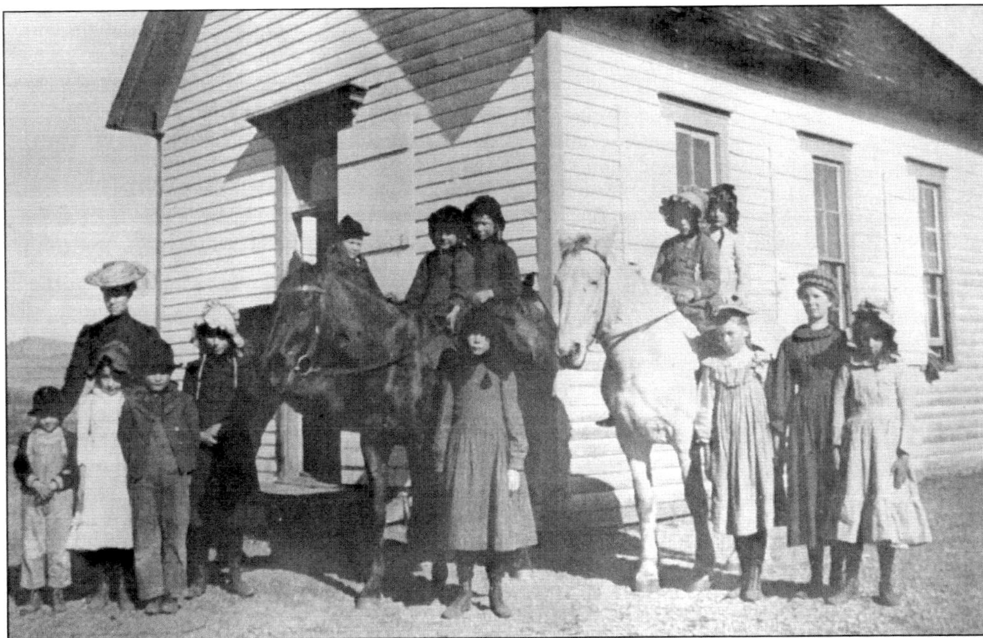

Pine Grove School. Pine Grove School had students from both El Paso and Douglas counties. In 1912, parents along the county border were concerned about the distance traveled by children to schools within their respective counties and petitioned the state for a joint district. The Aubuchon family donated land on the El Paso side, and the Dutton family donated a bunkhouse for use as the school. (Courtesy of Jim Sawatzki.)

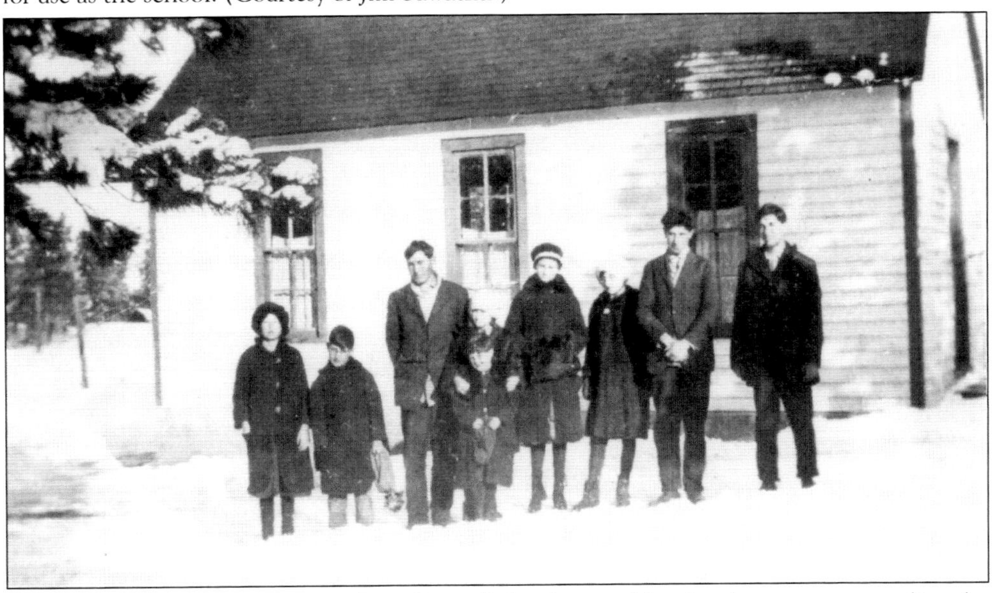

Pine Grove Students, c. 1918. Pine Grove School, named for the pine trees surrounding the building, had two outhouses, shelter for horses, and a coal shed. Out front was an American flag where students and teachers would recite the Pledge of Allegiance. Pictured from left to right are Leone Aubuchon, Homer Aubuchon, Steve Lavelett, Adele Aubuchon, Glen Aubuchon, Gertrude Dutton, Bertha Aubuchon, George Aubuchon, and Clarence Lavelett. (Courtesy of Evelyn McCune.)

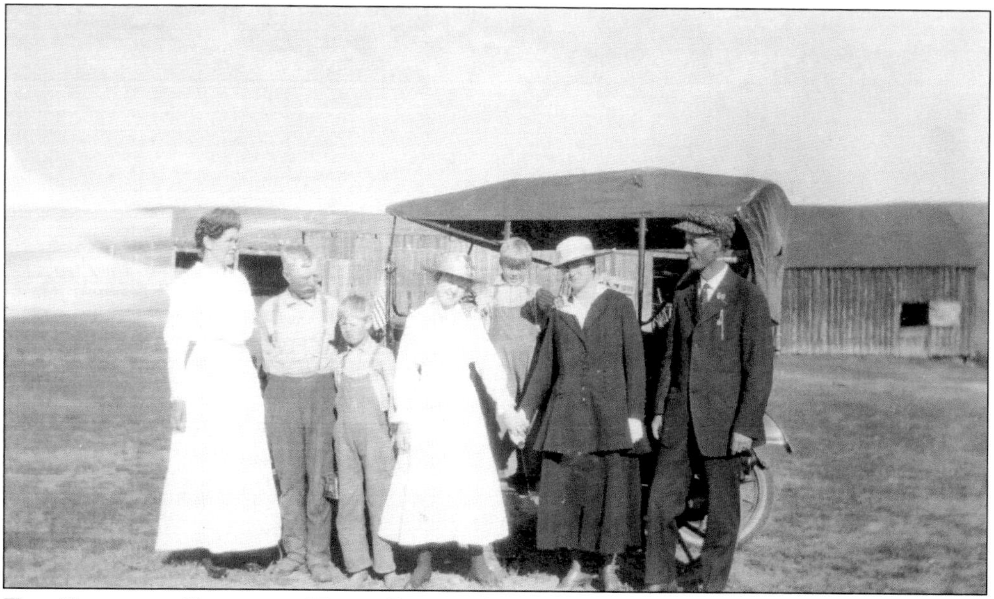

The Thompson Family at Table Rock. Like most pioneering families, Eva and Thomas Thompson and their six-year-old son Earl came west in a covered wagon. In 1890, they journeyed to Denver from Kansas before buying the Taylor homestead at Table Rock, where some members of their family still reside. From left to right are Eva, Thomas, Arthur, Hazel, Wilbur, Ethel, and Earl Thompson. (Courtesy of the Thompson Family.)

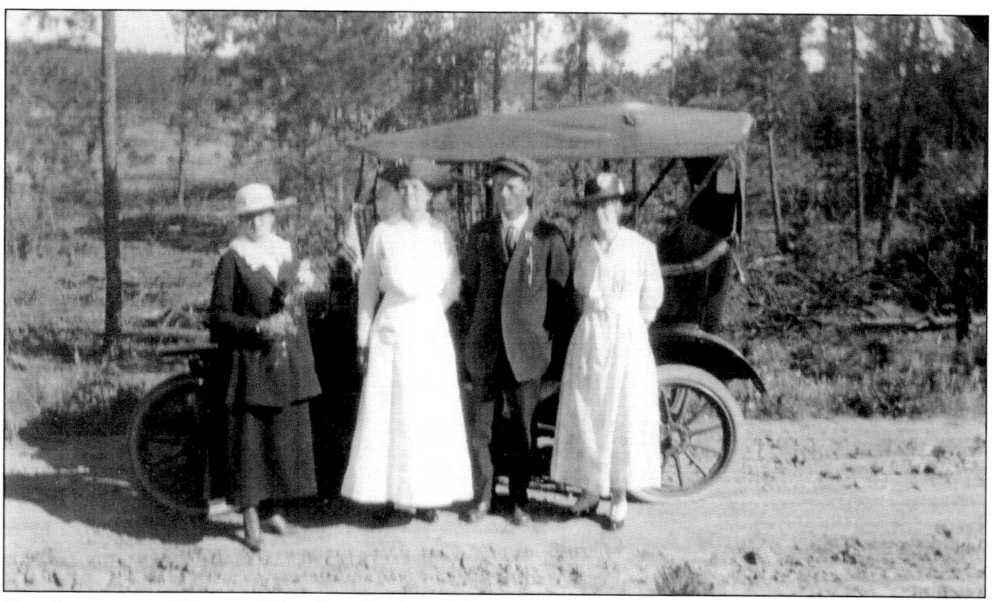

Eva Learns to Drive. After her husband died in 1924, Eva Thompson had to raise the two younger boys by herself. She had to learn many things for herself, including how to drive. She drove through the area, nursing sick neighbors, and even drove back to Iowa to visit relatives, which was unheard of for a woman to do in the 1920s. Pictured from left to right are Ethel, Eva, Earl, and Hazel Thompson. (Courtesy of the Thompson Family.)

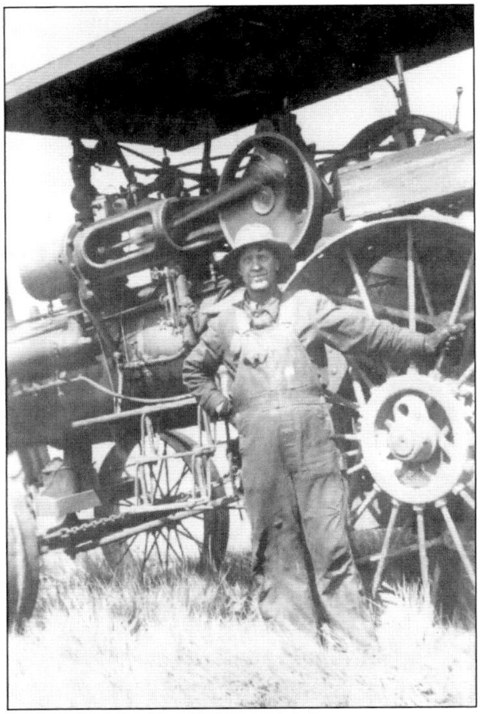

Earl Thompson, c. 1930. Earl Thompson stands next to the thresher steam engine that he operated for L. H. Gaunt and Son. At harvest time, the threshing machine traveled from farm to farm. Thompson married a neighboring girl, Nora Hodgin, for whom Hodgen Road was named (with her name inadvertently misspelled). He raised his family on the Thompson ranch. (Courtesy of the Thompson Family.)

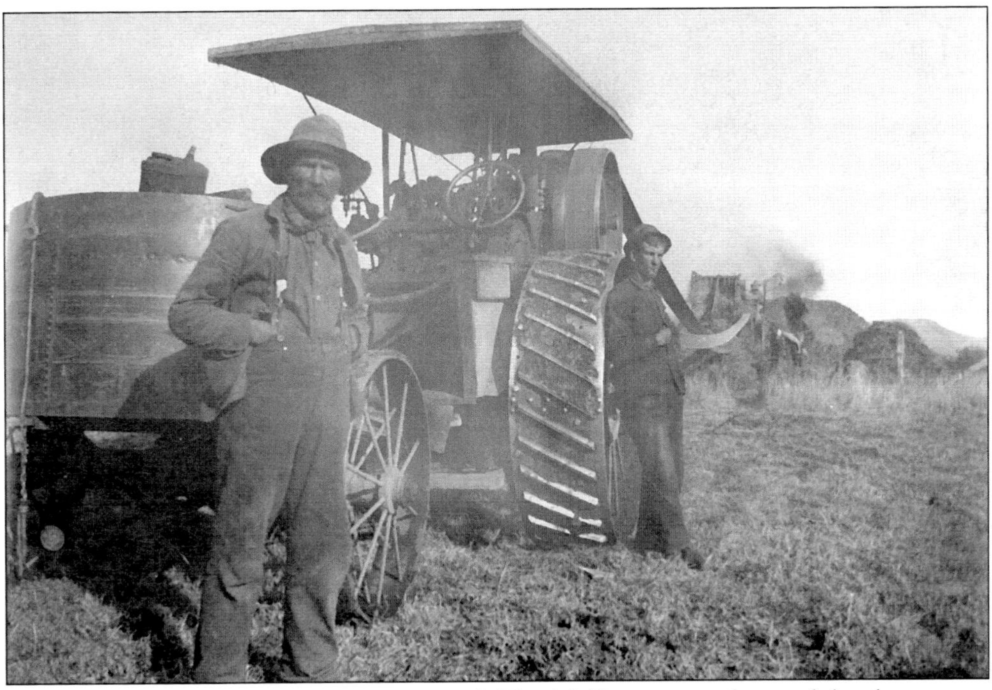

Albert McShane and Son, Dave, c. 1915. The McShanes owned one of the three steam threshing machines in the Palmer Divide area. Hugo Schubarth and Sons and L. H. Gaunt and Son owned the others. Lucille Lavelett wrote, "Threshing day was a big exciting, happy, hardworking time for the entire family." The faces of McShane and his son suggest the exhausting reality of farm and ranch work.

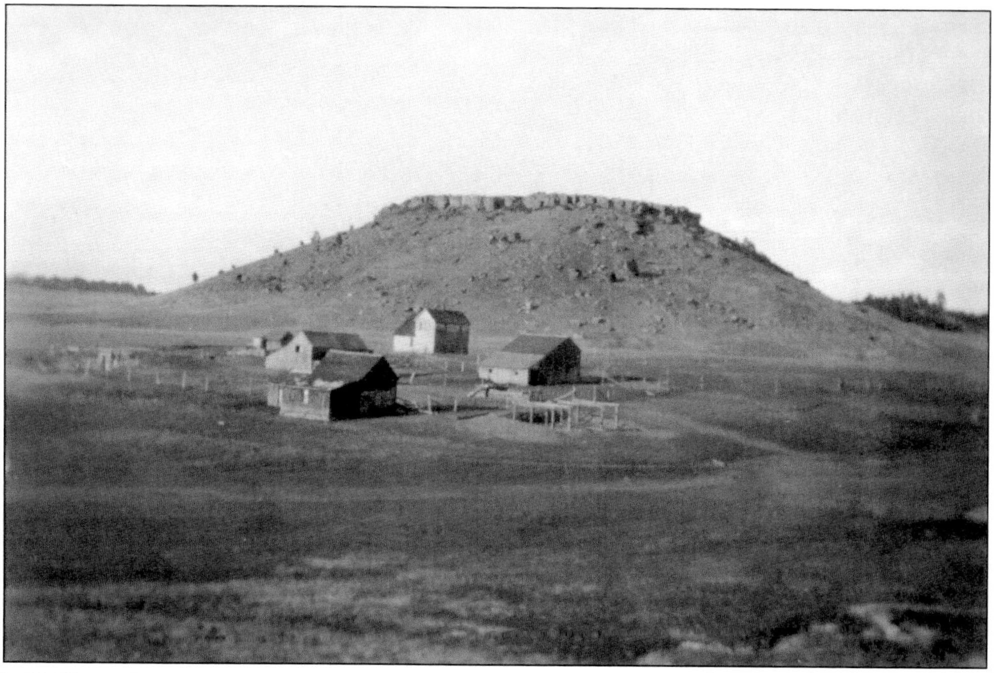

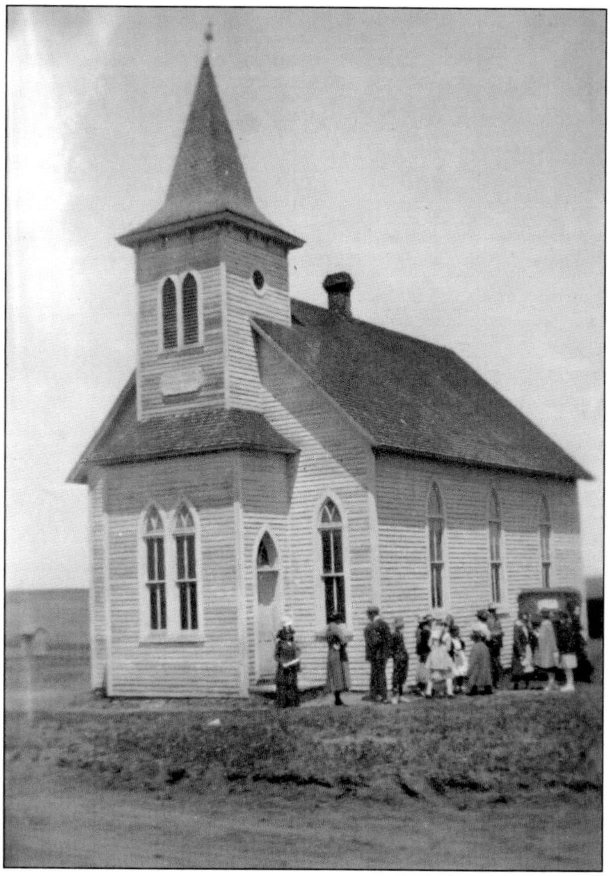

Table Rock Area. Table Rock Ranch was situated in the far eastern section of El Paso County, bordering Elbert and Douglas Counties. The ranch, seen above, had a store, a Presbyterian church, a school, a creamery, a blacksmith shop, and a post office. Pictured at left is the church. The ranch was named for the flat mountain in the background. Evidence of Native American activity has been found in the area, including a medicine wheel, arrowheads, and projectiles. The Russell family, early Table Rock pioneers, suffered a chain of tragic events, including a drowning, sickness, a lightning strike, and suicides. The family was buried in the small Table Rock cemetery that was in use from 1872 until 1910. (Courtesy of the Thompson Family.)

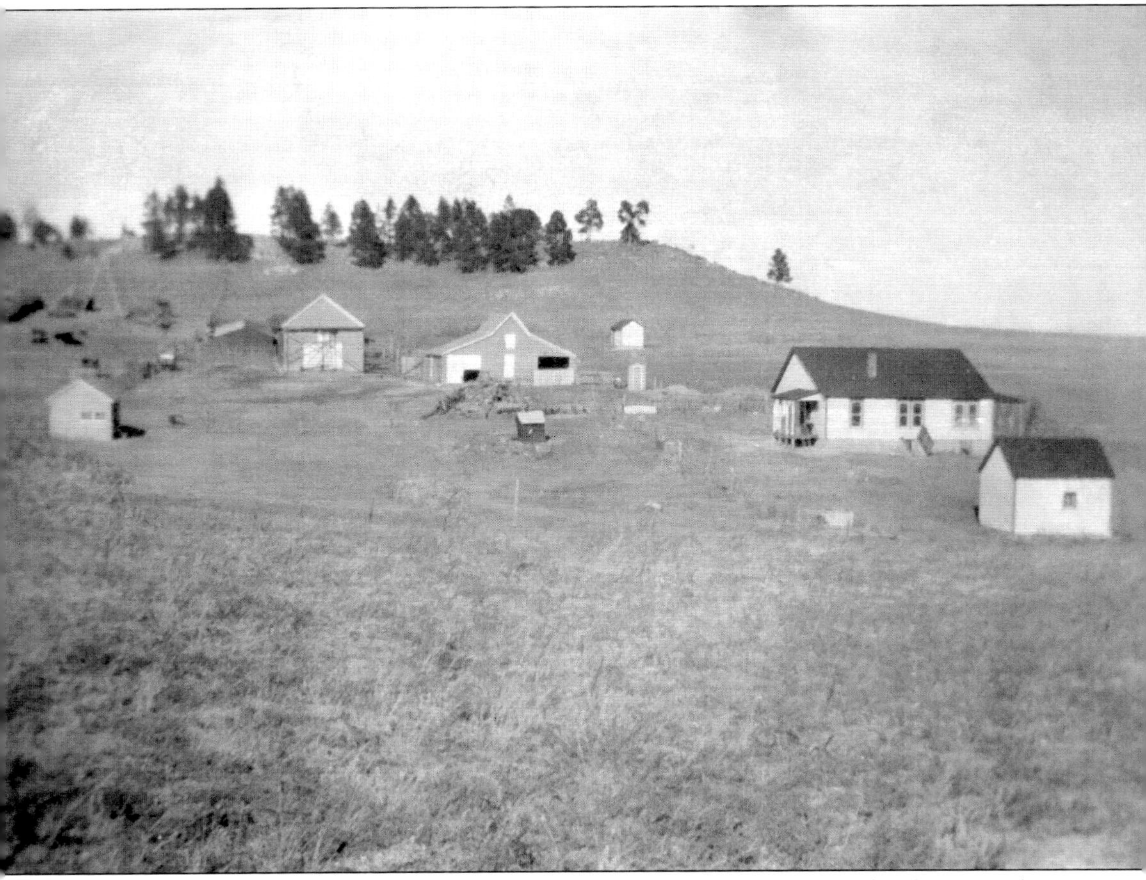

The Younger Ranch with Elliott Livery Building. The Younger family is another pioneering family of note in the outlying areas of the Palmer Divide. William and Grace Sears Younger and siblings came to Colorado from Knox County, Illinois, in 1884. William operated a livery in Palmer Lake before heading to Alaska in search of gold. Their son Charles (C. J.), married Lucy Elliott in 1895. Her father ran Elliott's Carriage and Wagon Repository and Elliott's General Store in Monument. The repository, which was moved from Monument out to the ranch, is the second building from the left. The Younger family bought property in Gwillimville and purchased two homesteaded ranches from the Aubuchon family. The Younger ranch, well known for its Hereford cattle, grew to about 2,000 acres. A large portion is still owned by the family. Five generations have lived on the ranch. (Courtesy of Dee Younger.)

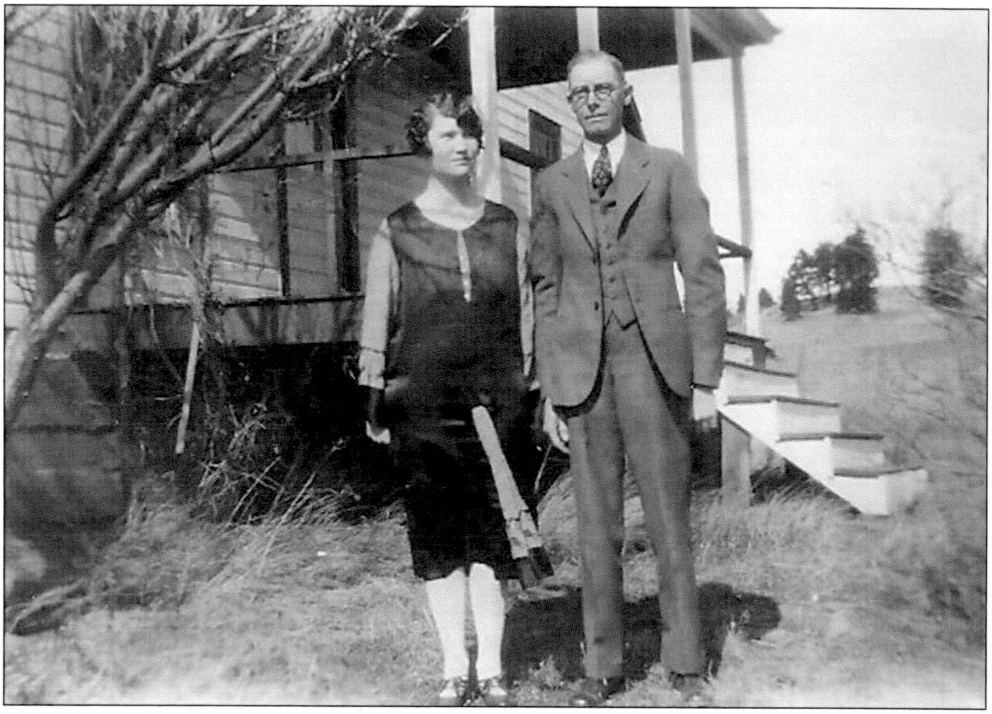

Bruce and Deane Younger. Charles and Lucy Younger's son, Bruce, chose to ranch with his father after completing the eighth grade instead of going to high school in Pueblo. He married Deane Hiatt in 1926. This photograph was taken on their wedding day in front of the Aubuchon Ranch house where they began their life together. (Courtesy of Norma Lavelett.)

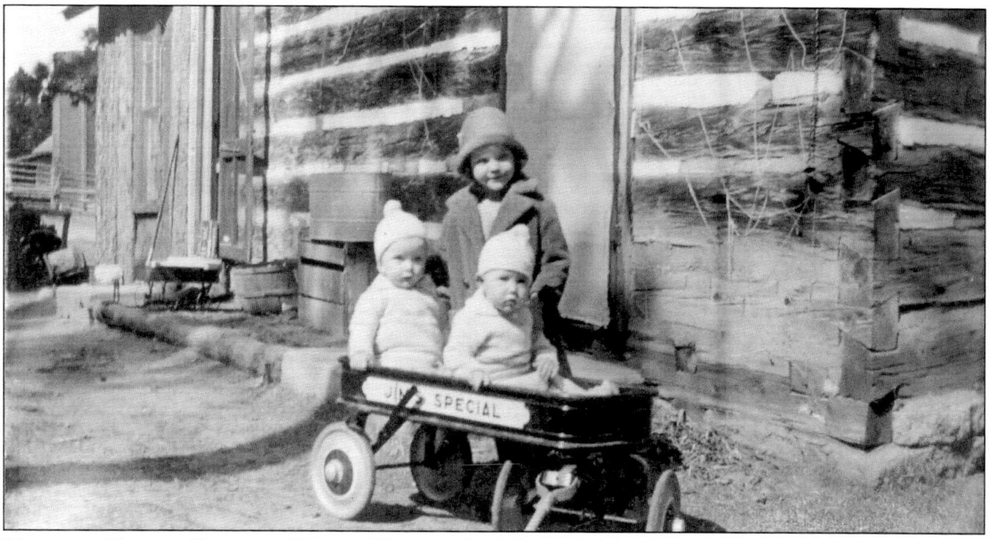

Younger Family. Bruce and Deane Younger had three children. Born first in 1927 was daughter Ruby followed by twins Norm and Norma, who were born in 1932. When Deane Younger went into labor in 1932, she was completely unaware she was about to have twins. Pictured in front of the Ruell Aubuchon cabin, the twins are piled into a wagon along with big sister Ruby. (Courtesy of Dee Younger.)

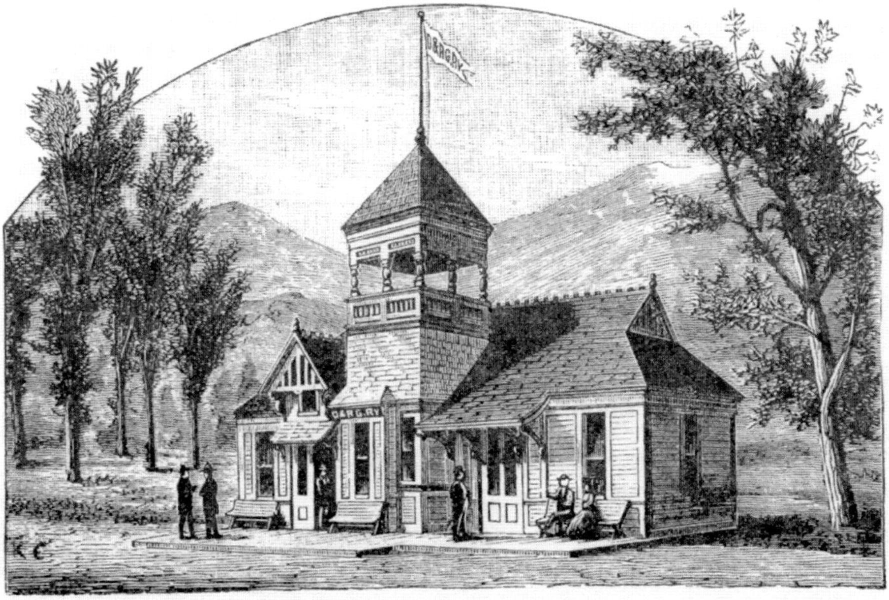

DEPOT AT PALMER LAKE.

PALMER LAKE HISTORICAL SOCIETY. In 1956, a group of citizens recommended that a manuscript written by Marion Savage Sabin detailing the founding of Palmer Lake, entitled *Palmer Lake, A Historical Narrative*, be published, and that a historical society be formed to continue the preservation of the area's history. The Palmer Lake Historical Society was subsequently founded by Marion McIntyre-McDonough. The society established the Lucretia Vaile Museum and expanded the society's scope to collecting the history and artifacts from the Palmer Divide area. The society promotes, preserves, and protects the history of the Palmer Divide area of Colorado, and sponsors, maintains, and is responsible for the activities and commitments of the museum. The primary goals and objectives of the society are to assemble, preserve, interpret, and display (as feasible) historical objects and printed material pertaining to the Palmer Divide area. This area includes Palmer Lake, Monument, School District 38, the U.S. Air Force Academy, and as far east as Table Rock.

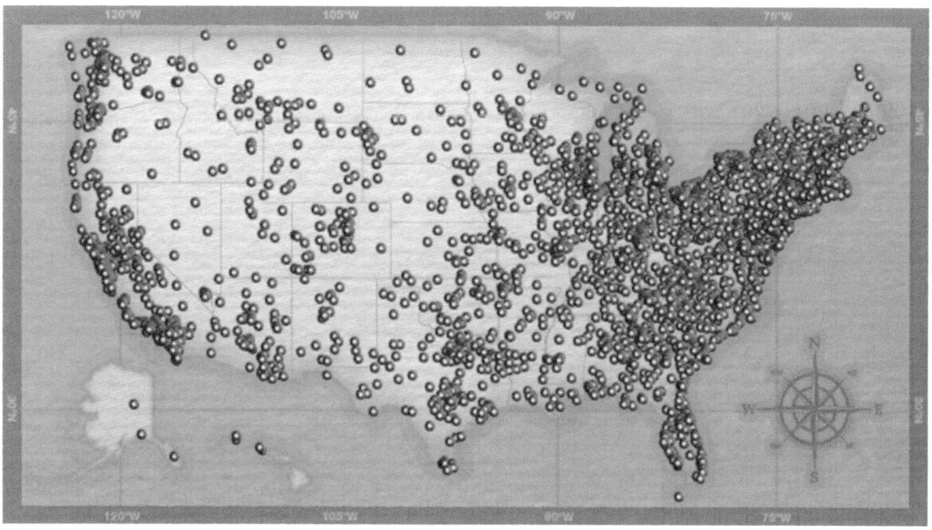